On the
Trail of
M
Polo

ALONG THE SILK ROAD BY BICYCLE
BRADY FOTHERINGHAM

McArthur & Company
Toronto

First published in Canada by McArthur & Company, 2000
This paperback edition published in 2001 by
McArthur & Company, 322 King St. West, Suite 402,
Toronto, Ontario, M5V 1J2

National Library of Canada Cataloguing in Publication Data

       Fotheringham, Brady
       On the trail of Marco Polo: along the Silk Road by bicycle

       Includes bibliographical references.
       ISBN 1-55278-168-2 (bound). – ISBN 1-55278-253-0 (pbk.)

1. Fotheringham, Brady – Journeys. 2. Silk Road – Description and travel.
3. Asia—Description and travel. 4. Bicycle touring—Asia. I. Title.

      DS10.F68 2000   915.04'429   C00-931342-7

Design and Composition: *Mad Dog Design Inc.*
Cover and Photo f/x: *Mad Dog Design Inc.*
Printed in Canada by *Transcontinental Printing Inc.*

The publisher would like to acknowledge the financial support of the Government of Canada through the Book Publishing Industry Development Program (BPIDP) and the Canada Council for our publishing activities. The publisher further wishes to acknowledge the financial support of the Ontario Arts Council for our publishing program.

10 9 8 7 6 5 4 3 2

Contents

For my brother Kip, who has supported
me in everything I have done.

I am grateful to my parents, Sallye and Allan, for giving me the courage and curiosity to explore the world. Moral support came from Elena who has never stopped believing in me. My late grandmother Carmen and my sister Francesca — in fact, all the women in my family — were initially cautious in their travel advice but well rewarded in the end. This is for them and, of course, my publisher Kim McArthur.

This book wouldn't resemble its present form were it not for the unofficial editing work of Nick Heron. Nick edited many drafts, gave me better advice than I deserved, helped shape the style and tone of the manuscript and put up with my constant whining. This book originated as a dozen articles in the *North Shore News* in 1997–98, thanks to News publisher Peter Speck.

Patrick Jennings, who only writes when he travels, was instrumental in helping fact-check the chapters on China (having travelled there himself) and designed the web site where additional photos from my trip through the Silk Road appear at
www.greymattermedia.com/BradyFotheringham
Thanks also goes to input from Logan Abassi, Sohail Kiani for his pointers on the way of the Islamic world, Monika Tang (who was there from the start), my official editor Pamela Erlichman, the Feckos and my best friend Kristina Walcott and her husband Marek Welz for his help with excerpts.

The Journey Is the Destination

Nothing so spurs a man upon a journey as the cautions of his friends: 'dangerous,' 'impossible,' 'when you get there nothing worth seeing,' and the like, All show you plainly that the thing is worth the venture…

R.B. CUNNINGHAM, *Mogreb-el Acksa*,
19th-century North African explorer

It all started with a letter from England…

It was an invitation to ride across 3,000 km of desert and mountain terrain from northern China to northern Pakistan. Not your usual letter. My British friend Tony had written to 13 cyclists he knew, hoping to interest them in an epic bike adventure. The plan was to ride a mountain bike through Central Asia, retracing the legendary Silk Road — the trade route made famous by Marco Polo, where caravans once carried silk and spices across the heart of the Asian continent.

Any of Tony's friends who could take the time off work and who were physically up to the challenge would begin preparing for the trip. Our plan was to start near the Mongolian border inside China. We would pass by Kazakhstan, Kyrgyzstan and Tajikistan through the heart of Muslim China. Switching from the desert plains of China, we would ride the great 1,300-km-long

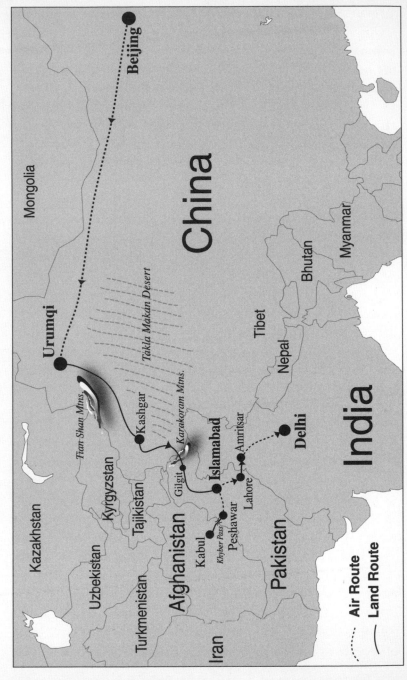

Central Asia route ridden by the author July 10 – Sept. 26, 1997

Karakoram Highway into the mountainous confines of northern Pakistan. My cycling mates (later whittled down to two Brits) and I would wind our way through lush river valleys into the blistering heat of the Indian subcontinent and on to the Pakistani capital, Islamabad. From there, they would fly home to England. I would continue on my own into Afghanistan (without my bike) and then on to India where the country was celebrating its 50th year of independence.

I was ready to embark on a journey across four nations, two deserts and five mountain ranges, most of it with my two British cycling companions. Much of the Silk Road comprised people whose names I couldn't spell, towns I couldn't pronounce and food I didn't recognize. Many places had little more than roadside stalls selling melons, mutton kebabs, bread and watered-down pop. I had to go.

I had cycled with my biking pal Tony through the Atlas Mountains and Sahara desert in Morocco a few years earlier and had a feeling that the North African trip would pale in comparison to Central Asia. I couldn't pass up his invitation. I refused to stay home and miss seeing a part of the world many people only read about. I wanted to live near the edge again and experience the desolation and bleakness of the mountains and desert. I wanted to take a holiday from the filtered, pasteurized and preservative-laden society I lived in. I was hoping to turn everything I took for granted in life upside down. Few things do this like travel in faraway places, especially rigorous travel.

I wanted this Silk Road pilgrimage to sharpen my senses by enduring challenge. I wanted a taste of things foreign and incongruous. I wanted to take my ignorance and my knowledge, erase a stack of preconceptions and start from scratch.

It was the spring of 1997. After nine months of preparation, many questions still lay unanswered — particularly my accreditation into Afghanistan. I had received a letter from the Embassy of the Islamic State of Afghanistan approving, albeit with a long list of conditions, my access into one of the most repressive regimes in the world. Afghanistan was undergoing a violent civil war between two Muslim factions — student rebels calling themselves the Taliban were trying to overthrow the government in Kabul.

The embassy staff had issued me a single-entry journalist visa, obtained with the assistance of my newspaper editor. However, there was the distinct possibility that some 15-year-old kid with an AK-47 would deem the stamp in my passport worthless once I got to the border. Tourist visas hadn't been issued since 1979 because of ongoing wars. First Afghanistan spent a decade fighting the Soviets who bombed and gutted villages and raped the Afghan people. Now the Afghans were fighting themselves, one Muslim faction killing the other.

When applying for the media visa, I had to acknowledge in what amounted to a dissertation that I understood all the subtle machinations of the Islamic holy war being waged in this fundamentalist state. I had to promise in writing that I wouldn't sue the Afghan government if I stepped on a landmine and blew my legs off. The most amusing part was the requirement to provide the name and address of a relative who could cough up $50,000 US if I were kidnapped and held for extortion. Complying with the request, I scribbled down someone's name. I never told this acquaintance of their fiscal obligation and I'm not going to now. Afghanistan, however, was just the icing on the cake of a much larger trip.

To travel you must first dream. Travel is not so much about where you go as what happens to you when you get there. By understanding others and the way they live and how you interact with them, you learn more about yourself. Travel would let me see how people survive outside my small North American bubble. To borrow the title from the travel journal of a young photojournalist stoned to death in Somalia — *The Journey Is the Destination*.

Travelling lets us leave our work and families behind; we can flamboyantly disregard our everyday obligations and become irresponsible for a brief period. We can immerse ourselves in other cultures, in other times, to see how we measure up against places we have only dreamt of. Travelling tests our resourcefulness, energy and patience as we cope with foreign customs, agitated stomachs and frustrating border officials. We are entirely at the mercy of our own judgment when away from home, be it good or bad. I knew this from experience. I had been thrown in jail in Morocco in 1995 for photographing the interior of a military barracks near the Algerian border.

Today, more and more people take adventure trips. They swim in cages with great white sharks off South Africa, climb Mt. Kilimanjaro, hang-glide over the rivers of Nepal. You name it — the trip is there for the taking. Many guided tours let you see regions of the world, safely pampered in the back of luxurious tour buses or escorted by guides who cook up five-course meals at Everest base camp. This was not the way I wanted to see Central Asia. Unlike travellers on bike tours through the south of France or the Napa Valley in California, where Sag wagons follow to pick up stragglers and fix flats, I was self-sufficient. Everything I needed for three months I had to carry on the bike.

I knew little about where I was going — something about China and Afghanistan and even less about Pakistan and India. Asia was a mystery to me; its eastern cultures were enigmatic. My association with Asian cultures in my youth had been limited to my schooling and visits to Vancouver's Chinatown — largely a commercial affair. My minor at university in Southeast Asian History helped me understand things a little better, but that was just books and term papers. I still didn't know the people.

I had been brought up in a comfortable, upper-middle-class neighbourhood with the usual two parents, dog, cat and a brother or sister or two. I thought of those families in the developing world — the truly poor — largely in the abstract. They made the news headlines but never affected me. I didn't have to include them in my life. In a way, I never had a chance — until now.

By my mid-20s, my city Vancouver was changing. A mix of central and South Asian immigrants turned one of the most staid and boring cities in North America into something stimulating and cosmopolitan. I had always despised the subtle racism of many Vancouver residents of European descent who viewed themselves as the only true qualifiers of Canadian citizenship. Jokes about "Hongcouver," a play on the number of wealthy immigrants from Hong Kong, had become acceptable by some.

Throughout the early 1990s, many of these wealthy Asian families moved into large houses in my neighbourhood. Their children excelled at school, giving me a one-sided view of their culture. I knew that the average citizen in Bangkok, Beijing and Seoul didn't drive a Mercedes-Benz or BMW, but that was all I saw. The Asians were among the best and brightest in Vancouver, but the flipside — for me to be part of the minority in Asia — beckoned me.

In Asia, I didn't want to rush from point A to point B by bus, truck or car like a backpacker. I wanted to spend as much time travelling between villages as in them. I would be meeting people who had never seen a foreigner on a mountain bike in their entire life.

Forget that this cycling trip was a chance to test and enhance my endurance. Forget that the Karakoram Mountains in Pakistan would put the Canadian Rockies to shame. Forget that the mystique of the Silk Road, where thousands perished in desert sandstorms, was an alluring proposition. These were all enticing aspects to the trip, but I knew from other excursions overseas that it is people who make a journey memorable — people's willingness to bring you in and feed you, to help you find your way, or simply to enquire about that peculiar exotic country you came from. That's what this kind of trip was about.

Trying to get a sense of the distances, the remoteness of Chinese Central Asia, was a challenge in itself. Riding new terrain and singletrack, whether in Utah, the Sahara or the Himalaya had always been an incredible experience for me and was a major reason for deciding to travel by bike to a foreign country. I had spent thousands of dollars on bikes over the past decade, living on Vancouver's North Shore where some of the continent's steepest and craziest trails were maintained by equally insane trail builders.

Now I was going to load up my gear and pitch a tent in the

desert. Like backpacking, cycling wasn't the only inexpensive way to travel through a country. There was one big difference, however — pace. A bike affords the luxury to do just that, to pace oneself and see the details of another society at leisure. You can see people working in fields, yaks grazing in marshlands and river gorges dropping steeply into oblivion. Some people attempt to see the world in antiseptic air-conditioned tour buses, elevated high off the ground. They whiz through oasis towns and mountain passes missing out on many things. To me, that's akin to experiencing the barrios of Mexico from a Club Med resort. You can't connect with the people who actually live there. I never did understand those who go on a vacation to France, and then head to Disneyland Paris. What's the point? I had to see things firsthand.

An added responsibility for me that other travellers gladly do without was the task of keeping my bike safe at all times. I had three choices: ride the bike, lock it up or keep it within sight, 24 hours a day. I couldn't cart it around on my back like a backpacker, and if I lost it, unlike a camera or passport, it couldn't be replaced. If my bike was stolen, I went home. It was that simple.

Packing was another challenge for me. I had accumulated 50 kg of equipment and supplies. Overkill. I had everything from state department travel advisory warnings to maps detailing water springs in the desert. I bought malaria pills, altitude sickness medication, water purification filters and a first aid kit. I had several vaccination shots. I needed gear to help me deal with the 45°C heat of the desert and the cold of camping in the Karakoram Mountains at elevations over 4,800 m. I packed clothes for warm, cold and wet occasions and a waterproof bivouac sac (a small tent) for the monsoons in Pakistan. Throw in a down sleeping bag, a Whisperlite stove with fuel canister and a half-dozen water bottles and I was almost ready.

Then came the heavy stuff: my steel-frame Rocky Mountain Fusion (borrowed from my brother Kip), bike tools, 36 rolls of film, two cameras, a tape recorder, a few books, gear cables, and a bicycle computer complete with altimeter. All I needed was food, water and money.

On top of all this was the baggage of my own beliefs and value systems. I was going into a part of the world that was entirely different from my own. It's a funny experience when you travel someplace where teenagers wear Chicago Bulls and Nike baseball caps backwards, just like in Toronto or Chicago. Only when you look a little closer do you realize that, stripped of the hats, all similarities vanish. Without the pop culture symbols, the kids are as distinctly Han or Hindu, Muslim or Mongol as the rest of Asia.

Before my trip, an accountant, stunned by my adventurous itinerary, asked me, "Why would you want to go to Pakistan, China or India? It's so crowded and they pee in the streets." I felt I couldn't answer this question for the number cruncher. Anyone who would understand wouldn't ask the question in the first place. The journey is the destination, sir.

In July of 1997, I left Beijing with two British companions to rediscover Asia's ancient Silk Road. Three months later, I arrived in New Delhi, minus the Englishmen, 5,000 km away from my departure point. I had been arrested numerous times, argued the merits of Islam with Afghan tank commanders, dined with Pakistani royalty and discussed the finer aspects of hashish with local police. I had seen the New China, the beauty and poverty of Pakistan, war-torn Afghanistan and the world's largest democracy in India.

CHAPTER ONE

The Silk Road

From Rhubarb to Ruin

Hundreds of years ago, camel caravans a thousand-strong disappeared into this barren Central Asian wasteland — the brutal Chinese desert. Now their skeletons lie buried forever in vast ravines of khaki-coloured sand. Market towns with mystic names like Bukhara, Samarkand, Tashkent and Kashgar once thrived as way stations and supply depots for weary travellers. Goods were bartered, ideas exchanged and technologies discovered in bazaars where as many as 20 languages filled the air. It is history's most famous trade route.

This is the fabled Silk Road where Genghis Khan marched through the steppes of Asia and Marco Polo journeyed east, bringing news of a legendary Middle Kingdom back to Europe. The Silk Road is not one route but many. It was in reality an amalgamation of several routes, many of them nothing more than mule tracks, stretching over 6,000 km from China to modern-day Turkey. It wasn't until a German geographer, Ferdinand von Richthofen, coined the phrase *Seidestrasse* in the 1870s meaning "Silk Road," that the moniker stuck.

Two thousand years ago, parochial Asian empires, weak from infighting, were suspicious of other nations far beyond their own borders. Although the Roman Empire traded sporadically with various Persian dynasties and kingdoms, not until 200 BC did

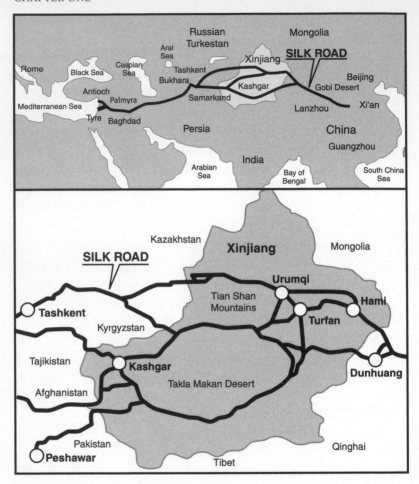

The Silk Road routes connected the world's five great cultural centres –
Greek and Roman, Arabic, Indian and Chinese.

China (then called Cathay) start to investigate what lay beyond its western borders. By the end of the 9th century, the Silk Road changed many of those insular attitudes. Explorers sent by Chinese emperors met with those from Western civilizations in exotic places that have gone by many names: Chinese Turkestan, Sinkiang, Kashgaria, Chinese Central Asia and High Tartary.

Trading became a hazardous business. Tribes often pillaged

each other's possessions in the quest for coveted commodities and territory. One warrior even decapitated his enemy, making a drinking cup out of the skull to celebrate. Men and some women would ride horses and two-humped Bactrian camels for months from Rome and Persia, bringing wool, ivory, glass and Tyrian purple dye (the colour of royalty) to the Orient. The first pomegranates and dates used by the Chinese came from Persia, while pepper and cotton came from India. In return, spices, precious porcelain and silk unique to China flowed west to the Mediterranean along with figs, spices, walnuts and gunpowder. Everything from exotic plants to gold, silver, alfalfa and rhubarb (to relieve menstrual cramps) traded hands.

Where did the silk originate that made these trans-Asian trading routes so popular? The Parthians, who lived near the Caspian Sea, had used large brightly coloured silk banners to blind the Romans during battle: the shimmering fabric reflected the desert heat. The Romans were sure the silk hadn't come from Alexander the Great, who never got farther east than the Indus River. At first, they thought it grew on trees. They doubted that the Parthians, astute as they were, or any other culture could have invented or grown this shining material. Later, Parthian prisoners captured by the Romans revealed that the exotic material came from the Seres or Silk People — the Chinese.

The Romans, at times straining their economy, often paid for silk in gold. Until the 4th century, everyone from trades people to aristocrats in Rome wore the soft fabric, and then the material became synonymous with decadence and was temporarily banned by the empire's elite. The Roman scholar Pliny lectured against the decadent silk as "rendering women naked." He was the first one to indicate to the Roman elite that the material grew on trees.

The Seres are famous for the wool of their forests. They remove the down from leaves with the help of water...

PLINY, 1st century BC

Ancient Asian history written by Chinese scholars reveals that the Chinese may have used silk to make garments as far back as the 27th century BC. Archaeologists continue to discover the origins of silk and found traces of it in Egyptian tombs in archaeological digs of the early 20th century.

The most significant commodity carried along the Silk Road, however, was not silk but religion. The religions introduced on this trans-Asian highway had a more lasting effect on society than anything else. Buddhism from India was introduced to China, later followed by Islam, which dramatically altered the cultural, artistic and ethnic makeup of the Orient.

The Silk Road started in Xi'an in central China, home of the famous terracotta warriors near the Yellow River valley. One route passed between China's Tian Shan Mountains on one side and the northern edge of the enormous Takla Makan desert on the other. The first leg of my journey would start in the midst of these mountains, taking me west across northern China before plunging into the blistering and parched earth of the desert. A parallel westward route (the actual route of Marco Polo) arced around the southern side of the desert, meandering past ancient Buddhist cities like Khotan and Dunhuang. These oases are some of the only cultural reminders of a great Buddhist past, preserved forever in the dust of the desert. Vestiges of the odd remaining caves, grottoes and frescoes now serve as centrepieces on the tour bus circuit.

Both desert trade routes reconnected in Kashgar on the northwestern edge of China. This was the resting spot for me where I would stop travelling west and turn south. The Silk Road diverged in several paths again, crossing over the Pamirs and Hindu Kush Mountains of present-day Afghanistan in a westerly route that pushed on to Persia. This giant Oriental trading autobahn continued through Central Asia via Tashkent, crossing through Samarkand and Bukhara, and both now in Uzbekistan. The route finally ended around Mediterranean cities such as Damascus and Constantinople — the nexus of the Byzantine, Roman and Ottoman Empires.

Other minor routes of the Silk Road went as far as the Caspian Sea and Persian Gulf. The southernmost leg of the Silk Road in Asia branched over the Karakoram Mountains in Pakistan to Leh and Srinagar in Kashmir. The Karakorams would be the last leg of my route, where I planned to cycle down through Pakistan to Afghanistan and into India.

Transportation along the Silk Road occurred in stages. Camel, horse and yak caravans transported merchandise through regional territories. The traders in a caravan would take their wares to the nearest central market and trade them away before returning home. Then another group of merchants would travel the next arduous leg of the route reselling the goods. Caravans exchanged their goods and supplies between Syrians and Persians who resold to the Greeks and Romans. In this way, food staples and new ideas made their way from Rome to Persia, Persia to Turkestan and Turkestan to China and back to Europe.

As the use of the Silk Road routes increased, so did the costs of warding off bandits and invaders, whether by building fortifications or hiring warriors to defend caravans. Simply put, the cost of building forts and walled fortifications such as the Great Wall of China were indirectly passed on to the very people who bought the tin, silk and spice goods at market. One of those Silk Road travellers became more famous than all others for bringing to Europe the attention of the Orient. His name was Marco Polo, an Italian from Venice.

Marco Polo

Without the benefit of Marco Polo's chronicles of strange people, exotic foods and new religions, the Far East would never have spurred Western curiosity as soon as it did. Marco Polo's maps from the late 13th century were considered strikingly concise and rich cartography. They represented in minute detail most of Japan and the Indian subcontinent. They also revealed the degree to which China was thought to control East Asia. Up to 1850, archaeologists were still using Polo's references — the best around

— to mark small towns along the Silk Road.

As a young man, Marco Polo feasted with Mongol emperors and escorted princesses, leaving descriptive records of his tales. He brought back news of a place called Cathay (China), a land where census-takers kept scrupulous records and where cities were connected by intricate canals.

Years after his travels to China, while fighting as a captain on a galley for the Venetians, he was arrested as a prisoner of war. Lying in prison in leg irons, he dictated his tales to a romance writer, Rustichello of Pisa, in the cell next door. The writer first published the fascinating tales in French. The world, seen by many as a cloistered fiefdom of the noble rich, soon began to unravel.

What must be the most famous travel narrative in history was now bound in two volumes, and later translated into English as *The Travels of Marco Polo*. Although many couldn't believe the stories of the cultures and foreign lands that Polo recounted in his book, Christopher Columbus thoroughly scrutinized his own copy before venturing off to Asia almost 200 years later. Poor Christopher, thinking he was headed to Asia, sailed the wrong way, ending up in the West Indies. The rest is history.

Marco Polo's ventures started when his merchant father and uncles were summoned by the Mongol emperor Kublai Khan. The elder Polos, Niccilo and father Maffeo, had just returned to their homes in Venice from a trading expedition to China when the emperor Khan sent word to them to bring back missionaries and papal letters from Europe. The great Khan, then residing in the new capital of Cambulac (later named Peking and then Beijing), wanted to know more about the Roman Catholic Church, Pope Clement IV, and the Holy Sepulchre in Jerusalem.

Young Marco was only 17 years old when the family left in 1271 on a courageous overland trip to see the Khan in China. It's remarkable how anyone could have travelled such lengthy distances so long ago. The Polos first sailed to Palestine and then passed through eastern Turkey to the Persian Gulf (then called the Sea of India). Travelling to Tabriz and Meshed in northern

Iran, they encountered the Curds (Kurds), a race of people Polo called "an evil generation, whose delight it is to plunder merchants." The Polos put to sea again in the Persian Gulf, re-entering at Hormuz, only to head back north to Armenia, and then east through the arid conditions of Afghanistan and onto Cathay, travelling over 9,000 km from their home in Italy.

The Polos went east into Cascar (Kashgar), the crossroads of Asia (and where I would stop for three weeks), reaching China after traversing the Pamir Mountains. There they hooked back up with the main Silk Road. There's some speculation that the group made a detour south into present-day Pakistani Kashmir and even north to Siberia. Four years after setting out from Italy, having survived desert heat, sandstorms, mountain passes and altitude sickness, they arrived. They had made it to Kublai Khan's summer capital, Shang-tu.

Kublai Khan, grandson of Genghis Khan, saw in Marco and the elder Polos a chance to send learned men to the outer regions of the Chinese empire. Kublai Khan soon came to favour this young foreigner who spoke Italian, Turkish, and some degree of Persian and Uyghur, but no Chinese. Marco could be trusted, unlike many of the Khan's self-serving attendants. When Marco befriended the emperor, Khan gave Polo's uncles high-ranking assignments as military advisors, an unusual act towards outsiders. During an earlier visit, Kublai Khan had presented the Polos with a foot-long golden tablet or *paiza* in Chinese, inscribed with words instructing anyone they should meet to give them horses, lodging, food and guides. The emperor assigned the young Polo as an ambassador to the courts of Tibet, Southeast Asia and Burma, where he spent two decades travelling and gathering information.

Marco witnessed and recorded everything from the work of women to the sport of falconry to the life of Kublai Khan and his stud of 10,000 speckless white horses. But Polo's observations were not always astute — he referred to coal "as stones that burn like logs." On the moon-like expanse of the Takla

Makan and Gobi deserts, Polo commented:

> *This desert is reported to be so long that it would take a year to*
> *go from end to end; and at the narrowest point it takes a month*
> *to cross it. It consists entirely of mountains and sands and valleys.*
> *There is nothing at all to eat.*
>
> MARCO POLO, *The Travels of Marco Polo*, 13th century

By 1295, Europe's most important traveller had just spent an amazing 24 years glimpsing inside imperial dynasties and nomadic tribes never before seen by Europeans. Having discovered many new lands for the emperor over the years, the Polos, eager to return to Italy, eventually convinced a reluctant Khan to allow them to escort a beautiful young Mongol princess to Persia. They left with a fleet of 14 three-banked galley ships and crew of 600 for the arduous sea voyage home. Hugging the Malay Peninsula and coastlines of Ceylon and India, they passed through the Arabian Sea on the final leg to Persia before reaching Italy. Disease, famine and hardship killed all but 18 people. Among the survivors were Marco, his family and the princess.

Despite the remarkable accounts of Polo's journeys, several prominent historians dispute whether he ever set foot on Chinese soil. A British librarian, Frances Wood, has postulated exactly that in her book *Did Marco Polo Go to China?* As fascinating as Polo's book was, there are huge oversights about Chinese culture and architecture. Travelling as much as Polo and his family did, how could he omit any mention of the Great Wall or the ideographic scripts of the Orient? Albeit, the wall was in disrepair during Polo's time and not prominent until centuries later. Other omissions stand out. Polo's journals lacked any reference to feet-binding, the ancient practice of tying up the feet of young women so that they would be submissive and wouldn't have to work.

As well, Kublai Khan's record keepers made no known notes about visiting Italians, an omission that raises more questions. Italian missionaries in China, however, were often given Chinese names like the Polos, and that may help settle that dispute. Some postulate that Polo recounted the tales of other travellers as well as those of his own family instead of setting foot in China. If Marco Polo ever had an unacknowledged source for his questionable epic tales, history is unlikely to verify it. Was he the biggest fiction writer of his time? No one will ever find out.

China's Technical Superiority and the Decline of the Silk Road

Before planning my trip, I really had no concept of how the Silk Road affected Western civilization. I knew the goods and ideas exchanged thousands of years ago made their way to continental Europe from the Orient. I didn't know how that ancient era had affected my life and those around me.

One of the most important contributions to the West from China was the secret of papermaking, which was in use for at least a thousand years before it reached Europe. For centuries, Chinese books had been written on bark, leaves, silk, tortoise shells and then on paper. In 1907, the Diamond Sutra, the world's earliest block-printed book dating from AD 868, was found in the desert in Dunhuang.

Western science and technological growth may be decades ahead of the Far East today and Galileo and Thomas Edison may have kick-started the New World out of the dark ages, but the Chinese, like the Greeks, were geniuses well before anyone.

Chinese society advanced scientifically and culturally from the early BC years to AD 1400 and is credited with inventing everything from gunpowder, fertilizers, veterinary medicine and ploughs to hydraulic engineering. Other innovations included the abacus (using bamboo chips), porcelain production, playing cards and the writing brush made out of weasel or white goat hair.

A Chinese blacksmith and alchemist, Pi Sheng, invented a clay moveable-type machine in the 11th century. Three hundred years before Johannes Gutenberg, Pi found a way to speed up the printing process and allow for better artistic results, though it is not known to what extent Gutenberg's printing press of the 1430s was influenced by examples from China. Because Pi was restricted to using ideograms (Chinese characters), the press didn't flourish until it was employed in the alphabet-oriented culture of Europe.

Three decades after Gutenberg's invention, the printing press became one of the chief means by which the Renaissance transformed Europe. The medieval world made way for the modern world. The printed book became the technological impetus to disseminate ideas that resulted in the democratic revolutions of the 18th century. In time, ideas from one culture to the next led to political changes around the globe.

Trade along the Silk Road made China the wealthiest and most powerful nation in the world through the early centuries of the second millennium. By the late 14th century, the Silk Road started to decline when China's Tang dynasty favoured using the sea routes popularized by the Europeans. Goods passed through fewer hands and this kept prices low. Pillaging Mongol aggressors like Genghis Khan could easily be avoided by using the maritime trade routes. Bales of silk began to arrive from India, a less costly journey than the overland routes through the deserts and mountains. Silkworm eggs that produced the material as translucent as ice were finally smuggled out of China by Nestorian Christian monks. This led to Persia discovering the fine art of sericulture (silk making), demystifying the source of the miracle fabric previously available only from China. The oceans became the new trading highways and the secrets of silk and papermaking had been revealed. The greatest days of the Silk Road were over.

But this chain of Asian bartering centres and market towns needed one final push into oblivion. As empires came and went, the Egyptian, Mesopotamian and Roman cultures, along with the Indus Valley farther east, all developed in isolation from China. In the West, this societal evolution led to an appreciation of differences. In the Far East, the lack of it led to an attitude of superiority and arrogance.

The Chinese believed they were peerless, unsurpassed in wisdom. Just like the Excited States of America who navel-gaze, smug in the assurance they will eternally be the world's mightiest economic power, the Middle Kingdom clutched at the same illusion. The Chinese were convinced they lived in the hippest, coolest, most righteous place on dear Mother Earth. And they were probably right, albeit for a half-dozen centuries.

One of the problems intrinsic to China's trading attitude toward the outside world was how they valued the goods they swapped with other states. From the perspective of the Middle Kingdom, the rest of Asia was simply an amalgam of inferior vassal states. When envoys from tribes brought warhorses and other goods for the Chinese, the gifts were viewed as offerings from a more barbaric or primitive people. The goods sent back west were regarded by China's emperors as greater in value because the Chinese thought themselves a superior race.

By the 15th century, after Marco Polo had visited Asia, the technological head start that China had exhibited over Western civilizations slowed to a snail's pace. China became xenophobic and fell behind. The Middle Kingdom shut out foreigners and their ideas after years of internal dissension and marauding invaders. China's rulers, always suspicious of foreigners, became increasingly more so. China fell behind. The country's outlying regions fell into disarray, leaving much of the desert and northwestern provinces unguarded.

Pre-eminence by a culture can flourish only if the ruling elite of that society responds to new ideas. Science alone cannot push a nation forward. When overseas explorations were throttled back by new emperors, the status quo in China prevailed. Exploring beyond the nation's borders ended. The Great Middle Kingdom was stifled.

Three things determine the progress of one culture over another: social values, political rivalry and economic modernization. In 1215, the Magna Carta gave individual property owners in England a stake in their own work. They could realize a small profit. In China, the mandarins and servants of the state served a centrally controlled government with a stagnant economy. The pluralistic West and the isolationist East were at odds. One aggressively enforced imperial trading practices, the other turned inward like a confused child.

By the 1800s, the great powers of the West, Russia and Great Britain were engaged in a turf war. This conflict reinvigorated some of the old Silk Road towns. The British wanted to explore the territories north of India on the other side of the Karakoram Mountains to add to their empire. To the west of Chinese Turkestan, as the region was still called, the Russians were watching with similar ambitions. As if on a huge chessboard, cartographers, geologists and spies were manoeuvred into China in a game of cat and mouse. Consulates were set up in Kashgar, the very spot where Marco Polo and camel caravans had travelled hundreds of years earlier. So began the Great Game.

My travels over these ancient trade routes were not so much a cycling excursion as a cultural odyssey back in time. I knew the food wouldn't always agree with me, my budget would be shot to hell and my itinerary wouldn't always work out as planned. I tried not to create too many expectations for myself. I always left myself a way out — a plan B. If the food turned my stomach inside out, then I was better for the experience. If I careened around a corner on the highway and came face to face with an erratic Pakistani truck driver, then I would hopefully be more in tune with how fragile my own destiny was. If I were stupid enough to argue with someone holding a gun in Afghanistan — well, by that point the situation would be hopeless.

Ominous and forbidding, enthralling and educational, this ancient trade route, or rather the remnants of it, beckoned me to seek out the cultures and mysteries of a land that had drawn Marco Polo away from his home hundreds of years ago. Off I was to one of the world's ancient capitals, a city of many names — Cambulac, Peiping, Peking and Beijing.

Beijing and the Great Wall of China

CHAPTER TWO

A Stranger in Beijing

Like many travellers before, I had come to China to be whisked back through time. I came to discover a land of contradictions where concubines, feet-binding and brutal massacres were part of a fascinating 4,000-year history. Beijing was a bold, austere-looking and mysterious city; its striking features withheld a thousand ancient secrets.

Beijing was both a beginning and an end for me. Months of planning, preparation and anticipation were at an end. Finally, I could begin my journey across Central Asia and the Indian subcontinent. I would spend the next three months retracing the Silk Road on a mountain bike through barren deserts and snow-capped mountain ranges. When I arrived in July 1997, billboards everywhere proudly proclaimed "Visit China. Experience our one government, two systems." Hong Kong had just reverted to Chinese control 10 days earlier as the last vestiges of Pax Britannica disappeared into the bowels of the world's oldest civilization. China was bracing for change. But it didn't know how or in which direction to turn.

With 1.2 billion people, the People's Republic of China is the world's most populous nation, similar in geographic size to Canada — but there the comparisons end. The country is still suspicious to this day of the foreigners who stroll through its gates.

When I entered Beijing, China was being pressured by dissidents, foreign leaders and Chinese students to change. The country was on the verge of testing a new hybrid economic system based on socialist values and the capitalism of Wall Street. Whether this great socioeconomic experiment would work was still uncertain. Some say it has to if the country is to become an economic powerhouse or quite possibly a world superpower in the next century.

China is still very much a feudal society. With developing-world living conditions, it has been trying to catch up to the West. Unlike Europe, China hasn't had the benefit of an Industrial Revolution. Europe had gone through this necessary transition in order to change from an agrarian society to a mechanical and technological one. China had not. It lacked the proper educational infrastructure, scientific expertise and social cohesiveness necessary to jump into the 21st century. The difficulty of pulling the squalid shantytowns and overdeveloped East Coast cities out of poverty was immense.

During my Vancouver–Beijing flight I was surprised at the wealth of many Chinese passengers whom I talked to. Diamond rings, Sony Discmans, Yves Saint Laurent handbags and white pumps galore seemed to be *de rigueur* for many of the tanned passengers. Our shared journey to the 700-year-old capital city soon came to an end; I was on my way to eight-hour days of cycling and they to their families, friends and businesses.

The small Beijing Capital Airport where I landed reminded me of the one in Casablanca during a trip to Morocco — decaying and decrepit, but functional. Unlike the tourists departing my plane, I would not seek the amenities of the air-conditioned hotels and ventilated tour buses. When I stepped onto the tarmac, the stifling 33°C heat hit me like a sauna, quickly turning my cotton shirt into a wet rag. The muggy air quality and humidity was a major adjustment for me being from the "Wet Coast" of Canada. Now it was time to check through customs, a process that could turn into a paperwork nightmare.

I had heard horror stories about other travellers who had tried to bring bikes into China and were denied. Once off the plane, they were told that bicycles could only be brought into the country at certain entry points — namely Shanghai. How much of this information pertained to the China of old? How much was the attitude of a single stubborn bureaucrat? I didn't know.

The two British cycling mates that would join me on my trip, Tony Shenton and his friend Tim Edwards, had doubts about getting their mountain bikes through customs successfully. In Britain, they were informed that Beijing was not a designated place for importing bikes. Maybe they were given the bureaucratic runaround because they flew into Beijing on Air China rather than the Canadian airline that I had chosen.

Tony and Tim had encountered some difficulties at the Chinese Embassy and Air China office in Britain during the planning stage of their trip. The two Brits were repeatedly questioned where they would be staying. This posed a problem since we would be constantly on the move on our bikes, staying a few days in villages to rest at most. Their plans were left in limbo until two weeks prior to their departure date. They didn't know whether they would be permitted to bring a bike aboard their Air China flight — again, another downside to organizing unsupported bike trips in foreign countries.

Each year China opens up a little more, but the attitude of the police remains very narrow-minded. Tourists spend a lot of hard-earned currency in China and are still looked upon with suspicion. Independent travellers, those backpacking or even more infrequently, biking without the support of a guided tour company, are especially mistrusted.

The Chinese bureaucracy, especially the police, does not necessarily follow the law consistently. The same officer will give two different answers over two days. It all depends on the officials, their education and whether they got out of bed on the right side that morning. Line up five Public Security Bureau officials (the Chinese police) and you'll get six answers.

It seems whatever a police officer says is the law of the land —

that day only, of course. Never make the mistake of arguing with the Chinese, whether it be the citizens or the police. Let them save face. Honour is coveted above all else in Asia. If you back someone into a corner in an argument, you will never get your way. Give them a way out. Don't embarrass them and they will make you a friend.

Either way, I think I was prepared for customs. I brought all the proper documents for my trip translated in triplicate. I had papers in Mandarin, Urdu and Pushtu for Chinese border officials, Kashmiri tribal chiefs and Afghan warlords respectively.

I was initially worried that bringing in several thousand prescription pills for my epilepsy might pose a problem at customs. If the pills were seized as drugs (amphetamines and barbiturates were part of my medication), I could be detained. If some bureaucrat decided to confiscate the pills, I would have to go back to Canada. My own street smarts or tragic lack thereof would be put to the test: when to barter, when to be diplomatic, when to be confident or simply when to drop to my knees and beg. There would be a time for each on several occasions.

In the end, getting my mountain bike and medication through airport security went without a hitch — probably the last time things would be so smooth. Thousands of kilometres from home in the cultural and intellectual capital of China, I realized that all my plans were coming to fruition. The feeling was a little premature, but the alluring desolation of the Silk Road seemed very close now.

Tony and Tim, who had flown in from London a day ahead of me, were waiting for me somewhere among the masses in the airport lobby. I noticed there were relatively few signs in English as I gathered my gear and bike box. No French, Spanish, German or even Japanese signs, let alone any other conventional languages found in most overseas airports. I soon met up with my British cycling mates as I was chatting with a group on holiday from Olympia, Washington. The two Brits and I outlined our bike route to the Americans, and one of the women quipped facetiously, "Not much into Third World countries, are you?"

Tony and I had cycled the Atlas Mountains in Morocco in 1994. Tony was a very fit 57-year-old private school teacher from Hertfordshire, England, who had cycled many times throughout Iceland and Morocco. He and I knew what to expect from each other when on the road together. Our North Africa trip with its winding passes and mountain descents helped us sort out each other's strengths and weaknesses.

Tim, 10 years younger than Tony at 47, complete with earring and full arm tattoos, taught English Literature at a local London university. He and I had never met. With our limited cycling wardrobe, we would all get used to seeing each other in the same one or two sets of clothes for the next 12 weeks. Tim was dressed in his University of Firenze T-shirt and purple sweatpants, me in my shorts and sleeveless polymer nylon shirt and Tony in his cycling jersey and Aztec jogging pants (or that's what I called them).

This was the first time any of us had travelled to Asia. Either you were of Han descent or you were not. The Han Chinese are the largest ethnic group in China comprising 93 per cent of the population. Everyone else fell into that other group — the non-Han, Tibetan Buddhists, ethnic Muslims, Scandinavians, English, Americans and Ugandans — everyone.

If you weren't born in China, forget it. You were the *lao wai*, the Foreigner. Even the overseas Chinese, those of Chinese ethnicity born in the West, are treated as second rate. They are above the foreigners but below the Han. And if you went shopping you were labelled the *wai bin*, the rich foreign guest who would be charged twice as much as the locals.

We purchased our plane tickets (foreigner price, of course), for the forwarding flight to Urumqi. Urumqi was a large city 2,000 km northwest of Beijing near the Mongolian border. It would be the starting point for our cycling trip after spending a few days in Beijing. We left our bikes and gear at the airport baggage centre and headed outside to the airport cabstand where we had our first lesson in being fleeced.

Unless you instruct the Chinese to do something or ask them

a question, they will rarely anticipate what you want. The Chinese react to situations rather than acting or expecting, hence, they can come across as being rude. In a taxi, don't expect to be asked where you want to go. You have to tell them.

If you are in a store shopping, you will most likely think the Chinese are ignoring you if all you're doing is browsing. Having your money out on the counter indicates intent to purchase to the merchant and doesn't waste their time. The idea of customer service (assisting the browsing shopper or asking "Can I help you?") is an alien concept. Actually, they aren't ignoring you; they're just being efficient business people. I was in a foreign place embarking on a bike trip over the top of the world. Customs were likely to be different here.

"The Tian Tan Sports Hotel, please," said Tony to one of the drivers standing next to a long line of cars.

"Two hundred yuan," the driver shouted back in herniated English.

After much questioning and gesturing as to the cost of the ride, we agreed like lost tourists that what we were being told was a fair price. I vaguely remembered something about red and yellow cars being the only authorized taxis as we stepped into an unmarked blue Nissan. With neither meter nor commercial markings, we were hardly off to an auspicious start.

The 25-km air-conditioned ride into downtown Beijing was uneventful until we realized we were being driven to the wrong place. Tony had booked us into an inexpensive place called the Tian Tan Sports Hotel. It turned out to have a very similar name to a nearby four-star hotel — the Tiantan Hotel. Guess where our driver took us? Not the cut-rate budget hotel.

As we pulled up in our freelance taxi at the Tiantan Hotel, I muttered something about the opulence of the place with its concierge staff and bellhops. It all seemed a little out of place. No sooner had we filed into the air-conditioned lobby of the 20-storey building than we found out it wasn't our hotel. Walking back outside, we realized the taxi was nowhere to be seen. It had vanished. Live and learn.

Luckily, our Tian Tan Sports Hotel was within walking distance and the three of us left on foot, bruised egos and all. The next day we discovered we had paid double the going rate for an airport cab. Upon arrival at our hotel, the one-hour room negotiations began. First there were no single rooms, and then no rooms for three. After much bartering (a skill learned in Morocco) and a price reduction, we put into our beds to rest.

At first, Beijing looks like any other cosmopolitan Asian city. Large modern-looking office buildings with glass façades are nestled among ragged apartments and row houses. From the small towns in rural provinces to hotels like ours in Beijing, the city and people with their TVs, satellite dishes, pagers and cell phones give the impression of a modern China. The truth is anything but. Many of the new buildings such as our hotel are falling apart, their shiny exteriors just candy coating on otherwise decrepit interiors. Plumbing systems leak, foundations crack and drywall chips. Things are not what they seem.

The satellite dishes serve large American hotel chains, entire apartment blocks and, more rarely, individual homes. Most electronic goods are just cheap versions of consumer products readily available in the West. Much of this is due to the purchase of technology from American and European companies. They sell outdated manufacturing plants to the Chinese to make steel beams or computer chips, but don't give them the patented processes to produce a quality product. The results are instruments with tolerances that aren't as precise, engine parts that wear out sooner and electronics that break down.

When we settled down to watch the first day of the Tour de France on TV in our room, China's technological backwardness soon became evident as we tried to tune in the channels. The television, however, flickered away, its intermittent signal fading out every few minutes. We knew that the likelihood of seeing a working TV set where we were headed, let alone one that carried the BBC and the latest football matches from Liverpool and

Manchester, was next to nil. Tony and Tim hunkered down for a few hours in front of the boob tube after endlessly fiddling about with the antennae. The Brits were addicted to cycling, rugby and football and were intent on getting a final glimpse of this last symbol of civilization. Frustrated with the TV, we decided to explore the streets of Beijing after the sun went down in the hopes that the temperatures would be more bearable.

Karaoke Brothels

It was humid, like a hot summer night in Ottawa except muggier. I had taken to wearing walking shorts, a T-shirt, Teva sandals (a gift from my landlords back home) and a black Barenaked Ladies baseball cap — a favourite Canadian rock group of mine. As the three of us walked through the streets, we discovered that half of Beijing had also gone out for a stroll, many of them now sitting by the roadside cooling down. The other half of the city seemed to be sweeping the garbage in front of their shops and homes into neat little piles. Everyone was being so tidy, leaving the piles of leaves and garbage in the middle of the sidewalk.

Beijing has many six-lane streets divided down the centre by white metal gates, and bordered on the outside by wide pedestrian and cyclist lanes. Cars, trucks, mopeds, buses and people moved in organized anarchy. They all seemed to be in a constant state of near collision, continually missing each other by inches. No one had discovered the turn signal switch on the automobile. I never once saw a car signal in advance. Any obedience to traffic laws as practised in the West was lost on a newcomer like me. I darted through the chaos of vehicles and people to the other side. Sensory overload had begun. In this vehicular melee, I recognized a great entrepreneurial opportunity — driver education schools. Someone could make a fortune trying to teach Beijing's 11 million residents how to improve their driving skills.

Walking through the narrow *hutongs* (alleyways), we stopped at the Carol Club, an innocent-looking karaoke bar. The first floor was a dimly lit lounge, the second level was full of karaoke rooms and the fourth was a nightclub — all relatively quiet. The third floor, however, was where all the activity was. Rock and roll music boomed down the hallways. Tall young Chinese women smartly dressed with immaculate makeup went in and out of private rooms; some were carrying drinks and others were taking away linen and bed sheets.

I made my way up to the third floor where singing could be heard from behind glass doors. When one of the doors opened, I caught a glimpse into this tiny microcosm of mini-stag parties. Most of the rooms had several men inside; their neckties loosened as they were entertained by two to three women. This was China's version of the Mustang Ranch except a little subtler.

I later found out that businesses like this were quite common around Beijing. Most had karaoke sound systems set up to entertain young Chinese men. The emphasis was on racking up the bill with overpriced drinks, appetizers and lots of friendly chit-chat. Women would at first entertain the older businessmen or college kids before splitting off to separate rooms where money changed hands and sex began. Booking a room to have sex with one of the ladies of the night was rarely the sole purpose of the visit. This was an evening affair. These karaoke brothels were not the pay-by-the-hour type. They were almost like Swedish massage parlours except by group appointment. What was a little lovemaking with an Asian princess unless you laughed and sang songs for four hours first?

I looked around for Tony and Tim. I concluded this wasn't a place where we could sample some of Beijing's finest food. Then I heard Tony yell to me from the other end of the hall.

"It's a brothel, just a bloody brothel, Brady. Don't waste your money," he said.

I didn't.

Another habit of the Chinese that can take a bit of getting used to is the inclination to spit on the ground. Anytime, anywhere. Even if you're crossing right in front of the mucus-hurling person, don't take it personally. They're not trying to see how close they can get to your sandals without hitting your feet. Depending on the surfaces, sometimes it can become quite slippery if enough people unload their saliva in a given area. This was a particular problem in front of our hotel.

Spitting is a common practice throughout many parts of Asia. You're just in another culture and have to get used to it. It is the little differences like this that separate the tourists from the travellers. Travel means finding out that other cultures are more than the sum of their museums. If you don't like it, you can go back to Las Vegas or Cincinnati or wherever you're from, but there's probably somebody from an Asian country horking on those streets, too.

Barbarians at the Gates

The day after our karaoke experience, Tony and I awoke to find that Tim had been out since dawn for a walk. Tim had gone to Tiananmen Square to watch people fly their kites and practise martial arts. Meanwhile, Tony and I were getting acquainted with the shower facilities that seemed to have not one, but two, hot water taps. We all wanted to visit the Forbidden City in the few days we were in Beijing before traveller mode occurred and we started to cycle the mountains and deserts.

Tony and I had found a bike rental shop next door to our hotel with full suspension frames and high-end Japanese Shimano parts for sale. We wanted to check it out and take some bikes for a spin — but first, Chinese tea. Soon Tim returned for our morning tea ritual. Every morning, the chambermaids dispensed tall silver canisters of hot water to our room. Green tea or *cha*, is served in all restaurants and hotels in these containers. Only in expensive American hotels in large cities will you find the black tea Tony and Tim were used to back in Britain.

Being British and all, Tony couldn't pass up advising the hotel staff on the particular requirements of serving tea the English way. Tony would insist that sugar and cream be brought to our rooms. The staff wasn't accustomed to this, as green tea in China is taken plain. Tea strainers are not widely available in China and the tea is often weak by Western standards. The leaves often float at the bottom of the cup. This bothered Tony to no end. The Brits liked their tea and they liked their football. Don't mess with either. Tony and I had yet to drink anything in China that matched the fresh mint tea leaves of Morocco. During that trip, we would drink this amazing tea each morning before cycling through the mountains. Chinese tea was definitely different.

After hiring crude three-speed bikes for $1.50 a day, we headed off for breakfast to McDonald's. The breeze in our hair was the only relief from the sapping humidity. We crossed roads with names like Changwenmennei Street and West Chang'an Avenue, cycling through the wide boulevards. McDonald's may have been a perverse choice on this polluted haze-filled day, but almost every traveller seems compelled to stop at one when abroad, whether in Moscow, New Delhi or Budapest. I can't explain it, but the attraction is almost as novel for a Westerner as it is for someone in Beijing.

Pizza may be the most popular food on the planet, but McDonald's hamburgers are the most ubiquitous. The Happy Meal signs and the clerks' red-and-white uniforms are the same everywhere. Even the buns look like they came from the same bakery. As we succumbed to eating our American-style breakfast like obedient foreigners, a shouting match erupted between some of the staff and a Chinese customer.

One of the managers, a woman, came out from behind the kitchen door and started to berate a female customer. In front of everyone, the two women went at it for over five minutes yelling back and forth like a bitter married couple. Maybe the coffee was too cold or someone left a hair in a Big Mac? I can't imagine what caused the quarrel or what it would take for a Canadian McDonald's employee to step from behind the counter and confront a customer like that. Outside near the front entranceway, oblivious to the public spat going on inside, a little boy sat in the lap of a plastic Ronald McDonald statue. McDonald's, the home away from home, was now a sign that we were in a foreign land.

The golden arches were only a few minutes away from Tiananmen Square, a huge expanse of concrete built in the 15th century that sprawls four city blocks. Behind the immense square is the Forbidden City, with enormous entry gates 20-m tall mounted on massive balled hinges. Off-limits for 500 years to the public or "old hundred names" as the Chinese say about the common folk, the Forbidden City was the exclusive domain of emperors and mandarins. At one time, drums were beaten to signal the arrival of visiting dignitaries.

Now the Forbidden City is open to view for a small fee. You can stroll through places with jovial names like the Hall for Cultivating Character and Halls of Medium and Supreme Harmony. The roofs of the Imperial Palace and temples inside are painted dark crimson red — the colour of prosperity. Guides and vendors at souvenir booths compete for your money by selling audiotapes, lapel pins and pamphlets boasting of the treasures that once adorned the many palace rooms. Everything from Kodak film, Buddhist statues, Coca-Cola and bottled water are flogged out of street-level stalls, reducing the whole experience to one big cultural tourist attraction.

As I stood in line for tickets at the entrance gate to the Forbidden City, I noticed we weren't getting anywhere. There must have been over 200 people in front of us. The line seemed to actually be getting longer. The Chinese don't queue I discovered. They assault a ticket counter, crowding it in a wedge shape, everyone trying to get to the front first. Queuing is a foreign concept, something for polite unobtrusive dull Canadians to do as they line up for their Starbucks coffee. The result is hectic ticket booths and train station lineups that turn into free-for-all crushes near any counter or person in uniform.

Centuries-old artwork was scattered about inside this huge walled inner city. At the Garden of Peace and Tranquillity, the statues of two gold Chinese unicorns with wavy spiked tails and evil-looking claws sat watch. After wandering through the endless maze of pavilions and temples, I was lost. Tony and Tim were nowhere in sight.

Then I bumped into a German woman and her mother near one of the Chinese unicorn guardians. The daughter Ruth taught German Literature at the Danish University of Odense and was on a month-long trip with her mother. Like me, Ruth had never quite fathomed the enormity of China or appreciated the depth of its cultural riches. Over the next five hours, we wound our way through the ancient sanctuaries and temples where gossiping mandarins once advised enigmatic emperors. Golden ceramic dragons and celestial horses lined the edge of many of the palace roofs. The temple's architecture with its imperial yellow trim and immense wooden doors stood eternal in time.

The entire site within the Forbidden City was for centuries home to state ceremonies. From these walls emperors and Mao Zedong addressed the masses. The student demonstrations and massacre in Tiananmen Square in June 1989 was but one of many gatherings where those critical of government policies shouted their indignation to autocratic regimes. Unfortunately, many of those demonstrators, both before and after Tiananmen Square, were sent to labour camps never to be seen again.

The People's Armed Police, a crack paramilitary division of the People's Liberation Army, was responsible for most of the deaths in Tiananmen Square in 1989. Soldiers chased down civilians in the streets, shooting them in the back. Others raked apartment buildings with gunfire and shelled demonstrators with artillery from tanks. In the end, hundreds to thousands died. The exact number is not known because many of the dead were taken straight to their families instead of hospitals. If the government found out who the parents or family members of the demonstrators were, they might be interrogated, jailed or tortured.

Like the German women in the Forbidden City, I met others visiting Beijing for the first time. Back at my hotel later that night, I decided to go out dancing with two Swedish girls who were staying down the hall from us. The two Scandinavian backpackers, Lisen and Joanna, were making their way through South Asia. It was their first time away from their native Stockholm and they wanted a male companion to chaperone them at night in this unfamiliar city. We decided to go for a burger-and-fries binge at the Hard Rock Café. I was determined to have one last night by myself before committing to travelling day in and day out with Tony and Tim.

Joanna in her green and yellow sarong, Lisen with her little backpack-purse combo strapped to her shoulders and me in my sandals and shorts headed out for a night of dancing. The bands at the Hard Rock Café were playing your typical top 40 Western hits. The three of us loved to dance and spent the next four to five hours eating, drinking and thrashing around the dance floor. After the restaurant closed, we walked the dark streets, poking our heads into the late-night shops and eateries. By 4 a.m., the girls and I were almost out of money and exhausted from an evening of dancing. We took a taxi back to our hotel and collapsed in our separate rooms.

The following sunrise came all too early for me. My head hurt. Then I had that sinking feeling you get when you know something is amiss. Where was my money? Looking over at the bedside table, I saw my debit card and some Chinese notes. Good. But where was my credit card? I turned my bed sheets upside down. My Visa card was missing.

I quickly regretted going out dancing with the Swedes. I had only brought $1,500 for the first month or so of travel. I had access to a second credit card account, but that didn't become valid until September — eight weeks away. I felt like I was back in university having an anxiety attack with an overdue term paper. As usual, Tony calmed me down, helping me retrace my steps that night. It proved futile. The Visa card was nowhere around and the hotel and restaurant staff hadn't found anything. This would prove to be some sort of trip karma that would plague me for weeks.

Had I let it fall out of my wallet while I was walking with Lisen and Joanna through the dark streets at 2 a.m.? Or had someone stolen it while we were on the dance floor? I couldn't even be sure if Lisen or Joanna might have taken it. I doubted it. I walked down the hall to their room but neither of them could remember anything. The Swedish girls, the Brits and I had one more day together in Beijing before checking out. Maybe we could find my credit card before we flew out of Beijing to Urumqi.

That afternoon the five of us were going to see the Great Wall, a trip planned the previous day. I wanted to hire an extra taxi with Tony and Tim to take our mountain bikes so that we could ride down the hillsides beside the wall. Our bikes, however, were still packed in boxes at the airport and it wasn't feasible to go get them for this short trip. Instead, we took two vehicles and Lisen and Joanna came along.

Now one of the world's great medieval wonders, the Great Wall is divided into three renovated sections, much of the rest decaying in ruins. The closest and most crowded section is at Badaling, a two-hour drive north of Beijing, where we were headed.

The Great Wall

The Great Wall of China is massive, majestic and grand. At one time it stretched for 5,000 km, though some claim it was much shorter. Poetically, the Chinese call it the Wall of 10,000 Li. One li equals a half a kilometre. It is impossible to photograph its full length. It isn't one place but many, stretching from the mountains of Korea to just south of the western deserts. It's visible from space — one of the greatest engineering achievements of all time.

Of all the shrouded mysteries of the Middle Kingdom, the Great Wall is the most amazing. For many, it's a dream come true to see the wall, to climb its granite steps, some more than a metre high. It's wide enough to drive a tank over or land a Cessna on if you dared.

The Great Wall was initially a series of walls built by different dynasties over one thousand years to ward off raiding nomadic tribes such as the Huns and the Mongols. As the wall expanded, it became more sophisticated in design. More importantly, however, it became inexorably linked to the success of the Silk Road. By the 16th and 17th centuries, the wall was a

huge defence mechanism. Where the wall peaked over moun-
taintops, crenellated ramparts and granite or rammed earth
watchtowers were added.

Everyone from peasants to soldiers captured from invading
tribes was forced to labour away, building and maintaining the
wall. Workers burned piles of dung and straw to stay warm during the cold winters. Others signalled those in far-off guard towers if invaders were spotted. Narrow trails winding through the
mountains along the wall were the only supply routes for food and
building materials. Today, virtually all sections are still only acces-
sible by gravel roads.

One peasant, Meng Jiangnu, as Chinese folklore goes, was worried that her husband would freeze to death during the harsh
Chinese winters as he slaved away on the wall. To keep him warm,
Meng sewed a padded jacket made from cotton and climbed the
rough hillsides for days carrying the finished coat. She arrived at
her husband's campsite only to be informed that he had died.
Falling to her knees, Meng wailed so loudly that 20 li (10 km) of
the wall collapsed in pieces. In front of her lay her dead husband
buried among the rubble. Her grief was so colossal over the loss
of her husband and the horrible working conditions he had to
endure, that she proceeded to drown herself in the ocean.

Here at the Badaling section where thousands like Meng's husband toiled in misery, the wall stretches from east to west, rolling
up over small green bushes and tree-laden hills. There must have
been at least 5,000 people on the wall that day. We walked past
workers sweeping up construction debris who were dressed in
white shirts and wide-brimmed hats to keep the sun off. After two
hours of sweating profusely in the midday sun, the five of us
reached the end of one section. We dipped into a turret tower to
catch some shade and rest from the blistering sun.

Tony, Joanna and I wanted to walk to the end of the wall. Up
ahead a little way we could see that the wall was crumbling, but
this last section was closed to the public. The steps beyond were
impassable; a metal gate barred further access. Off to the side of

one walled section, a small military-style underground bunker with green doors lay built into the hillside. Cable cars led out one end of the underground berth down a chairlift system that followed a shallow ravine through the surrounding hills.

When I was a little boy, my father went to China in an era when Mao was revered like god. You couldn't even buy a souvenir or can of Coca-Cola at the Great Wall. The Western-style tourist kitsch souvenirs hadn't permeated the far corners of the Middle Kingdom — yet. Today, the entranceway to the wall is an open experiment in government-sanctioned lapel-pin souvenir-hawking capitalism. Camels with bright red canopies covering their backs parade around the entranceway. A 360-degree amphitheatre shows 15-minute films on the wall's history. Chinese girls sell "Memento of the Great Wall" pins and "I Climbed the Great Wall" T-shirts for ¥20 to ¥80 (yuan, the formal unit of Chinese currency), which converted to $3 to $13 CDN.

As the Great Wall slowly commercialized, China began to change, as well. Like the pioneers who had wandered the Silk Road, it was time for me to see Chinese Central Asia. Time to ride its historic roads and discover the legacy of an exotic land, a new people.

Muslim China: Urumqi

Central Asia at Last

Forms, forms and more forms.

When travelling in China, I could never seem to avoid the omnipresent Chinese bureaucracy. Travellers and citizens alike are inundated with paperwork that follows you everywhere. Bureaucracy pops up at check-in desks, hotels, border checkpoints and bank wickets. I even began to fill out documents, applications and questionnaires when waiting in lines to fill out additional forms.

My British cycling mates Tony and Tim were headed with me to Urumqi (pronounced O-room-chi), the Muslim capital of Xinjiang (pronounced Shin-jang) province in northwest China. It was here that we would begin our bike trek across the Tian Shan Mountains down into the great Takla Makan desert where the Silk Road traverses Central China. As we gathered our bags and bikes together at the Beijing airport, we realized our flight out of the Imperial City would involve paying more than twice the baggage fees charged to local Chinese (¥1,000 each or $166).

Credit cards aren't accepted when paying for transportation costs within China. I had to adapt to this, as did Tony and Tim, so off to the currency exchange counter we went and with that, more forms. We were expecting to stretch our initial cash draw much further and hadn't anticipated expensive luggage surcharges.

We frantically pushed our way through the chaotic scene of shrieking passengers after triple-taping our bike boxes and putting our panniers and equipment in duffel bags. Our plane was an old blue-and-white Soviet Ilyushin Il-86, first built in 1976 and used by Aeroflot. We walked across the tarmac to board our ungraceful-looking airliner. Like most of the regional Chinese airlines, China Xinjiang Airlines was creatively managed, frequently late, but surprisingly, the biscuits were remotely nourishing. For the first time in my life, I had actually found something better than Air Canada food.

While filling out my departure card mid-flight (yet another form), I noticed from the rivets and metal rollers below my seat that the wide-body jet had been converted from use as a military transport plane to civilian service. As I passed out some Canadian souvenir pins and stickers to the kids seated across the aisle from me, a recording came on with emergency instructions in Mandarin and Cantonese. The man sitting next to me told me that if the plane crashed, the Civil Aviation Administration of China guaranteed a full ticket refund and ¥20,000 in compensation (roughly $3,300). Some deal!

The hair-raising trip was making me wish that the airline stewards sold Valium, but soon the flight was over. I quickly ventured into the cockpit up front, as my two British companions disembarked. I gave a children's book in English to the co-pilot who I had been talking to earlier on the flight. I had brought along several souvenirs to distribute as presents throughout my trip. I knew about the importance of hospitality in Asian cultures and wanted to kind of pre-emptively thank any people who befriended me on our trip. I didn't want to carry the books and other heavy gifts on my bike so I was parting with them now. The pilot was my first real connection with this immensely complex country and he graciously accepted, promising to read the storybook to his kids.

Landing in Urumqi for us was like visiting Las Vegas in the '50s without the neon lights and voice of Old Blue Eyes. Arid hills surrounded the city of one million people while dreary concrete buildings and large co-op housing and apartment units pocketed the core. These faceless buildings, several of them 10 storeys high, are a common feature throughout many of China's larger cities. We thought we had come to the heartland of Muslim China, but realized this was just another urban centre. How interesting could any city be that had a Holiday Inn and Lego-like buses for people movers?

Spartan hotels and desert oasis towns — those that still exist — are no longer visited by camels. Instead, truckers, traders, travellers and tourist groups come by plane, train and bus hoping to catch a glimpse back into history. Most head across the mountains to the southwest and then westward across the desert. Like the tourists, Urumqi would be our gateway to ancient Chinese Turkestan and the northern Silk Road, now a trans-desert trading route for trucks.

On our airport run, Tony and I decided to be a little more judicious with our money than in Beijing where the taxi driver had taken us for the long ride home. Using the bartering skills that we had perfected on our visits to the souks and markets of Morocco (but forgotten in Beijing), Tony put his best phrasebook Mandarin to the test in front of the terminal building.

"Duo shao qian?" enquired Tony of the cabbie, asking how much for the ride into central Urumqi.

Blank look from driver.

"How many renminbi (the official foreigner currency)? How much yuan?" Tony repeated.

Tim replied with a little better accent and got a response. We were in.

Although the three of us were not dressed in the usual tourist configuration of walking shorts, knee-high white socks, Tilley hats and wash-and-wear polyester shirts, we were obviously from the wealthy West. An endless array of corrugated blue-and-yellow steel signs and dumpsters dotted the city streets on our ride in. The roads were noticeably devoid of traffic save for bright little red Suzuki taxis and red-and-blue–striped buses. On the outskirts of

Urumqi, factories with belching smokestacks were interspersed among tenement apartment complexes. Driving on streets with names like Healthy and Bright, we passed colourful billboards in Mandarin and Arabic.

Zella

Smack in the middle of nowhere, 350 km from the Mongolian border, Urumqi is home to 13 of China's 56 ethnic minorities. Most are Muslims of mixed Turkish descent: Uyghurs, Kazakhs, Kryghyz, Uzbeks, Taranchis, Tartars and Persian-speaking Tajiks. The Uyghurs (pronounced Wee-gurs) of Turk and Mongol heritage are the dominant Muslim group in China and have spoken their Turkic language for the past 500 years.

The taxi driver was Uyghur and as it turned out, so was our first Muslim friend. We checked into a local nine-storey hotel and met the first of many people who would double as guides and advisors. We had gathered in a small room where guided tours were booked, set off from the poorly lit lobby, when a young Uyghur girl dressed in a blue-and-white checked shirt introduced herself.

"Hello?" she said in English. "Where are you come from?"

"We are from Jianada," I replied, using the Mandarin word for Canada.

"These two are from London, you know, England?" I said.

"Yes. I am Zella," she said.

Whether courting our business for a trip through the country-side or genuinely curious, Zella Kader became our friend for two days. Zella's curiosity about the West was matched only by my own about her country. What did she think of the Chinese government and the return of Hong Kong to her country? What was she studying at the local university? What was good to eat? Did Muslims feel discriminated against by the Han Chinese? Like most Uyghurs, Zella had broad high cheekbones and dark hair — a little Turkish ancestry mixed in with Asian.

Before letting Zella show us around town, we needed to unpack our gear and take stock. It was time to ration. In our room,

I spread out my belongings; the first aid kit, cooking and clothing supplies, spare bike parts, additional reading material on Central Asia, plus two cameras and a tape recorder. Sprawled on our tiny single cots, Tony and I sorted out our belongings. As the wise elder statesman on this trip, he suggested, actually demanded, that I show him everything I had brought. Tony had seen me cart souvenir after souvenir through the Sahara desert in North Africa on the back of my bike and knew my propensity to gather stuff.

He thought that if I could buy a large enough set of panniers (saddlebags), put enough racks and fanny packs and other carrying cases zip-tied, taped and strapped to the bike, I would lug 500 kg around with me if possible. My philosophy seemed to be, if you're willing to pedal the bike with extra weight, that's your business. Just keep up with the rest.

Tony was right about the weight. We weren't on a three-week jaunt across Morocco's Atlas Mountains. This was a much longer trip. It made no sense to carry more than the absolute minimum. The seven extra sets of white socks, a two-foot-long plastic yellow floor pump, enough Capilene long underwear and clothes to outfit an Everest team, prepackaged camping food, a stove, fuel canister — all of it — was deemed unnecessary. We donated my bike pump, all the extra bike parts and a bit of Tim's stuff to friends and co-workers of Zella. I had brought along a large first aid kit with enough hypodermic needles, syringes, sutures, band-aids, gauze and altitude sickness pills for five people. We consolidated much of our bicycle repair tools, for these were some of the heaviest items in proportion to their size. The less metal, the better.

After sorting out my gear, I headed to the washroom to air out a few clothes. I was in for a little culture shock. Unlike the washroom in our hotel in Beijing, rows and rows of doorless concrete stalls with pit toilets in the tiled floor lined one side of this washroom. On the other side of the room, curtains hung around cubicles used for showering and washing. Everyone from janitors to backpackers to repair workers used the sinks — the same sinks. You wash your face, I'll wash my mop and next the toilet plunger!

It wasn't hard to get used to crouching over the pink tiles in the stalls. Morocco had been the same. These stalls came complete with foot imprints to help guide your visit to sanitation heaven. The squatting position was made hazardous by the wet slimy tiles. You could slip and break your neck falling over backwards with your pants half off, while you tried to keep your clothes from the mire on the floor. "Keep the clothes away from the sludge" became my mantra when using the pit toilets. God knows when they were last cleaned but then again, so what? I was in China, not the Sheraton or even a Motel 6. What else did I expect?

Many Chinese flush before, not after using the toilet — that is only if the flushing system works. Chains hanging from an over head reservoir manually operate most flush systems. Other washrooms have plastic buckets full of water where you have to purge the evil deed down the hatch. If you're lucky, you will find the leftovers of a toilet paper roll in the stalls, probably left by another traveller. In China, nothing is consistent except the inconsistency of everything — even the bowel-shattering food.

Later that night, Zella knocked on our door for a visit. She stared in shock at the walls as she entered our tiny room. We had pinned up several large maps of the desert. They had been formerly used by the US military and I had bought them from a map retailer in California.

"What are those? Where did you get them?" asked Zella, pointing to the maps.

"Close the door, Brady," said Tony in his protective manner, not wanting to attract attention.

Without access to such detailed information, the average Chinese citizen such as Zella was stunned. We didn't exactly come across as the ordinary Canadian or British tourists. Zella's perception of us as three lost souls, stupid enough to attempt to cross the mountains and desert, quickly dissolved. We didn't want her to get nervous and call some Public Security Bureau official to come by and question our travel plans.

We had spent nine months meticulously planning our trip,

co-ordinating schedules, visas and holiday time. I didn't want to raise questions, particularly since we weren't travelling with an organized tour, the norm for most foreigners. We hoped Zella would be our confidante, translator and saviour all in one, helping us get our trip successfully on the road. In the end, we explained to her that we needed the maps to find our way in the desert, to search for settlements that might carry water and to gauge how far we could cycle before camping. This helped calm her down, as she recounted what little she knew about the few towns outside Urumqi.

For the rest of the evening the four of us talked, each as excited by the other's stories as the next. Zella was taking Economics at Jiangxi Economic College. Sending a female family member to postsecondary school was rare in China. Many families don't see the value in educating a daughter who will eventually have children and be unable to work full-time. Zella was in her early 20s and knew that if she wanted a career in a technical or scientific field, fluency in Mandarin was a must, especially for those lucrative government jobs. As a Muslim, things wouldn't be quite that easy.

In China, the ruling Han subtly discriminate against the ethnic Muslim minorities. The Han occupy all major positions of authority in this Muslim province, from top administrative officials to police and immigration jobs. They get preferential bank loans, cheaper homes and better education. Subsequently, the ethnic Muslims ever so gradually have become the have-nots.

Hanification: Muslim–Han Dissent

When the Communists came to power in China in 1949, only 8 per cent of the population was ethnic Han in Xinjiang province. A half-century later, they comprised 38 per cent. The assimilation of the Han into the region, at a rate of 200,000 a year, is referred to as regional "Hanification" in this Alaska-size province.

The swing to Han domination was helped by the Great Leap Forward in the 1960s, a radical program to experiment with agricultural communes under Mao. In the 1950s and 1960s, 360,000

Muslims were executed, half a million Muslims were interned in labour camps and 29,000 mosques were closed. During the Cultural Revolution, Muslims were prevented from learning their written Arabic language under Mao's leadership. This distanced the Muslims from their religion. Billboards and posters were put up in major cities calling for the abolition of the Islamic faith.

The Uyghurs called it cultural genocide, viewing the expulsion to the desert gulag camps as attempts to pacify Muslim dissent. Over 10,000 Uyghurs starved to death due to repressive cultural policies. More than double that number fled across the border to the Soviet Union where a quarter million Uyghurs live in present-day Kazakhstan and Kyrgyzstan. Some Uyghur radicals who promote independence for their region through armed means claim that they have had to put up with forced sterilization and interracial marriages, all of which further inflames anti-Han sentiments.

Since Mao's death in 1976 and the end of the horrors of the Cultural Revolution, Beijing has greatly liberalized its policies toward Islam. It has reinstated the Arabic alphabet for educational use with the Uyghur language. There are even eight different translations of the Koran in Mandarin, as well as translations in Uyghur and Kyrgyz available in state-run libraries. Despite these changes the animosity remains.

The constitution in China guarantees the right of a minority group to be educated in their own language. In reality, Mandarin is indispensable in everyday life. It is not uncommon to see slogans in classrooms stating "You must learn Chinese to master technology" even though the minority of students in Xinjiang are Han.

Religious policy, or rather religious suppression by the government, periodically leads to separatist clashes with Chinese troops. This spoils any apparent co-existence between the two races. The influence of the Han has caused problems for centuries in the region. Beijing, however, would have you believe otherwise. As in Tibet, the Muslims in China would like to separate.

Chinese leaders and those of the former Russian republics have always been concerned about the prospects of an independent

Greater Turkestan — an allusion to an ancient Central Asian Islamic nation. Unfortunately for the Muslims, their independence movement is not as well known overseas as the plight of the Tibetans. Without the publicity in the West, political pressure will never come to bear on the Beijing authorities as it has in Tibet.

It seemed while I was in Xinjiang province that any armed insurrections were unlikely to happen. Five months before my trip, however, a Uyghur rebellion in the town of Gulja resulted in 200 injured and 9 Uyghurs dead. Han shops were vandalized and the Beijing press reported the arrest of 30 Muslims. Twenty more secessionists were later executed and hundreds detained. If the government-sanctioned press published these figures, it's anyone's guess what the truth was.

Amnesty International has suggested that criminals sentenced for execution are part of a government-run organ-donating scheme. The human rights organization claims that many prisoners are often kept alive well beyond their planned execution dates so that their bodies can be harvested for corneas and kidneys. When the much-needed organs are finally requested for transplant, the poor soul in some backwater desert prison cell is, well, let's just say recycled.

Fellow Muslim nationalist groups in neighbouring Kazakhstan and Kyrgyzstan have fuelled acts of rebellion since the fall of the Soviet Union. Charges by China that nearby Afghanistan is training Uyghur nationalists in terrorism further exacerbate the situation. The ongoing feud with the Han and Muslims makes the separatist movement in Quebec seem like a squabble between two impudent children.

The distrust between the Uyghur majority and the Han is often written about with questionable accuracy. Skewed agendas are rife on all sides. The Chinese claim that this area of Central Asia has always been part of China. They also claim that, as in Tibet, the Uyghurs are descendants of the Han Chinese who have lived there since the 7th century. The Beijing government argues that entire farm regions of Xinjiang have been developed specifically for the benefit of the Uyghurs. These projects include the railway extension to Urumqi from Lanzhou and a highway across the Takla Makan desert. The educational system in China boasts that those living in Xinjiang are free to practise their own customs and language.

Archaeologists, however, have discovered that skeletons with high cheekbones of Caucasian descent were buried in the desert long before the Han started to settle there. When government museums mislabel ancient artifacts, deliberately misrepresenting the origins of skeletal remains in favour of a dominant Han culture, what are the Muslims to think? How independent can a population feel when military troops routinely parade through Muslim and Buddhist towns?

Urumqi Markets

As one of China's many ethnic Muslim minorities, Zella's family was given flexibility in complying with the government's one-child policy implemented in 1979. Ethnic Han families who only have one child are given certificates redeemable for preferable housing, money, maternity leave benefits and day care. Many people are penalized when they don't comply with the one-child policy, but the need to keep birth rates up among some of the smaller ethnic groups has created an exemption in Beijing's policy. Zella was, in effect, a microcosm of China's attempts at population control.

Many credit China for taking its population explosion problem by the reins and bringing it somewhat under control unlike India. However, there has been an unfortunate side effect. There are not enough workers or young people being born because of the one-child policy and it is hampering the country's growth. China is getting old.

Amid all our talk, Zella had told Tony and Tim about the Hong Shan markets where cheap Muslim food is served, or rather deep-fried to death, all day long. As soon as we got up the next morning, we decided to sample some spices and increase our proficiency at bartering.

If the city's architecture was a bit Spartan for my liking, the markets were not.

A market bazaar is an amazing thing. Fruit vendors quickly rearranged their produce after each sale to maintain attractive displays. Pillbox hats with gold brocade trim, elephants and prancing horse figures made of brass were for sale alongside medicinal herbs, nuts, apricots and potatoes. Lamb kebabs, yoghurt and basted dough sticks were peddled on street stalls beside large bagel-size breads with poppy seeds on top. The eclectic cuisine more than made up for the coldness of the pencil-pushing administrators.

Nan bread, noodles, and dishes with names like *shashlyk* (kebabs) and *pulau* (fried rice) could be sampled amid live Uyghur music. I wanted to savour the food and see what exotic things were up for barter. So far nothing beat the bear's paws and dried rodents (all available for eating) that I saw on one table. The markets were full of carpets, wool caps, tartan skirts and the region's famous Yengisar knives. From 3 to 12 inches, the stainless steel blades were encased in elaborately carved leather pouches with tiny buckles, often engraved with animal figures.

Reading racks lined the entranceway to most markets where Mandarin Chinese, Arabic-inscribed books and Muslim newsletters sold side by side. The Islamic writings — the books at least — seemed to be bound in the more old-fashioned leather styles. The Chinese selection offered the staid daily newspapers churned out by the state to the "independent" papers also censored by the state. Take your pick.

In addition to the broadsheet newspapers were smaller fiction publications like *Selected '97 Stories* or *Traditional Chinese Fiction* that seemed aimed at the younger Chinese reader. One magazine of collected stories featured a blonde Western woman's head thrown back, eyes closed in desire mode. Her lips were slightly open, displaying gleaming white teeth, her face featuring a Marilyn Monroe–like birthmark. The hair may have been à la Farrah Fawcett from the late 1970s, but the "sex sells" message perfected in the West was not lost on Chinese publishers. Other colourful covers featured Jackie Chan–like action figures with guns.

After a few hours of this, we all needed an escape from the drab concrete cityscapes and sought the unusual. Zella had the answer. We would take a day trip to Heaven Lake.

Heaven Lake

When I heard about Tian Chi, the Chinese name for Heaven Lake, reputed to be a Lake Louise–like sliver of water nestled in the mountains, I had to go. As usual, Zella was the perfect host, ringing us up first thing the following day to get us ready for our trip to the lake.

Our little blue Toyota Hi-Ace van with its blue floral patterned bench seats was typical of the Japanese-made runabouts in Urumqi. If you're on the streets in any large Chinese city, you will inevitably be deluged with minivans and buses. The buses are mid-size by North American standards and are painted with large route numbers on the side. Because it's so expensive to own a car in China (in 1999 the country had only 1.3 million cars), most of the vehicles are econoboxes, either Suzuki taxis usually in red, or Volkswagen Santana sedans (similar to Jettas).

We left from Renmin Park in the middle of town for the two-hour drive to the glacier-fed water retreat. We headed outside Urumqi packed four per row in the van, driving past factories spewing their fumes from burning and smelting operations. Like Eastern Europe, China has neglected its environment to the point where logging bans are placed on entire forests. Over three-quarters of China's pollution comes from burning low-grade coal, not to mention the cars whose emission standards are 10 to 15 times as bad as those in the United States.

Many small and medium-size farms were virtually devoid of all vegetation. Farms were often nestled between coal factories where acid rain, not to mention industrial waste, was destructive to wheat, rice and corn crops. Planning didn't seem to be a factor in locating factories away from agricultural areas, many of them now just barren farmlands, their topsoil useless. According to the World Health Organization, air pollution in northern China is 500 to 900 per cent above acceptable levels. Despite declared attempts to improve the situation under president Jiang Zemin, the government has had a tough time enforcing more stringent emission standards on factory owners.

Closer to Heaven Lake, Zella, Tony and Tim and the eight others with us stopped on the shoulder of the winding gravelly road, a sheer granite wall lining one side. The concrete mileage markers (there were no guard rails) acted as the only barriers to the river below. We knew we were near the mountains by the canvas tent-like yurts that started to appear along the roadside. Yurts are small canvas homes shaped like native teepees about 5 m high, fortified with long two-inch wide wooden lattice panels to support a domed roof. Nomadic mountain herders use these small homes, complete with stove and rugs to sleep on.

Two male Kazakhs passed us on horseback, each headed in the opposite direction. One of the men, with his canvas sneakers, wore a windbreaker jacket; the other wore a suede jacket with blue tassels. The tiny horses, almost shorter than the men, slowly trotted around the corner. Thick red blankets with white-and-yellow embroidered designs lay underneath the horses' saddles that were a mixture of Australian and Western styles — the horns being metal U-shaped bars. This was Kazakh country, the land of the nomad.

A small footbridge provided access to the river below us for a breath of fresh air — a noticeable change from the smog back in Urumqi. Zella soon began to develop a good rapport with Tim as she told him about her schooling in Urumqi. She was still a little bit shy when some of the other passengers started to take photographs, but her coy attitude made up for it.

As the road wound its way up the river towards the lake, the land turned from large, lush fields of sunflowers to a small rapid stream surrounded by conifers. At Heaven Lake, 1,800 m up in the foothills, the scenery actually did remind me of Lake Louise in

Alberta. The forested alpine slopes were not as steep as the Rockies but the view of Mt. Bogda behind the lake was my first picture-perfect look at China's wilderness. The area around the yurts for the overnight guests was crammed with booths where Kazakhs peddled postcards and Kodak film. Small square caps with feathers often rivalled for space alongside multicoloured Nike baseball caps. The marketing wasn't that sophisticated, but everyone who had anything to sell had an earnest sales pitch.

Long, wide, low-slung boats escorted visitors out onto the lake while a tiny red-and-blue gondola tram transported mostly Han tourists up one side of a hill. Underneath the gondola cabs, small horses carried young children and the odd adult around a winding trail that circled the parking lot and lakefront. My official Silk Road bike pilgrimage was still one day away, so I participated in this tourist stop and rode one of the horses for a few minutes. It was like I was back at the petting zoo.

One little Han boy in a nylon blue jacket and Puma running shoes waited in line for the next horse tour as his sister and younger brother played a game of roll the dice. It was a schoolyard game, similar to marbles played in the West — the two children amusing themselves with the marble-like spherical stones. Over at the concession booth, four Uyghur police officers, dressed in their finest blue, sat chatting at a table on orange plastic chairs. Everything was relaxed and tranquil despite the obvious commercial appeal of the site.

The litter around the edge of the lake and behind the shops was something else. Cows munched on old milk cartons and rotting watermelons in one forested section that had turned into a provisional Smithrite garbage bin. The smokestacks and polluted rivers that ran through major urban centres were one thing, given China's poor environmental record, but I expected a relatively remote area like Heaven Lake to be kept clean. I had discovered the reality of the rest of the world.

Tony and I climbed over some rocky outcrops down through the woods that eventually led to a beautiful five-pillared pagoda.

Away from the other sightseers, overlooking the lake, two little white goats grazed nearby as we finally got a sense of the pristine alpine forest, unfettered by the litter and garbage back at the parking lot.

Over at the yurts, Zella had pulled out a pink dress and white headdress from one of the Kazakh homes. The Kazakhs, with their vests and hats, had turned the whole lake into one giant Kodak moment. They were the real entrepreneurial driving forces behind the makeshift shops. One guide, Rasheed, who spoke Japanese, English and Mandarin, was pitching overnight stays in a yurt. An old Kazakh man shaving in front of his yurt provided the one moment that made the day trip worthwhile. Sitting outside on a small wooden stool, red plastic mirror in hand, he gingerly pared away his whiskers like a circumspect barber. Lathered up, he used hot water from a tin teapot, oblivious to passers-by.

A Kazakh family served us soup and noodles, melons and fried rice for lunch. Everyone from North America seemed to be visiting the lake that day as we sampled the boiling hot food. Tony and I bumped into some Americans from Pennsylvania who were busing their way westward to the Karakoram Highway. By late afternoon, it was time to go as the day trekkers packed back into the buses and the others stayed overnight in one of Rasheed's yurts in the forest.

Several Chinese on bikes passed our bus, returning to Urumqi and holding onto huge multistriped balloons 2- to 3-m high. The balloons, almost like large beach balls, were coloured green, red and yellow. I asked Zella what they were for, but she wasn't sure. Most likely, a ceremonial parade of some sort she theorized.

Back in Urumqi, I wanted to use the fax machine and computer facilities in the Holiday Inn. The Holiday Inn was built to accommodate the Han business clientele, high-end Western travel groups and the odd Communist party member. I wanted to write the first of several articles on my travels for my editor at a local newspaper in Vancouver, especially after meeting Zella. Faxing back home was proving more difficult than I thought. It was hard at times to get an international operator. Often I had to rely on a smiling face in a telephone office who exercised god-like powers by letting me know if a connection was successful — usually through indecipherable Mandarin or wild hand gestures.

Between arriving in Beijing, crossing the desert and cycling the Karakoram Highway into northern Pakistan, I only managed to find out a few places where English was spoken in advance of my trip. Few inns or hotels had fax machines. I had three chances in China (Beijing, Urumqi and Kashgar), three in Pakistan (Gilgit, Islamabad and Peshawar) and none that I could be sure of in Afghanistan. India had a fairly good telecommunications infrastructure and would not be a problem.

After typing up my story in the Holiday Inn, I let Tony read it. He feared that the hotel staff might screen any use of Zella's name before being faxed to Canada. Given the Uyghur-Han tension, my fax might backfire Tony thought. The police could harass Zelda.

"You can't fax that story, especially from here. All the staff are Han. You never know who they're going to inform," said Tony.

"Don't be paranoid, Tony," I replied. "I know the government and police are a bit authoritarian but they can't keep track of everything that is faxed or e-mailed overseas."

Neither of us knew the truth. Did I seem overly naïve or was Tony overly cautious?

Big Brother wasn't everywhere in China I told him, but in the end I relented after Tim chimed in, agreeing with Tony. I omitted Zella's name from the story but the whole exercise proved fruitless. After spending $63 on typing and fax expenses, the faxes did not print out legibly in Vancouver on the other side of the Pacific Ocean. My editor would have to wait.

Tian Shan Mountains

The Cycling Begins

It was 4:30 a.m.

"Leave in an hour and hide your bike boxes," advised Zella.

"Put the cardboard in the closet in your room. The police are very strict about foreigners travelling alone, especially in remote mountainous areas," she said to Tony, Tim and I. The Brits had had enough bureaucratic hassles getting their bikes into China that we decided to err on the side of caution and stealth.

With Zella's warning and adieu, I gingerly wheeled my trusty Rocky Mountain bike, stuffed with gear, down seven flights of stairs. Our hotel elevator wasn't operating during these early hours and we had to take the bikes downstairs one bump at a time. Several hundred steps later, I lugged my bike out across the lobby. As the three of us rolled our Rocky Mountain, GT and Diamond Back bikes past the sleepy desk clerk, his head jolted upright. Where were these foreigners going? the look on his face said in bewilderment. What time is it anyway?

We were ready to leave the hotels and good food of the last five days for the next 2,000-odd km. Our immediate goal — cycle over the Tian Shan Mountains.

Outside, as the sun began to rise over the horizon, we began our first day of cycling one of the ancient Silk Road trade routes. The three of us each had two rear panniers attached to our rear bike racks. After a few minor adjustments, we were all set to go. We spread suntan lotion liberally over our arms, legs and faces, secured six litres of bottled water to each of our bikes and were off.

I tuned in my Sony Walkman and let the mellow sounds of Sarah McLachlan drown out all other thoughts. Simply put, this was the beginning of a trip of a lifetime — as rich and exotic a journey as I could imagine. A part of me didn't really care to return to Canada. Sure, I had a job to go back to — albeit at a bookstore going bankrupt — and of course family, but no other substantial ties.

Why settle down and have children when you can travel the continents and see the world's children? For me, as for some others, travelling can be a kind of high. I came to get away — to sever all links with home. Even the word *home* made my skin crawl.

I was free at last.

We crossed the outskirts of Urumqi heading for the foothills of the Tian Shan Mountains in 30°C heat. The Tian Shans (meaning "celestial mountains") run 2,415 km long, about the same length as the Rockies in North America. The Tian Shans separate the Gobi desert and steppes of Kazakhstan to the north and the Takla Makan desert to the south. The steppes, treeless plains meticulously cultivated and farmed by nomads, dominate much of the foothill terrain that lie between the mountains and desert. On the south side of the Takla Makan, China's largest desert, lie the plateaus of Tibet (China's other more infamous autonomous region).

At first we passed through lush cornfields lined with poplar trees, about the only type we ever seemed to see in the countryside. Then we began the climb into the mountains, which were a stark contrast to the arid hills of Urumqi. Canyon walls and a windy dirt road marked our entry into the ever-upward ascent to the mountains. Although the temperatures were a little cooler now that we were climbing above the treeline, we took off our helmets. It was just too warm and the traffic was too light on the roads to warrant any danger.

A few motorcycle sidecars scooted past us carrying goods from the city markets. The blue-and-white Chinese-made motorbikes with their Uyghur drivers, many wearing wool caps, often had huge bales of hay strapped down with bungee cords. It was an amusing sight to see, these archaic two-wheelers putting along poplar-lined roads. Westerners might think that a motorcycle made in the '50s still in use today is behind the times. Unfortunately, it's the only thing available for many in China.

The reality is that many Chinese-manufactured trucks, cars and bikes far outlast anything made in Japan, Germany, Sweden or Detroit. If something breaks, the old give-it-a-whack with a hammer know-how comes into play. If the chassis is corroded through to the floorboards, so what. Everyone keeps driving these rust buckets because they have to.

Like night and day, life outside Urumqi here in the mountains contrasted sharply with the towering office and apartment buildings in the provincial capital. I knew we were entering the mountainous areas where the Kazakhs lived when we started to encounter the occasional flock of sheep. Some Turkic-speaking Kazakh and Kyrgyz herders even shepherd camels, bringing out the real exotic nature of Chinese Central Asia.

Meeting one group of Kazakhs at a construction road site, I took advantage of a weigh scale they were using, putting my bike on it to see how much stuff I was carrying. My handlebar bag, rear panniers, several litres of water, both racks and bike came to 57 kg (125 lbs.). We figured it would take four to five days to cross the mountains, most of which we hoped to ride in warm sunshine under crystal blue skies. We were planning to rest on average every fourth or fifth day. I hadn't lost much weight since leaving Vancouver, but expected to lose more, now that I would be cycling 60 to 90 km a day on the flats.

Our first day went rather quickly as we rode 50 km by noon. After our lunch break, we hit our first descent into a valley, my Canadian flag sticking out of my right rear pannier, flapping in the wind. As we turned a fork in the road, the lush green vegetation on the mountainsides suddenly ceased. We had entered

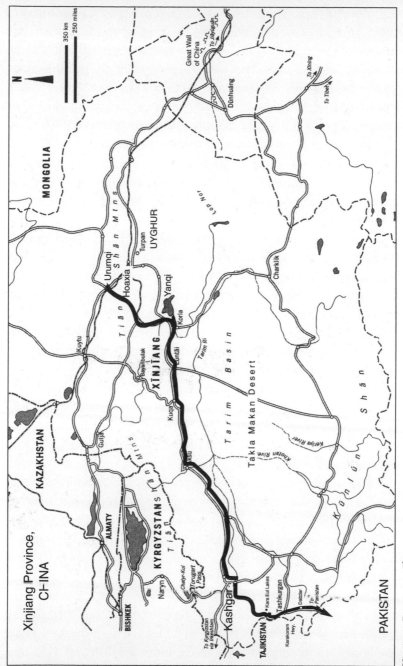

Xinjiang Province, China

the town of Hoaxia, a steel town 2,000 m up in the mountains with huge rusting smokestacks billowing thick black coal fumes. Brick houses with wooden thatched roofs were scattered throughout the town. The white smoke from the steel factory filled the nearby canyons and valleys. The hillsides around town had a white tinge on the soil; all land was stripped of vegetation. It looked just like Sudbury, Ontario, in the 1970s.

The polluted "white valley" made me realize how bad China's environmental problems were. Coal is cheap and plentiful throughout China and supplies 70 per cent of the country's energy needs. The coal is of such low quality that high carbon dioxide and sulphur dioxide emissions contribute to millions of respiratory diseases in China and a third of South Korea's acid rain problem. Our lungs burned a little from the exertion in such congested air, the blue skies a few kilometres back now nothing but thick white and grey clouds. I thought Urumqi and Beijing were bad, but this town made any pulp mill in British Columbia look pristine.

Much of China's current economic boom has come at the expense of the environment. Outside major Chinese cities, water is scarce and many rivers are fully maximized for irrigation and agriculture. Logging is rampant with stickmaking factories and lumber mills contributing to much of the deforestation. China has now implemented a "Green Great Wall" campaign in an effort to combat the destruction of natural resources, but it may be too little too late. What we saw certainly wasn't encouraging.

As we pulled in for the evening to Hoaxia, we stopped at the local police station to ask directions about the availability of staying overnight. One of the two Uyghur officers in the building left to get someone who could help us. In a few minutes, he returned with a Han woman dressed in a red-and-white gingham shirt with white collar.

The woman's name was Wong Ani, a 29 year old who ran a small guesthouse down the road. She showed us to some Spartan rooms with wooden slat beds where we locked up our bikes. Then she invited us to dinner. Wong spoke a little English and soon was telling us that the meaning of her last name was glory, something she seemed very proud of. After hearing this several times, we nicknamed her "Glory" as she told us about her English tutoring in Urumqi. Every weekday, Glory travelled to Xinjiang University by truck, the same route we had ridden that day, where she stayed with her boyfriend.

The four of us talked back and forth over our first Chinese meal in the mountains, my *Lonely Planet* phrasebook on the table for quick reference. It was our "bible to better eating" just like the publisher said. The menu tonight — Mandarin. We filled up on spicy pepper chicken and pork, rice and piss water tea, by now the standard drink served in Han restaurants. Different noodle combinations (*tangmian* and *chaomian*) peppered the Chinese menus. We used rice as filler between main courses. As you go westward in China, the Muslim and Chinese dishes are more peppery and hot. Even in the Han restaurants, the vegetables were spicier, the muted Cantonese dim sum now only found in the east. Beijing had been an introduction to authentic Mandarin cuisine and at that, some of the best in the world.

Dining in China is more of a social event than in the West, where many gladly gobble their Subway or Pizza Hut meals alone in front of the TV. The multitude of dishes served at Muslim and, in particular, Han Chinese restaurants are just part of a cultural extension whereby several people share many dishes. There is no tipping in China and service is something you have to learn to do without, unless you're in the larger hotel restaurants that cater to Western tourists. As always, we were discovering the subtle nuances between what a tourist would naïvely expect for dinner and what we as travellers wanted to learn as distinctly Chinese customs.

We always had our bottled water with us to keep the drinking as safe as possible, hoping to limit any bad eating experiences to the food at hand. Tony hadn't quite got used to which spicy foods he needed to avoid. He would spend the better part of the night making nine bathroom visits. Tim and I seemed to weather the herbs and spices a lot better, but we were all very careful with the water. Bacteria in poor-quality water was the quickest way to put us out of commission for a few days, not something we could afford given our rigorous cycling schedule.

A lot of bone seemed to be left in with our meat dish. We all avoided the seafood because we knew it couldn't be fresh since we were as far from the ocean as you can get. Urumqi (70 km away from Hoaxia) is probably best known for the small trivial fact of being the most landlocked city in the world; namely, it is located farther from water than any other city. The Indian Ocean lies to the south, the Yellow Sea to the east and the Arctic Ocean to the north.

Uyghur food differs from Han Chinese cooking by emphasizing lamb instead of pork. This is a standard convention to suit the Muslim diet. Noodle dishes with lots of meat kebabs, meat buns and meat pies (all greasy) dominated the menus in Urumqi. I had never tried Muslim dishes before in Canada and looked forward to delving into them, fingers and all, over the next few weeks as we cycled deeper into this Muslim province. Forget cutlery, forget clean fingers.

One of the differences between the two cultures was that the Uyghur places had menus painted or scrawled on the walls, whereas the Han restaurants were cleaner — complete with linoleum floors, Formica tables, laminated menus and cushy chairs. In the Han restaurants, red-and-white checked plastic tablecloths were standard fare. Many of the Muslim restaurants often used the same dirty dishwater to clean the dishes and the pots.

Chowing down was becoming one of the best parts of our trip. One can see the archaeological digs, the monuments and other cultural trappings, but until you savour the food, you haven't truly experienced another civilization. Full from a large meal and pleased with the distance we had covered on our first day, we all passed out after dinner on our tiny cots in Glory's little guest-house, ready to tackle the mountains the next day.

Leaving our hardened beds at dawn the following morning, we were a little sore but rested. I gave some of my Canadian stickers and pins to Glory and a Han woman police lieutenant in a navy blue jacket with gold epaulets. Glory took some group photographs of us before we began our daily water bargaining exercise at the local store. A myriad of underwear, cigarettes, bathroom products, drinks, snacks and film filled the store's blue wooden racks. Glory bartered with the shopkeeper in Mandarin, helping us get a good rate for 20 litres of water and Sprite (my sugar fix for the day).

Adequate water supplies are essential on an unsupported bike trip. We had consumed eight litres of water each on our first day out of Urumqi. Bottled water would be our single biggest expense on the road. Despite the illusion of the cool mountains, we had to drink a lot. If we became thirsty when cycling, we knew we weren't drinking enough water. Hydrate or die is the golden rule of cross-country mountain bike racers, and I adhered to it religiously.

The steel factory and Glory behind us, we headed up a valley full of spruce and fir trees into the mountains. The smog followed behind us for a few kilometres until we were back above the tree-line. Hills lush with greenery surrounded us as the road dipped in and out of steep gorges. It was a quiet ride. The occasional off-road vehicle and city bus heading to Korla would pass us by in a trail of dust. This was our second day of cycling and my bike legs were finally kicking in. The trip wasn't a race, although the day before I had felt like I was keeping the group behind. Not today.

Through the Tian Shan Mountains

Tony and Tim had a little rivalry going on this day that started to disrupt the trip. Tony was the most level-headed of the three of us, Tim the most stubborn. I was the most adventuresome. Tim liked to motor on ahead without waiting for Tony and me. Sometimes, Tony would stop to take the occasional photo or to stretch and I would stop with him. None of us was any faster than the others — we just hadn't set into a routine where we all stopped for a break at the same time in order to minimize our downtime.

Then Tony started calling Tim "The Colonel" behind his back for being belligerent. Now, I thought this jesting animosity seemed a bit much for two British friends who had cycled together for years. I hoped it didn't get any worse because Islamabad (our final goal as a threesome in southern Pakistan) was still several thousand kilometres away.

Things progressed rather well for the rest of the day until one of our breaks. Tim decided to chastise me for playing the music in my Walkman through the speakers for all to hear. I had a small front bag mounted on my handlebars with two side pockets. One of the pockets had my Sony Walkman cassette player where I played my "Silk Road tunes" without headphones. The music carried for several yards and Tony would often ride beside me listening to my recordings of Sheryl Crow, The Tragically Hip, Alanis Morissette, Sarah McLachlan and Garbage. To Tim that was not Garbage the band, but garbage music.

"You've come all the way to the mountains of China and you're playing this fucking European techno-pop music," yelled Tim after four hours of the music.

Enough said. He had a point.

We were a team and had to get along, so I turned the Walkman off and enjoyed the scenery without the tunes. We cycled up into the mountains passing the 2,600-m mark and encountered our first brief rain shower. Out came the rain gear. A half-hour later when the temperature went back up to 30°C, the rain gear was packed away. Something I was getting used to. It changed back and forth like this all day.

Out of nowhere the jingle jingle could be heard coming over the hill in front of us. It was an ice cream truck, of all things. The truck stopped to give us Chinese-made Popsicle sticks just like when I was a kid. We fumbled for our tiny mao notes, the Chinese equivalent of dimes, and stocked up on sticky blueberry, pale pink raspberry and other assorted flavours. In the searing heat, this was a blessing from the Bike Gods.

Our route had been running near the Urumqi River for the past day and a half as it cut its way through the mountains. Suddenly, the river turned to a raging dark green. Alluvial deposits and boulders were scattered by the riverbed, signs of low water levels. One abandoned bus, stripped of all its parts, lay rusting by the riverbank. It had fallen off the cliff farther upstream and been washed down with the current.

The river veered closer to the road as we climbed higher and higher, the steep valley walls dropping sharply away to the water below. Cows and sheep grazed on 65-degree slopes, oblivious to the fact that one false step and they might cartwheel down the hill, plunging into the river. Higher up in the mountains we could hear marmots whistle, their echoes rebounding off the valley walls.

It had been a tough haul on a steep gravelly road for a meagre 30-km day. We started to look for a place to camp. We were between towns and needed a place to put down with soft dirt or grass, neither of which was in any abundance up here in the mountains. We finally found a grassy mountainside ledge overlooking a 300-m drop-off into the river. We pitched our gear and bikes and hooked up Tony's tarp, stringing it around some large boulders in case it rained. Two young Kazakh children, not more than 10 years old, came climbing up from the river to talk with us.

The kids had seen us from the opposite side of the river below. They had walked down a goat path to a small footbridge and crossed the river before climbing the steep hills up our side. The boy and girl had brought some food and bread and something that looked like a potato mix. The boy knew a bit of English, though much less than Glory back in Hoaxia. We couldn't really understand what they wanted. They didn't ask much. They just stared and giggled.

They wanted to touch our pannier bags but we were fearful that they might accidentally let one of them roll down the hillside into the river. Between "expensive bike," "Canada," "Britain," "the Queen" and "we go to Pakistan," our efforts to communicate failed miserably. But it was fun trying. After figuring out that we had a breakfast invitation to the local yurt the following morning, we convinced the kids we would be their guests. Then they climbed back down the hill and went home.

Just as we were going to sleep in our bivouac sacs and tents, four Kazakh herdsmen came down from the road above. The Kazakh men were on these cute little horses that looked like Shetland ponies. We had specifically camped behind some rocks with the purpose of remaining hidden from view, but the kids had seen us from below and had told their parents. The herdsmen made similar hand gestures as the kids before them. They seemed to want us to stay for dinner and sleep at their yurt. We politely declined. We were already settled down in our sleeping bags. Across the river, high up on a mountainside meadow, some goats grazed.

Here I was in the mountains in China, all warm in my down sleeping bag, not a care in the world. Everyone else I knew back in Canada was probably at work or taking care of their kids. I was in heaven, staring out at the stars. This is the life I thought. I just hope I don't roll over the edge at night into the river. That would bite.

Over the Tiger Pass

We discovered the next morning that our breakfast invitation was a little farther away than we had thought. We would have to ride back up the road, go down to the river and cross the footbridge before hiking up a hill to get to the Kazakh yurt. It wasn't worth the time and effort to go get the tea, bread and soup that would probably be fed to us.

On the other hand, this meant we had to do without any food that morning and quite possibly the whole day until we hit the next village. The next town, Ulastai, was 50 km away on the other side of the mountain pass. That didn't sound like much, but we still had the top of the Tian Shan Mountains to cross. And it was all uphill. We had run out of our own bread and cookie supplies, evidently mismanaging our rations. With no food, the town might as well have been 150 km away.

Even worse, our water supply was quickly running out. The

Urumqi River, a thousand metres below, was too treacherous and too far away. A water purifier would solve the problem of clean water, but only when the hill wasn't too steep to climb down to the river. We set out cycling up the winding gravelly road, only to have our water supplies run out in a few hours. I soon regretted passing up the Kazakh yurt for tea. Then I found out that Tim had some dried soup rations. Unfortunately, the soup needed to be boiled. Without access to water, the soup was useless.

By late afternoon, the Urumqi River began to thin out as we reached its upper limits. In the distance, we could make out the top of the Tian Shans and the Tiger Pass that went over the top and down into the desert on the other side. The pass was 3,660 m high — 12,000 ft. This was going to be one long sufferfest.

I began to doubt my abilities to ride the whole way to the top. It was packed with switchbacks zigzagging their way up one side of the mountain face. It seemed as though we would have a little walking to do unless there was a McDonald's around the corner or some other miracle. I looked back where we came from. I could see Kazakh herdsmen and cows along the roadside 5 km away. In front of me, the canyon flattened out into a broad plain, enormous glaciers surrounding three sides of the mountain. Their size was deceptive, their looming masses making everything seem so much closer. We were still about 7 or 8 km away from the base of the mountain pass.

The only food that we had managed to come by all day was some watery Chinese yoghurt at a lone yurt. Now we were up in the mountains with nothing to eat. I had pedalled 57 kg of gear with little sleep and less than 100 calories up to an elevation of 3,200 m. We had averaged 3 km/h over the past eight hours. A sluggish 25 km — that's all we had travelled the whole day. Our bodies were depleted of all resources, our spirit to press on the only source from which we drew energy. My body had bonked and my legs were seizing with cramps. I was exhausted. We were exhausted. Travelling unsupported like this had its rewards but this day was not one of them.

The Mountain Bike Gods must have been watching over us. Around the bend we noticed several structures at the base of the mountain pass. Finally, a place to sleep and maybe some food. The dilapidated green concrete buildings turned out to be a weather station complete with satellite dish. Any doubts that the Bike Gods were not looking over us were erased when a tour bus stopped, giving us some bread and bottled water. This satisfied the immediate hunger, though it wasn't enough to nourish us after a full day's ride.

A half-dozen Han geology students who occupied the station immediately invited us inside. Tony and I unpacked our sleeping bags, clothes and belongings. We lay them out in a bedroom while Tim went to chat with one of the students. Tony gave me his emergency dried soup ration and we cooked it over boiling water in the kitchen. Then Tim came back with the good news. We had been invited to dinner. Food salvation!

Despite wasting this emergency food, we considered ourselves lucky to have found indoor shelter and a hot meal.

Yu Pen was a hydrology student taking his doctorate in geology and had been at the station for seven months. There were seven glaciers in the area, all of which fed into the Urumqi River — the main focus of his research. The other two students, Zhang Minjun and Ye Barsheng, were studying botany and agriculture at the Xinjiang Agricultural University in Urumqi.

Food was brought up to feed the students each week from a hydrology station farther downriver where it was grown. They had rigged up a long white corrugated piece of PVC tubing that ran down the length of the central building. Ice-cold water from the glacier behind us, Glacier No. 1, passed through the plastic pipe serving as washing machine, sink and bathtub. The whole station was jury-rigged with electrical wiring and tape. Anything to make generators run, stoves cook and antennas send signals. The students were up here for a long time and had to be as self-sufficient as we were on our bikes.

The rooms were bare but freshly painted, green on the bottom half, white on the top. One of them served as our dining quarters, a damp room with a wooden yellow table and matching chairs. A second room acted as an alternative kitchen where the main food preparation took place alongside a rusty old black wrought-iron stove. Just like in many college students' kitchens, dishes were strewn over the only two tables in this room and more were piled up on a counter alongside rows of canned sauces, Sichuan chili pastes and powders.

We helped prepare dinner, washing the Chinese cabbage, bamboo shoots and spring onions outside in a steel pan under the running water. The students were making our favourite — spicy Chinese. They had enough to feed a football team. Salted soya beans, green peppers, white fungus (very chewy) and huge radishes that looked as though they were grown on steroids — it was all there. Fennel, cloves, hoisin sauce to season the meat and lots of cooking oil were added to our dinner feast as we watched the college chefs go to work.

As our tea boiled away and vegetables steamed in a large metal pot, for the first time we glimpsed China's intellectual culture. The students had an intense desire to learn as much about us as we did about them. Ye's English was fairly proficient as he helped translate most of the evening's conversation. Yu and Zhang depended largely on my phrasebook. Their questions went beyond Zella's and Glory's simple and predictable "Where are you from?" and "How much is your bike cost?" etc.

The students were pleased to have Hong Kong back as part of China. The changeover had occurred just 19 days earlier. Yu, however, stated if he were a doctor in Hong Kong he would like the city-state to remain independent from mainland China. They all wanted a better income and a career that would help them achieve that goal. They knew that English and a university education were the keys to a good career and financial success.

In such an overcrowded country with few opportunities, I couldn't blame them. Money seemed to be all they desired to pull themselves from the simple life back home in Urumqi. The

Chinese, like many people in developing countries, don't realize that a large part of an "exorbitant" Western income is distributed among various local, provincial and federal agencies to pay for roads, sewers and schools. They have no idea that Westerners have sales and property taxes to pay, capital gains costs and other expenses. Pension plans and unemployment insurance deductions don't figure into their train of thought. Gross versus net doesn't exist to the same extent as in the West. Hence, everything the students viewed about us was skewed by their perception of our wealth. When I told Ye that someone who earned $60,000 in Canada only takes home half that, he didn't believe me. Why doesn't the state pay for your education, your funeral expenses and your day care he asked?

Then there was the staring. Yes, the Chinese like to stare. They have an intense fascination with the West. I had become used to certain Asian idiosyncrasies like the spitting back in Beijing. I knew about it before coming to China. The staring was different. As one would stare at a cow sleeping on a road in downtown New Delhi, oblivious to traffic, the Chinese stare at foreigners. All they want to do is ask you a lot of questions. They are curious. Intensely so. How much money do you make, how much does your car cost and how many children do you have? You name it, they'll ask it.

I chalked up their curiosity about the cost of material possessions to the inundation of television and the Internet (still in its infancy). However, their questions about family life puzzled me. To be single in your 30s is unthinkable we heard repeatedly from the younger Chinese. The institution of marriage seemed to be very important to them. Maybe it was because of the restrictions on the number of children you could have — the one-child policy.

Our conversation with the students was interrupted when I began to get a little adventurous with the spices. I liberally spread chili paste on a piece of bread in the kitchen. After I took it back to the eating room, I wolfed it down. Then Tony and Tim gave me the "you asked for it" look.

Nothing.

For the next few moments, my strong constitution withstood a variety of hot spices. I ate more and more bread with no effect — or so I thought. Suddenly, my mouth started to burn. My face turned to tears. It felt like my head had burst into flames after swallowing a jar of jalapeños. The students and two Brits erupted into laughter behind me as I ran to my bedroom for my water bottle. Lesson learned.

Late that night, walking outside to the brick shithouse under a full moon to do my thing, I seriously reconsidered the wisdom of spices. I hadn't come all this way from North America with its staid boring food to surrender to the Spice Gods and eat plain rice and noodles. I would adapt. Tonight, however, I felt like abandoning that culinary mantra.

The entrance to the outhouse was dark. I had to duck inside and turn a corner. Now it was pitch black inside. I couldn't make out a thing. The outhouse couldn't have been any larger than a queen-size bed. I navigated the pit toilet in the dark like a blind man trying to read Braille hieroglyphics on a wall. My hands touched the walls inch by inch. I felt like I was in a Chinese rendition of Edgar Allan Poe's *The Pit and the Pendulum*. I never knew how close to step to the centre, lest I plunge foot-first into the quagmire of the concrete toilet pen.

Normally, I would have brought my flashlight but it had run out of batteries. Although I managed to survive unscathed, you haven't lived until you've encountered a pit toilet at 3 a.m., squatting in total darkness.

As I walked back into the weather station, I saw a truck head slowly up the switchbacks to the top of the Tiger Pass. In the starlit night, I could make out its path as the headlights climbed slowly up to the right, then disappeared for a brief second before climbing slowly up to the left. It was freezing outside as cows meandered under a full moon. I watched the truck amble onwards, its diesel fumes drifting up in front of the moonlight slowly and surely. From this moment on, I knew I had the energy to cycle up those steep hills the next morning. I was not going to push my bike. I had eaten well and was replenished, my will restored. Eighty per cent of the battle on a trip like this is psychological; the other 20 per cent is physical. I had both.

We got up the next morning for an early breakfast at 6 a.m. The Brits and I quickly ate a noodle mixture before heading up the switchbacks to the pass. I was beginning to enjoy one of the breakfast delicacies that we had eaten in Urumqi. The steamed bread concoction called baozi was filled with meat, mutton or chicken and wrapped in a round dumpling about the size of a small tennis ball. Every time you bit into one you didn't know what was inside. Some even had sweetened pork inside, my favourite. This morning the carbohydrates may have felt heavy, but it was fuel. It would be burned in no time.

We tried to pay for our overnight stay and meals but were refused. This was typical of polite Chinese hospitality and was now becoming a ritual with anyone we met who was not a bureaucrat or police officer. As we packed our stuff back into our panniers and did some stretches, we exchanged phone numbers with the students. With overcast skies above, Tony, Tim and I headed out toward the first of the nine switchbacks that led over the top of the Tian Shan range.

Cycling in mountainous terrain with 57 kg of bike gear requires a lot of heavy breathing. Oxygen demand for this is much greater than trekking a similar grade with 20 kg on your back. I became aware of this as I climbed the switchbacks. My lips dried out and started to chap. The rampant shortness of breath made the task difficult. The Mouth of the Tiger Pass, as the top of the mountain range was called, was a 450-m vertical climb from the weather station to the top. Despite their excellent physical conditioning, Tony and Tim walked their bikes up most of the nine switchbacks. Tony had the build of someone decades younger than his 57 years. They were both older than me, but this was the first time that our fitness levels became apparent.

The switchbacks were a gruelling ride, the rocky roads absent of any metal barriers. Handmade piles of rocks formed crude barriers and makeshift walls on either side of the road, protecting to some degree falling rocks and landslides. Trucks would frequently pass by us, taking supplies to one of the desert oasis towns like Yanqi, Korla, Aksu, Kuqa or Kashgar. Swerving to avoid them was not always the easiest of things to do, given our weak legs.

As we rode higher and higher, Glacier No. 1 that had towered above us the day before, now loomed opposite the valley. I could see all the way down the valley to the weather station and river beyond, the cows, herdsmen and sheep mere miniature specks on the landscape.

One, two, three ... each switchback slowly became history. I slogged onward. My eyes were focused on the front wheel of my bike. The road slowly rolled by around the next switchback. Four, five, six, seven ... two more switchbacks to go and I would be there.

A cyclist who has done any serious riding knows that all hills are mental. Pure and simple. Mind games; nothing else. If you concentrate, focus and shut out all the pain that your body is sending to your brain, you will master the climb and conquer the mountain. My forte in mountain bike racing was not steep climbs, but endurance. As long as I paced myself, I knew I could climb the whole pass sitting in the saddle. If I succeeded here, I certainly had an excellent chance of making it over the 4,730-m-high pass that bordered China and Pakistan.

I stopped for several water breaks and the after-effects of the spices from the night before. I made my way around the last switchback. My legs felt like they were going around in slow motion. Up, down, up, down. A gerbil from a leper colony could have outraced me, but I pressed onward. Three and a half hours and nine switchbacks later, I stood up in the saddle, exerting what little energy I had left and slowly sprinted to the top of the pass.

I had reached the top of the mountains, high at last. I was 3,868 m high (12,896 ft.). It felt good not to despair and give up on my first big climb over a mountain range. Soon we would be headed downhill over the south side of the mountains, passing all those diesel trucks that kicked up dust in our faces.

Summiting the pass, a minivan stopped and let out its passengers to stretch their legs and take photographs. On the side of the van in large letters was the inscription "Don't Kiss Me, It's Terrible" and at the back "Come With Me, We're On the Same Road." Different. After I took several photos of the tourists, who immediately recognized my Canadian flag on the back of my bike, the bus broke down. Everyone had to push-start it until it got going again. That lasted about 10 m until the engine quit again.

Eventually, Tim and Tony reached the top. Their legs were more rested than mine because they had been off their bikes for a while, but even for them pushing all that gear was hard work. They were waiting at the crest of the pass ready for the long descent down the other side. I didn't stick around to see what happened to the tourists in the van. Then we were set.

After climbing through the mountains, we were ready for the quick descent into the desert and the fabled northern Silk Road. It's always worth the effort to spend days, even weeks, going up, in order to experience the thrill of bleeding off altitude at 60 km/h. This was our fourth day since leaving Urumqi and we wanted to ride into a small village and relax. We deserved it.

A rocky road awaited our bikes' tires as the three of us took off down towards the desert oasis towns. We pedalled around the first bend and dropped away into an arcing corner. My speedometer zoomed up past 30 km/h, then 40 and 55. Soon it reached 68 km/h. My flag was flapping so loudly that I thought something had broken on my bike. I wasn't really pedalling at all. None of us were.

The weight of our gear carried our momentum, like Eric Lindros ploughing a peewee hockey player into the boards. Tony and Tim were riding side by side ahead of me. Tim's scraggly hair was flapping in the wind. This was the only time it would have been prudent — no, make that wise — to put our helmets on. But this was China. The downhill time of our lives. There was no traffic. Just the goats on the hills and the occasional Kazakh horseman.

We had gone about 30 km when suddenly my frame began to convulse and shudder. Then the back wheel started to fishtail back and forth. The rear tire kicked up like a broncing buck. Something was wrong. Terribly wrong. I was losing control at a speed far in excess of my bike-handling skills.

Skidding sideways, the rear of the bike slowly came forward, my front wheel still pointing down the hill. The left pannier fell off, tumbling over to the edge of the road. I couldn't jam my foot in the ground because I was wearing sandals. Between the fear of shearing off my toes and flipping over and breaking my neck, I did nothing.

Then it stopped. Everything settled down — the dust, the bike and me.

I had a flat.

CHAPTER FIVE

Arrested

Hate My Bike Week

Things were going to hell.

My bike was falling apart over and over again — not once, not twice, but 11 times in two days. The tiny 6-mm Allen bolts that held my rear rack onto my bike were slowly working loose. They had started to unscrew on the left side of the frame during the steep rocky fireroad descent coming down off the Tian Shan Mountains. Compared to my rear tire, which was flatting every few kilometres, that was the least of my worries.

The familiar sagging feeling I had experienced so many times before as the air went out of my tire, was now becoming an irritant. I don't know if all the extra clothing, camping gear, books and note-taking material I was lugging around were the problem. Everything from pills and maps to a tent, first aid kit, repair tools, sleeping bag and 36 rolls of film was stuffed into two large waterproof panniers.

It just didn't make sense. The rim was new, hand-built back in Vancouver the month before at my local bike shop, Ambleside Cycles. Were the spokes poking through the rim tape into my inner tube or was the desert heat expanding the rubber and catching on some tiny metal burr? Did I have a snakebite flat (a double puncture caused by hitting an obstacle too hard or by underinflating the tires)? I had no idea.

I felt like chucking the whole Taiwanese-made steel frame onto the train tracks that ran along the road. Let it twist into a piece of useless junk. When you're so reliant on a single piece of equipment, you take it for granted that it will work — work all the time. It has to, until that is, it fails you.

Tony and Tim were understandably getting frustrated each time they had to wait for me to fix my flats. At first, they had no idea if I had careened off the roadside or encountered mechanical trouble, as they were often several kilometres ahead of me. By the end of my fourth flat they had it figured out.

Fixing a bike flat is a simple and straightforward exercise for the experienced mountain biker. If the front tire goes, the brakes are flipped aside, the wheel pops out and the rest takes about three minutes. When the rear tire blows, the procedure takes only slightly longer. This was all second nature to me, but when you're travelling with heavily loaded panniers and a rear rack, the process becomes a little more tedious. You have to take off the panniers, flip the bike upside down and access it from below. This allows you to free the wheel from the rear derailleur and chain.

Usually I would replace a punctured tube with a new one instead of patching the old inner tube. I had plenty of extra tubes (nine in fact), but was quickly running out. I soon realized that the desert temperature was so hot the glue was liquefying. This prevented the patches from sticking. And this entailed putting in a new inner tube for each flat. I strapped the old tubes onto my rack, intent on patching them in a cooler environment where the glue would have a chance to harden. But out here on the edge of the desert, I had to make do with what I had. This strategy worked until I ran out of tubes. Now I was at the mercy of borrowing Tony's extra tubes, something he shared with reluctance.

Becoming a burden to my bike mates was an unforgivable breach of cycling etiquette. Don't jeopardize your partner's well-being. Every cyclist must be independent and self-sufficient. This necessitated bringing a repair kit complete with inner tubes and spare spokes and knowing how to fix anything that could go wrong with the bike. To ask for another cyclist's tools is admitting defeat.

I temporarily contemplated that my Rocky Mountain Fusion was cursed; it was in greater need of reincarnation than fixing. But at this moment, I didn't care if I had to ditch it and turn to back-packing. As the bike problems persisted, we covered fewer and fewer kilometres, our mileage dragging down to less than 35 km a day.

We eventually settled into a riverside bunkhouse after two days of frustrated bike karma. The railroad workyard with its tent-like quarters housed the Chinese workers who were repairing the rail-way ties nearby. The cook at the worksite let us consume all the noodle soup and bread we could eat, allotting us canvas beds to sleep on for the night.

The entire section alongside the railway tracks coming down from the mountains was rich with parsley-green hills and well-irrigated streams. It looked like a page out of a book on the Irish countryside. Rolling bluffs and gentle hills gradually made way for the drier dustier features of the desert. As we passed Kyrgyz herds-men wearing tasselled felt hats, I gingerly picked my way around potholes, small depressions and rocks, fearful of another flat. At last we turned onto the main highway, paved and smooth, the past 48 hours of flats seemingly behind.

Arrested in Our Underwear

As we neared the oasis town of Yanqi the following day, six days and 250 km after leaving Urumqi, we were stopped abrupt-ly. We had started to gain good ground, picking up speed, when my bike decided it would let me down once more. Since we were on the outskirts of a major desert city, we attracted a lot of atten-tion when I stopped to fix my eleventh flat. Twenty to 30 people crowded around my bike, each wanting to take a turn inflating my tire. Everything was going fine as Han and Muslim alike took turns pumping a few strokes into my tire.

Tony, who was helping me change the tire to save time, sensed that we might draw the curiosity of the wrong person — namely the authorities. Then Tim called out.

It was the police.

A military Jeep had just pulled up and a Public Security Bureau officer was walking our way. The young officer, dressed in jeans with a uniform shirt and tie, proceeded to tell us that we were riding into town on a restricted road. He said there were two roads used by local residents to access Yanqi but only one was open to travel by foreigners. After looking at our plane tickets and passports and putting the latter in his breast pocket, the officer politely asked us to cycle behind the Jeep and follow him to the police station.

At the PSB station, a drab two-storey concrete building in Yanqi, it was made clear to us that we wouldn't be leaving soon. We were shown an English translation of what supposedly was the rulebook on crimes and misdemeanours. Tim suspected the worse. He thought there was a chance that we would be heavily fined and held up for days. Either way, none of us could afford a fine or worse, the attention by the police that came with being detained.

Tim and I differed as to what would happen to us. I tried to convince him that the officer would let us off easily. But I was wrong. The officer, in his kind, disarming, persuasive way, informed us that we would each have to pay a fine of ¥500 ($83), the lowest penalty permissible under the law. Typical of Chinese bureaucracy, receipts were issued to us after we reluctantly paid the fine.

"So sorry, sir. Law says you pay dollah. Beijing rule. America good. Canada good. Please come again," said the demure officer in his best English.

Since leaving Urumqi, we had only been spending about ¥35 to ¥45 a day ($6 to $8). The fine was like taking a week's spending money and burning it. This was the last thing we needed. Tony and Tim were low on cash and since my Visa card disappeared in Beijing, I had even less.

Tim paced the halls until the paperwork was completed and our passports returned. Tony kept quiet throughout most of the ordeal, silently acknowledging that it could have been any of us who brought the attention of the officer. Tim was just frustrated. We all were. We knew full well that the roads into Yanqi weren't restricted. None of the guidebooks or PSB offices in other towns indicated any restrictions in the desert with one exception — Lop Nor.

Lop Nor lay in the middle of the desert 300 km southeast of Yanqi. The salt lake was once used to refresh the caravans and animals of Silk Road travellers like Marco Polo. Today it is the central testing site for China's nuclear weapons program, the fourth largest in the world. Red Army troops are permanently stationed in the region as a show of force. Unusually high rates of deformity in livestock and children have been reported in villages near Lop Nor, where people have developed white splotches on their skin.

At the PSB office, I felt we were caught in a hopeless situation. Poorly paid officials were bending the rulebook to exact extra money from wealthy foreigners. We also knew that to argue with the authorities would only make our situation worse. Sure, we could have insisted on calling our embassies in Beijing, but we probably would have spent several days in town and twice as much money waiting. We had to let the officer save face. It was the Chinese way. Apologize and tell them we were just naïve foreigners. We would never commit the blasphemous crime of cycling in a "supposedly" restricted area again. That was the quick and easy way out.

We left Yanqi, our money belts a little lighter, with fresh legs after a two-day rest. We rode a quick 50 km south towards Korla into the Takla Makan desert, an impressive expanse of shifting sand. The desert lies in the Tarim Basin, a 1,600-km-long depression crossing northwest China. Out here between the Tian Shan Mountains and the desert, the climate began to transform. The terrain between Yanqi and Korla became drier and vegetation sparser. Huge temperature disparities characterize many of these oasis towns — the cold desert nights contrasting sharply with the dusty broiling plains. Although the oases with their poplar trees provided a false sense of relief from the barren expanses between towns, the tarmac on the highway was the worst. The road heated up (often above 50°C) to the point where small balls of asphalt would collect at the side, the changes in temperature cracking the pavement.

It was on this leg of the trip that one of our greatest challenges as travellers lay — how to find enough settlements to stock up with bottled water. The guidebooks were useless when it came to detailing the tiny desert towns, especially regarding a cyclist's needs. My maps revealed the region in detail, but they were surveyed in 1981. We couldn't be sure if the markings indicating small clusters of homes were accurate. We had no idea where we could get extra water if our supplies ran out, or if we could find streams that weren't dried up.

The surrounding desert region south of Korla, like Siberia's gulag and Australia's outback, has long been used to unload China's criminal element. Approximately half a million prisoners labour away in the desert *laogai* camps, working in factories and fields. Prisoners plant trees, make building bricks and dig coal. The camps are China's largest source of slave labour. This is where most of China's executions take place, estimated to be over 1,000 each year — more than the rest of the world combined. There are 68 punishable crimes by death in China, from robbing a diplomat to stealing panda skins. After our own little brush with the law in Yanqi, we had no interest in exploring northern China's prison system. Little did we know that we would be back in a police station the next morning trying to appease another PSB officer. Furthermore, this encounter wouldn't be as friendly as the one two days before.

In Korla, a town of 175,000, we had found a guesthouse for a considerably cheaper price than usual — around ¥20 ($3.30), almost too good to be true. We were low on funds and willing to take any breaks we could get. Guesthouses or *binguans* as they are called in China, are four- to six-storey government-run hotels, often managed by private operators. They include dorms and individual bedrooms, the walls usually peeling paint, the cracked ceilings and concrete floors signs of shoddy workmanship.

Pit toilets, cockroaches and an intermittent supply of hot water are also characteristic features of these desert accommodations. What's more, they are considered on the higher end of the accommodation scale for foreigners and wealthy Chinese to use.

Unlike Europe, Japan or Southeast Asia, China has no youth hostels. *Luguans*, as opposed to *binguans*, are the grubbiest places to stay and, short of a tent, are about as rockbottom as you'll find. The main difference between *luguans* and *binguans* is the quality of the showering and toilet facilities. Even by Western standards, I didn't find the *binguans* that bad for the purposes of our trip. After booking into our rooms and locking up our bikes, we headed out to gorge ourselves on spicy Muslim food.

I loved eclectic dishes. My favourite food often consisted of things sitting on my plate that looked completely foreign. The rope-like noodles, dough sticks, kebab dishes, rice gruel and leek dumplings were a refreshing change from the sweeter deep-fried North-Americanized regimen I was used to in Vancouver.

Armpit dives that masqueraded as restaurants and were located in back alleys beckoned for your business in towns like Korla. For me, the dirtier and grubbier the place, the better. Good health was low on my priority list when I could experience foods that were exotic. Among our little trio, Tim and I had appointed ourselves the food connoisseurs. We always sampled the new and unknown dishes on the menu, preferring the spicier entrees.

Out on the edge of the Chinese desert, I had to cross-reference my *Lonely Planet* phrasebook with the dining list and hope for some new exciting regional variation on a favourite dish. Heavy soups and the odd *bishtek* hamburgers — both Russian influences — were available in several Muslim restaurants. This was due to the Kyrgyz, Kazakhs and Tajiks living in the region — ethnic groups living in both China and the former Soviet republics. On the Silk Road, the historical and ethnic influences of this great trading route were still apparent.

Most of the time, eating came down to pointing and hoping. Point to the menu and hope you recognized the Arabic or Chinese character. Each time we thought we knew a key word like chicken or noodle, we were pleasantly surprised by something else on our plate. Usually, the restaurant owner or family member who doubled as waitress or waiter couldn't speak our language any better than we could theirs. We almost never left a meal unsatisfied.

That changed, of course, when Tony gave in and tried some spicy kung pow noodles for lunch. Tony shied away from the spicier Chinese and Muslim food, the latter having a particular tendency to upset his stomach. We had been in China two weeks and Tony had yet to try the best food. Each time Tim or I would order something we thought was new and delicious and spicy, Tony would pass it up. Tony had become accustomed to his own list of agreeable foods.

Today, however, was special because it was Tony's 58th birthday and we were splurging by eating to our heart's content. We thought it was time for Tony to try something a little different for a change.

"What's the harm?" I said to Tony.

"How hot can the noodles be?" I said pointing to the *tangmian* soup concoction.

"Just drink lots of water," Tim chimed in.

And then Tony swallowed ...

Tim and I laughed as Tony's face went bright red. Tony quickly drank every glass of water on the table, regretting he had trusted us. The spicier food of this Muslim province was obviously too much for Tony's palate.

The most interesting things I noticed after a few days in Korla were the hats. Hats, hats and more hats. Every young Uyghur, Kazakh or Kyrgyz male wore some kind of octagonal hat or skullcap in observance of his Islamic faith. Some wore the traditional caps — small white or black caps that resembled Jewish yarmulkes or kippahs. Other hats were more like flat berets scrunched over the head. They came in white and black, some even decorated with interlacing designs characteristic of Islamic motifs. White felt hats with tassels, so symbolic of old central

Russian life, are worn by many of the 170,000 Kyrgyz living in China.

In Korla, the most startling thing about the Kyrgyz to foreigners is their red hair and emerald green eyes. I had read about this, but when I actually saw it firsthand, it was striking and disconcerting. I was walking along, turning a corner in the market when I came face to face with a red-headed Kyrgyz man at a knife shop. For a second I questioned where I was. This was it — one of those regional oddities of Muslim China. With their pale skin, auburn hair and broad cheekbones (almost Finnish-like), these Kyrgyz market hustlers looked as though they were straight out of a Bulgarian market in Eastern Europe.

If hats were in abundance, then so were pears and mushrooms, famous export commodities of Korla. But the real economic value to the region were the mineral and oil deposits in the desert. Geologists, surveyors and other specialists from multinational petroleum corporations like ExxonMobil, had been coming to the natural gas fields deep in the desert since the 1950s. The city has since turned into a major transit hub for trans-desert workers and travellers.

That evening, after more cautious eating on Tony's part, we settled into our tiny little green room at 1 a.m., our clothes and gear scattered everywhere. We used these moments of relaxation to catch up on our journal writing since leaving Urumqi a week earlier.

I was just going to put some bungy cords on my bike downstairs when a rapid banging on the door alerted us. The three of us froze for a second. Who could be knocking at this hour? The Han woman who ran the front desk had long since locked up and gone to bed. Apprehensively, Tim opened the door. In front of him stood five Chinese police officers dressed in imitation Mao khaki outfits.

"Could I have passport?" asked the tall one of Tony.

"What is this for? We just went through this two days ago," I said.

It was pretty obvious what was going on. We were being arrested. I was wearing only my Calvin Klein underwear.

"Passport please," the officer repeated as the three of us stood in our briefs and T-shirts.

The senior officer told us that we were being arrested for staying in a hotel not approved for foreign guests. We would have to leave right now, pick up all our belongings and find another place in the next hour.

Welcome to China!

The officers took our passports and told us the directions to the Public Security Bureau office where we should go the next morning. We would almost certainly have to pay a fine for our indiscretion he said and gave us the name of his superior to talk to.

The officers queried where we were headed on our bikes and where we had come from. This line of questioning was headed into territory none of us wanted to go. China, despite opening up in the past few years to foreigners, was still very suspicious of those who weren't on guided tours. Mobile travellers like us were hard to pin down. No one likes a moving target.

We didn't want to outline our plans to cross the desert. On the other hand, we didn't know if they had contacted the PSB office in Yanqi where we were first detained. Did they know what direction we were travelling? Could we lie and tell them we were headed east towards the big eastern cities instead of west?

Several hours earlier when we had finished dinner, I had gone off by myself to make some international telephone calls from an office across the street from our hotel. Following the overseas call, I sat on the curb in front of our hotel and dictated my daily journal into my Sony Walkman. None of this was contrary to Chinese law, but a foreigner sitting on the street late at night might be cause enough to attract the curiosity of a passing police officer. That couldn't possibly be what caught their attention but then what had?

As we made multiple trips downstairs, carrying all our gear to be packed into our panniers, Tim launched into me. This was our second arrest and most likely our second fine. This time it was my fault. He was sure.

"Look what you did now, Brady," said Tim. He then commented on how we would have to bribe this guy to get our passports back.

"It's not my fault. I was only sitting on the curb dictating into my tape recorder," I replied. "How should I know that foreigners weren't allowed to stay here? The woman let us in."

"That's not the point. You attracted attention when you could have avoided it," Tim shouted. "You should have left that god-damn Walkman at home. We came to get away from everything."

On the legitimacy of staying in the hotel, we knew we had every right to stay here. In the old Soviet Union, foreigners were obligated to stay in government-sanctioned Intourist hotels. The situation for overseas guests in China was a little murkier. Where you could stay as a foreigner was often a function of how much you were willing to pay. Our hotel undoubtedly charged both local and *wai bin* (foreign guest) prices. We were charged the local rate, something the owner may have later regretted when confronted by the police.

China had recently outlawed this two-tiered system, but the reality of what the law was and whether people followed it was like night and day. It would take years to change old customs. Hotel operators would have to give up charging $35 per room to Westerners, whereas locals only paid $6.

Down at the police station the next morning, our suspicions about the fine were soon verified. Another $83 each and we were on our way. Or not quite. The commanding officer at this station wasn't as apologetic as the one in Yanqi. In fact, he was more interested in harassing us about our trip than making us pay the obligatory fine. I felt like a 10 year old in the principal's office.

Why are you going to Kashgar? he asked. How will you get through the desert? Do you have permits and reservations in hotels in every city? What are the exact dates when you will be arriving? And the best question of all, What tour group planned your itinerary?

The officer's attitude really sucked. He had our money (after a short trip to the bank), but still wanted to grill us on our trip. Not "How is Canada, I have friends there." None of the usual friendly Chinese chit-chat.

By this time, even Tony was showing a bit of resentment towards our situation. He was contemplating aborting our planned desert crossing and taking a bus all the way across the desert to Kashgar — all 930 km. That meant a week and a half of riding wasted because of red tape and stupid rules. China was a great beautiful country and the people were nice but they really needed to change their government. But then, part of travelling is dealing with the vagaries of divergent cultures — homogenous, colonial, autocratic, socialist.

Either we put our bikes on a bus as Tony suggested or risk that this officer would have other PSB stations keep tabs on us through each town — a serial shakedown. To take a bus or not to take a bus. That was the question. We had come on this trip primarily to ride some of the old Silk Road routes in northern China and down through the mountains into Pakistan. This chopped up our trip into three stages: China's Tian Shan Mountains, the Takla Makan desert and the Karakoram Highway. To forfeit one of the three was unthinkable.

Another threat to our trip was the possibility of infuriating the officer to the point where he would make us leave the entire province. We had heard of stories where others were forced to throw their gear and bikes on top of a bus and given a one-way ticket to the nearest border. That meant going either back to central China, if we had to leave the province, or all the way to the next country — the Pakistan border 1,500 km away. Our whole morning now turned into a strategy meeting. We took turns chatting with each other privately in the lobby while one of us was in the office talking to Mr. Big Shot Policeman.

I actually thought the chances of having our passports taken away a third time were relatively slim. Maybe it was a subconscious wish to ride across the full length of the desert despite our bad luck with the authorities. I had to take into consideration the feelings of my two travelling mates. The Brits were older and maybe more experienced when it came to making judgments under these conditions. We concluded, albeit not by a unanimous vote, to skip the next 10 days of cycling. The practical option won out over the ideal option.

We would take a bus instead, our bikes strapped to the top. How bad could the ride be anyway? It was probably just a short eight-hour drive and we would be relaxing in Kashgar drinking pop sooner than we thought. After buying tickets from a Kyrgyz man at the depot, we waited for the bus to pull in. We were ready to load our bikes and escape the bad fortune of the past few days.

While I was waiting for the bus, I met a young man from Japan who had cycled the entire 930 km width of the Takla Makan desert from Kashgar at the western edge — all on a one-speed bike. It had taken him one month. He was equipped with nothing more than a blanket and a wire basket tied to his handlebars. Nothing else. No rain gear, panniers, stove, extra clothes or sleeping bag. My family thought I was crazy for embarking on my little escapade across Central Asia, but this guy was certifiable. We had no concept of what the depths of the desert were really like. Its bleakness and boldness contrasted sharply with the mountains and cities of the east where we had come from.

Thus the Desert Is Crossed: The Takla Makan Desert

> But there is a marvellous thing related of this Desert, which is
> that when travellers are on the move by night, and one of them
> chances to lag behind or to fall asleep or the like, when he tries
> to gain his company again he will hear spirits talking, and will
> suppose them to be his comrades. Sometimes the spirits will
> call him by name; and thus shall a traveller ofttimes be led
> astray so that he never finds his party. And in this way many
> have perished. So thus it is that the Desert is crossed.
>
> MARCO POLO, *The Travels of Marco Polo*, 13th century

The Bus Ride to Hell (or How I Got to Kashgar)

We were on the bus to Kashgar crossing the Takla Makan
desert, packed in like sardines for what we thought was a quick
half-day trip. Our bikes were strapped to the top of the vehicle
along with burlap sacks and crops, suitcases and god knows what
else. Like semi-comatose patients, we passed in and out of sleep,
in and out of the stifling heat, stirring occasionally as the bus hit
another bump or stopped at an oasis town to unload passengers.
I was continually amazed at the bus driver's ability to stay awake
and take risks. Parts of the road were washed out from landslides
or flooding, but he sped onward through the night, oblivious to
the road conditions.

The seats were divided into two rows, three abreast in each.

I sat by the window with Tony on the far side and a fat Muslim woman in the middle, her jiggling flesh squishing me into the window frame. The Chinese love sunflower seeds and this woman hoovered them down like a vacuum cleaner. Out like a shotgun she spat the splintered shells, littering the floor below. I periodically wiped the sunflower seeds off my legs, eventually switching seats with Tony so that we could share the window as I tried to rest.

The woman's daughter was dressed in a bristling pink lace dress. She had a bowl-cut hairdo and huge earrings and sat across the aisle. The girl demanded our attention while we attempted to nap. She giggled, as all young children do, with whichever passengers would share eye contact. She was intent on having me appease her every playful whim, despite my need for sleep. She would smile or stick out her tongue. I would make a face in return. I secretly wished someone would hit me on the head with a tire iron and reduce me to a restful sleep. While her mother smiled, the daughter poked me in the side, taunting this strange foreigner with a beard and sunglasses.

We trundled on through the searing heat of the desert, the acrid smell of rotten food and body odours fouling the bus. The girl changed her routine to slapping my thigh as I tried to rest my head on Tony's shoulder. I couldn't turn my back sideways so I wasn't able to stretch in my seat. I was too tall. My legs and knees pushed into the seat in front of me. This continued hour after hour, our bus sauntering along the desert highway at what must have been the slowest speed for any Chinese-built vehicle on four wheels.

Tony tried to rest his head against me and had a little more luck. He was able to pass off into sleep heaven for an hour or two before someone walking down the aisle would bump us. Every few hours we would have the guess-when-we-will-arrive conversation. It did little to psychologically improve our suffering.

"We'll be there in three hours," I would say.

"Sure, not more than three or four," Tim would reply. "The bus ride can't be that far."

That made everything better, the bus seemingly closer to its destination. We all figured that 930 km divided by 60 km/h would be approximately 16 hours of travel, give or take a few food stops to stretch our legs. If the trip were longer, we assumed like complete fools that we would stay overnight in Aksu, the midway point between Korla and Kashgar. We thought the trip would take the better part of a day at most. We were wrong. Dead wrong.

Dawn turned into day. Day turned into evening. Evening turned into pitch-black darkness, the occasional light from camel eyes reflecting the bus's headlights. Weary and weak, we finally pulled into a town in the middle of the night, not quite sure where we were. At last Kashgar, I thought. We all started to gather our bags from the racks above the seats when we noticed we were the only ones doing so.

"Hotel stop? Finally, a place to lie down for six hours," I mumbled.

"No, they're fixing something under the bonnet," Tony said. "I don't think we're there yet."

Twenty hours had lapsed since we left Korla at the crack of dawn. My batteries had run out on my Walkman. Music no longer drowned my senses. How long was this bus ride? We asked a passenger. We gestured at maps and used vibrant hand signals that must have seemed more confusing than helpful. There may have been five or six languages spoken on the bus but we understood none. The passenger flashed forty fingers, our only indication of an answer. Forty kilometres or 40 hours? Which was it? Could our trip really be 40 hours long!

We had left on a Friday morning and wouldn't be arriving until late Saturday night. It was also the milk-run trip. Our bus would stop at every oasis adobe hut village, unlike the faster sleeper buses at twice the price. Had we only known! If you are ever in the Chinese desert and are trying to get to Kashgar, take the expensive bus with beds.

When you wake from a dream and are in that groggy sleepy state we all know so well, sometimes you utter incomprehensible words. If our trip was going to take over a day and a half, then surely that must include sleeping time in one of the desert towns. "At last I can unwind and lie on some mud floor or damp cot. Anything would be better," I muddled when the bus stopped two hours later.

Wrong again.

This was an unscheduled stop as the driver and his assistant, a young boy, got out at 2 a.m. to fix the engine. The engine was leaking oil and this was the first time we were allowed out of the bus to buy some water and stretch our aching bodies. The boy's usefulness became apparent when he crawled underneath the bus, squeezing between the muffler and crankshaft. Prior to our stop, the assistant's job seemed to amount to nothing more than sitting up front on the transmission next to the driver for the entire ride, collecting tickets.

Now we were in for the long haul.

Then began the lectures on why we ended up on a 40-hour bus journey sitting on partial metal seats with cloth headrests. The truth is, neither Tony, Tim nor I knew about the more expensive yet comfortable soft sleeper buses that would have made the trip bearable. Oh, sleeper buses. We had never heard of them. We weren't our usual astute inquisitive selves and hadn't asked around.

Later, I met some Westerners who made the same trip from Urumqi by sleeper bus at a cost of ¥199 ($24). The sleeper buses had individual compartments to doze off in. You couldn't escape the heat or stench of bodies but you could relax. The only complaint was that obnoxious Chinese music was piped through built-in speakers, blaring non-stop, even while people tried to sleep. The only way to stop it was to take out a penknife and cut the wiring, which many did.

I was certain that the first chiropractor started up practice in this very desert. Go set up a booth and charge a fortune for the weary travellers who stumble off, regretting they had not flown or booked a sleeper bus. Again, take the more expensive bus if you're ever going to Kashgar. Your body, soul and mind will thank you.

The rest of the journey through low desert plains was barely visible in the early morning hours. I was starting to love the desert and its shadows from the night. The heat of the day came again and with it the smell of three-dozen passengers who hadn't bathed in two days. We were one big happy family of four or five different ethni-cities, shacked up together in a tin can rumbling through the desert. We were tired and too nauseated to eat. Thirty hours passed by. Soon 36 hours had ticked away. We were closing in on 40. We were getting close to Kashgar, a lone outpost in Central Asia's hinterland cut off from the rest of the world — like the moon from Earth.

Only in the desert did I fully appreciate the vastness of China's wide-open spaces. I realized for the first time that China borders 14 countries with as many different dialects as religions and cuisines: North Korea, Russia, Mongolia, Kazakhstan, Kyrgyzstan, Tajikistan, Afghanistan, Pakistan, India, Nepal, Bhutan, Myanmar (Burma), Laos and Vietnam.

The last few hours into Kashgar were on a gradual downhill, the poplar trees that lined the road a welcoming invitation back to sanity. I'm sure the other passengers, the Uyghurs, Mongols and Kyrgyz, must have looked at Tony, Tim and I as though we had something wrong with us given all our squirming. What was so bad about crying babies, squawking chickens and people sweating profusely through their clothes?

Aside from learning to worship chiropractors and discovering the limitations of my back, I learned that people, who have nothing in common except a lone destination, could laugh and cry and endure each other's company for hours on end. We were respected on that bus as people from afar, as we turned our subtle bitching into cultural envy.

It was here on the edge of Central Asia's desert country — another land, another place, another time — that China began to change. Chopsticks became scarce, replaced by mutton kebabs. And the taxis, well, what taxis — everyone seemed to ride donkeys around here. The people were changing too, to the point where you wouldn't recognize you were in the Far East. Kazakhs, Uzbeks, Uyghurs, Tajiks and Hui. They were all here — the Han

Chinese slowly blending in with the ethnic Muslims.

"Toto, I don't think we're in China any more," my friend Patrick would tell me a year later after cycling a similar, but lengthier route across the desert.

If You Go In, You Won't Come Out

The Takla Makan desert is northwest China. To understand the hardships endured by those who travelled the Silk Road, one needs to understand the Takla Makan. Our bus had just rolled across one of the most inhospitable places on earth. A *terra incognita.*

Once a large fertile plain, the 1,300 km-wide Takla Makan is the dominant geographic feature of Xinjiang province — a beige sea of fine-grained sand roughly the size of Germany. It's like a giant sandbox stretching from Vancouver to Winnipeg or San Diego to Dallas. The rounded Pamir Mountains separating Afghanistan from China cradle the western edge of the desert; the treacherous jagged peaks of Tibet and Kashmiri India lie to the south. The smaller Tian Shan Mountains that we had crossed on our bikes skirt the north.

The desert spans a portion of China that Westerners wouldn't recognize if it hit them smack in the face, which it might if you get dehydrated and fall off your bike. Its name means "If you go in, you won't come out." The Chinese have a word for places like this: *gebi* meaning "wasteland." During the days of the Silk Road, men and the occasional woman, spent endless weeks and months crossing through unknown territory. They weathered desolate mountain passes and sweltering desert heat, pushing onward until exhausted.

Much of the Takla Makan doesn't look like a desert at all. By that, I mean it isn't sandy. Imagine Saskatchewan or Kansas stripped of all topsoil and crops. Now cover it with dust and cracked earth. It looks more like the moon. Its rocky outcrops go on forever, the occasional depression providing little relief for the weary traveller who is unfortunate and insane enough to try and cross it width-wise.

East to west, there are many oasis towns on the Takla Makan, strung along like beads on a necklace. Get to the next one and you are fine. If not, try to survive the Mt. Everest-like temperatures of the night or die of dehydration in the day. One route of settlements crosses the northern edge of the desert; another one runs along the south. Two highways cross the middle. They have only been built in the past decade (one for oil exploration companies, another for transport trucks). If you break down, that's it. You're on your own — alone with the vultures. It's a true test of survival. As Marco Polo, the first acknowledged European to cross the entire Asian continent illustrated, the desert renders a quiet sense of desperation for those hoping to cross it alive.

Centuries ago, at the Jiayuguan Pass near what today would be the Mongolian border, people who were rejected from Chinese society would be escorted through a remote sentry gate in the Great Wall. Fending for themselves on the other side, they were subjected to a barren solitude of nothingness. Those were the days when the Silk Road was at its peak. Traders trekked through the heart of Central Asia on their way to Persia or Xi'an in central China, braving the elements, hoping to strike it rich.

The hours passed at varying speeds. If it was warm and windless you fell sometimes into a meditation which blotted out a segment of the march, so that when you returned from the far-off things and places that had filled your mind you remembered the country you had passed through hazily, as you remember country in a dream. But if the wind blew no anaesthetic availed; for every yard of every mile you had your wits too much about you, and progress was a slow and wearisome route.

PETER FLEMING, *News from Tartary*, 1936

It would take months for these Silk Road explorers to skirt the desert on horse or camel with its hills and valleys of sand. Nothing to eat could be found anywhere until the trading caravans happened upon an oasis where they would fill up with food and water to refresh their animals. Sometimes they would stumble across a small oasis that wouldn't have enough water for the 50 or 100 beasts they were riding. Some animals were given water; others were left alone to perish. Inevitably, some of the horses and camels would die of thirst, unable to make it to the next oasis.

Many of these oases were former garrisons that watched over the caravans. They warded off highway robbers who traversed the Silk Road. Unlike India (later occupied by the British) or Hong Kong (later reduced to a colony), China was too large to conquer for most. The Mongols under Kublai Khan occupied greater China, but even his empire collapsed in time.

The First Silk Road Traveller

Fourteen hundred years before Marco Polo's 13th-century excursions, a lesser-known Chinese general trailblazed through ancient China's outer empire, exploring an unfamiliar land. China had never bothered to seek out those who lived beyond the great Middle Kingdom. The Chinese were superior. They were the centre of the world. What else could be of interest in the "lands of barbarians"?

Before the Chinese began to build walls to keep out the Huns and Mongols, stronger tribes from the north routinely attacked the weaker colonies that lived on China's outskirts. The peoples that lived in these outlying desert areas of China were only intermittently successful at warding off these assaults. They would lose miserably to tribes that would charge in on horseback and pillage, ransack and do all the nasty things that raiders do. No wonder the Chinese thought the rest of the world was barbaric.

Around 140 BC, one inquisitive Han emperor sent a general out to recruit some nomads called the Yuezhi. The Yuezhi, who lived beyond China's borders, were capable fighters and were thought to be worthy allies. The emperor needed to conscript them and forge alliances to help keep his empire intact. If China's outer boundaries weren't secure, what was?

The emperor sent General Zhang Qian, recognized as the first major Silk Road traveller, out to track the Yuezhi. Headed with a caravan and armada of 100 men, General Zhang trekked west through the Takla Makan desert in what is now Xinjiang province in China. He began to methodically explore the lands west of China. Eventually, Zhang and his men, all 100 of them, were captured by a nomadic tribe and held prisoner.

During the 10 years General Zhang was held hostage, he married a few times and had some children. Eventually he escaped with the few remaining men he had set out with and turned south. He tracked the Yuezhi down in northern Pakistan (then the early empire of India). But the Yuezhi never did turn out to be of much help. They seemed to be getting beaten up by invading clans as often as the Chinese. Zhang arrived back in the emperor's palace 13 years after his departure. Of the 100 men who started the Silk Road exploration with the general, only one survived the entire journey.

General Zhang recounted to his emperor tales of other peoples, ideas and artwork. Astounded by the cultures encountered on Zhang's massive expedition, the Chinese emperor immediately grasped the significance of this new knowledge. The political, military and economic intelligence Zhang brought back was invaluable for future missions.

Zhang and others who succeeded him returned from Chinese Turkestan (now Kyrgyzstan and Tajikistan) with the much-fabled Heavenly Ferghana horse. The Ferghana was a warhorse of Arabic stock that had the size and stamina to defeat the Huns and others with whom the Chinese often fought. China's own horses were small ponies, much better suited for pulling heavy loads on the farm than fighting in cavalry warfare. Today, small bronze versions of the famous Ferghana warhorses are on display in many Western Asian art museums.

Future Chinese emperors started to send forth greater numbers of caravans and men, decreeing religious artwork to be brought back to adorn their temples. So began the "borrowing" or stealing of other societies' belongings.

Lost Desert Artifacts

The Takla Makan desert in all its desolation and bleakness is home to some of the world's greatest archaeological spoils. The region is littered with Buddhist ruins, such as the Thousand Buddha Caves near Turpan and those found throughout oasis towns in Dunhuang and Kuqa.

China would be very different today if Buddhism had not been introduced along the Silk Road. Many local desert cultures adopted it, building monasteries, temples and artifacts. Later, other regions, such as Tibet, developed their own strains of this new faith. In Afghanistan, a 54-m-high sculpture — destroyed in early 2001 by the Taliban soldiers — was the second largest sculpture of Buddha in the world.

Buddhist artwork painted on grotto murals and sandstone caves dates back to the 1st century in Xinjiang and Sichuan provinces. Not for another 200 years were Indian Buddhist priests sought-after during Chinese missions down the Indus River. One Buddhist monk, who came north from India, amassed scriptures and helped spread the Buddhist doctrine throughout Kashgar and the Tian Shan Mountains. Another monk introduced Tantric Buddhism to Tibet, helping fuse Indian Buddhist art with the style of the Han imperial rulers. These two artistic methods eventually combined to form Serindian art, a Greco-Buddhist influence from the Gandharan school of Buddhism that came to China from Kashmir.

China's two million Buddhists weren't to last for long, as Arab traders and missionaries introduced Islam, the ultimate competing religion. Islam (Arabic for "submission to God") came to western China during the Tang dynasty at the end of the 9th century, supplanting Buddhism as the main religion along the Silk Road. Buddhists were eventually persecuted in large numbers by order of the Chinese state. A quarter million monks and nuns were forced into religious exile while their temples were destroyed. Over 4,500 sq. m of paintings in Dunhuang survived, but most of the ancient oasis towns are long since lost under the sands — cultures past lost forever.

Fifteen hundred years after Buddhism's ascendancy, Tibet still practises the most spiritual religion to penetrate the Middle Kingdom (Lamaism or Tibetan Buddhism). Unfortunately, the archaeological rape of the desert's Buddhist treasures began in the early 1900s. When the Russians, Japanese and Germans began to excavate, they found ancient Chinese scripts and Buddhist art works. Artifacts were quickly siphoned out of China into European museums. Like the art that was looted during the Second World War, many of these artifacts were simply lost during bombing raids on Berlin.

Sir Aurel Stein, a British-Hungarian archaeologist who dug up 24 boxes of buried art treasures in 1907 from the desert town of Dunhuang, known for its Buddhist frescoes, enriched the Asian art museums of Europe and India with his findings. Stein embezzled another 600 volumes of scripture books seven years later. The rest of the portraits and silk paintings from the desert caves and grottoes are in a dozen museums, the French alone having spirited away 6,000 volumes of handwritten books. The most valuable are in the British Museum in London and the National Museum in New Delhi. The Hermitage Museum in St. Petersburg houses over 18,000 ceramics and figurine objects from Dunhuang, many formerly owned by some of Russia's old Tsarist regimes. Silk paintings, scrolls and murals are also on display in other Western museums from oases like Kuqa and Turpan. Others still are in private collections.

If not for the Western archaeologists who stole the desert artifacts and squirrelled them away in foreign museums, they never would have been properly preserved. Preservation techniques used by Chinese archaeologists and curators have simply been inadequate. The Chinese, of course, did not look on the looting of their ancient history very kindly, although many Chinese curators admit that the methods used in their museums in the past were not up to the standards needed to preserve the artifacts.

In 1974, one of the greatest archaeological finds of the 20th century was discovered on the Silk Road when some Chinese peasants were digging a well outside Xi'an. Once the eastern terminus of the Silk Road, Xi'an became the site of hundreds of life-size terracotta warriors buried in a huge mausoleum during the Qin dynasty. Overnight the city became known for its rows and rows of life-like armour-clad infantrymen poised in battle formation. Bronze-painted horse-drawn chariots and burial tombs for slaves filled five acres of pottery masterpieces. Most of the clay warriors were sculpted individually right down to details differentiating their nationalities, class and facial expressions.

It was through these ruins, warriors and forgotten oases that I ended up in Kashgar at the crossroads of Asia. I was heading with trepidation through this great nation of China that once dominated the world and had such an effect on Western civilization. My bus ride with the Brits had taken us across the far reaches of the Takla Makan. We were now entering what was once the greatest trading town on the Silk Road — Kashgar, a Muslim outpost lost in time.

Kashgar: The Crossroads of Asia

Through the dusty sun-lit street donkeys trotted, as you had often watched them trot, loaded with grey lumps of salt or with bundles of fodder or of fuel. The same piles of bread and vegetables and fruits attracted, in the open booths, the ubiquitous but no longer overwhelming flies. The same Russian sugar, Russian scent, Russian cigarettes and matches preponderated in the wares displayed by more ambitious merchants. Strings of camels stalked through the city west-wards, carrying — at a gait and pace well known — bales of wool and other goods to the Russian railhead over the passes...

PETER FLEMING, *News from Tartary*, 1936

The Bus Arrives

I peeled my legs from between the metal seats of the bus from hell. I swaggered with drunken steps down the aisle, weak-kneed and sore. As women and children gathered their belongings from the racks above, I squeezed myself towards the door. I was so exhausted and bruised, I felt like a junkie going through withdrawal. A Swedish massage wouldn't have helped.

I stepped outside and sat my sorry butt on the loading dock. The bus terminal was a gravel yard with rusty tin-bucket vehicles parallel parked. Although a relatively small station, the depot was busy with a number of people milling about the yard. Departing passengers gestured wildly at weary-looking men seated inside the ticket booths. Others demanded tickets and shouted their complaints and frustrations in a myriad of dialects.

This was Kashgar.

At our bus, Tony was already negotiating with the driver's helper, a boy in his teens, to get our bikes and gear down from on top of our bus without forking over more money. Bus operators, seeing an opportunity to make some money, won't let foreigners put their own luggage on the roof. They insist on being paid to climb up the ladder (kept at the back of the bus during trips), even though we were quite capable of doing this ourselves. As the let's-rip-off-the-naïve-British-guy-and-charge-him-to-retrieve-his-own-bike charade developed before me, I let Tony fend for himself. Then I looked for Tim.

In 1936, the journalist Peter Fleming scribbled "to most people Kashgar must seem barbarously remote; but for us its outlandish name spelt Civilization." So true, I thought. Fleming was making an arduous trek from Peking (later to be called Beijing) to Kashmir, when he wrote those words. He never would have envisioned the polluting diesel buses that packed the depot today.

I experienced as much pain and discomfort on the bus as was humanly possible. With some sleep, I was sure to stop bitching about the tin-can- coffin-on-wheels trip. The bus ride, however, was an appropriate introduction to the slower pace of Kashgar, where Islamic architecture and customs dominate. The Han Chinese were now a minority in this Muslim province.

Feeling the need to collapse on the nearest bed, the three of us strapped our gear on our bike racks and panniers and cycled into central Kashgar for the short trip to our hotel. I was still unsure of whether my tires would flat again after the punctures in the desert. I knew that if something happened again, there were dozens of makeshift tire repair shops throughout the city.

Coaxing my bike past a huge 25-m-high statue of Mao Zedong, I thought about the symbolism of the venerable chairman in his long overcoat, one arm reaching out to the ethnic minorities.

Quite ironic, I thought. If the Muslim groups had their way with this symbolic statue of the Muslim massacres from the Cultural Revolution, it would be pulled down and used for building blocks in an instant.

Back in May, Tony had made reservations from England at a place called the Kashgar Guesthouse to pacify the Chinese bureaucracy and get his visa approved. He had to pick out some place that had a fax number listed in the *Lonely Planet* guidebook. We didn't know if the place was a dive, convenient to the markets or overpriced. We soon arrived on the eastern edge of town, a quick 15-minute ride from the bus stop.

The guesthouse was spread out over a sizeable area, its low-slung dingy buildings typical of Communist Chinese provincial architecture. The remnants of what must once have been beautiful circular gardens now lay overgrown and neglected. Tony and I checked out the rooms, plunking our gear on the beds, eager to take a break from riding.

"Where is everyone?" I said to Tony, noticing the hotel was largely unoccupied.

"The pool seems filled with swamp water," Tim interjected. "The place is dead. Go and see if we can back out of our reservations and take our kit someplace new."

The empty lobby and vacancy in most other rooms soon led us to the realization that the hub of activity was on the opposite side of town. If anyone ever stayed here, it strangely wasn't in late July at the height of the tourist season. The markets, bazaars, stores and most important, the much-heralded John's Café where foreigners gathered, were all on the west side of town. With that in mind, and badly in need of showers, we headed through the streets past a dull grey body of water called East Lake. This was Kashgar's only water refuge aside from the region's many irrigation ditches. Couples would often come here to have some romantic privacy at night or try their luck at fishing.

Changing our accommodation, we booked into the Chinese Overseas Hotel, a vast improvement over the Kashgar Guesthouse.

Tony was solicited by a prostitute outside a seedier shelter while picking up some peanuts on his way through town. The only indication of this profession at our new fancy Overseas Hotel was a chambermaid who opted to wear a revealing dress rather than the customary uniform. Without any sense of modesty, she threw salacious glances at the parade of male guests that went up and down the stairs.

Our three-bed hotel room was worthy of the ¥100 ($16) a night we were paying (dorms were cheaper at ¥10). It had a private washroom with toilet instead of the squalid communal pits on some other floors. Our room on the sixth floor overlooked several Muslim restaurants. It was an interesting view with cows in the back lots of restaurants, ready for the next group of dinner customers.

I unpacked my clothes and camping gear as Tim attempted to swat flies with a wrench. Tony fell asleep with my Canadian flag stuck between his toes. He was at peace. We were settled in to our cosy little hotel and didn't plan to leave our rooms until we all had a good day's rest.

The Muslims

Kashgar was one of the most important towns along the Silk Road; a bustling oasis city in China's far northwest corner, it was once the busiest trading hub in Central Asia. Kashgar is nestled within 200 km of Kyrgyzstan and Tajikistan, lying roughly on the same longitude with New Delhi. Although there may not be any tribal warlords on horses feuding over trade routes today, the disagreements between the ethnic Han who rule China and the minority Muslims living in Xinjiang province are just as confrontational.

The former republics of the Soviet Union have long flirted with the idea of secession, bonding in Muslim brotherhood with those Muslims in China. The collapse of Communism in 1989 freed those on the other side of the Chinese border. The relatively independent countries of Azerbaijan, Georgia, Uzbekistan through to Kazakhstan not only follow Islam within their own borders, but they also encourage Islamic separatists in Xinjiang. Many independence leaders for a free Muslim province fled to Istanbul in 1949 when Mao Zedong and the Communist Party took control of China. Mao set about dividing the Muslims into nationalities and encouraged assimilation with the Han.

The drastically different types of dwellings that the ethnic Muslim and Han Chinese live in are evidence of this cultural division. In the East, the cities are built to impress, but fail miserably with their drab grey crumbling structures. These large decaying cities are designed in true Communist style, the massive slab concrete apartments displaying little individuality. They look like the result of a 70-year strike by painters and cleaners. In the desert, the people stand out, the mud and brick buildings fusing into the backdrop. Kashgar evokes an Islamic spirit, its people and markets giving a distinctive taste found nowhere else in China. There's a sense that the town hasn't changed much in 1,500 years, since the days of warding off invading Huns.

In the midst of the ethnic tensions between the ruling Han and the country's 56 ethnic groups (13 of which are Muslim living in Xinjiang) falls another group — the Hui. The Hui are Chinese inhabitants of Islamic descent who have adopted the local dress and dialects of the Han. Although relations between the Chinese and Muslims can run from cordial to bitter, the Hui are not trusted by anyone because they have fought both for and against the Han. In the mid-1800s, the Hui effectively controlled the region around Kashgar after they revolted against the ruling Han. They are often ostracized by both Muslim and Han.

The Hui men can be distinguished by their white caps as they wander the back alleys of oasis towns like Kashgar bartering for goods. Hui women wear green caps to designate their status as virgins, and black caps after their wedding vows have been consummated. It is not unusual to see older Muslim women, Hui or Uyghur, dressed in brown woollen shawls draped over their heads, even in the 32°C heat.

The women walk about the markets in pink taffeta dresses and carry fake leather shopping bags. They all wear dark nylon stockings and some sort of white shoes or sandals. I would see these women on the roadside hitchhiking a ride out of town, dressed in what looked like wedding dresses, except they weren't bridal gowns — just their versions of stylish clothes.

The younger Uyghur women in their 20s, dressed in miniskirts, look almost Japanese or Korean with their beautiful broad cheekbones and attractive faces. They have striking, brilliant, icy blue eyes and dark complexions, in marked contrast to the Han. Those not familiar to the region would be baffled by their origins: China? Kazakhstan? Japan? Their eyes are Central Asian with a hint of "the Orient." Different, exotic. Even the word *Chinese* doesn't mean much out here. It's hard to imagine that when these girls grow up, they will no longer be wearing brightly coloured silk blouses or flowing dresses. Instead, they'll cover their heads and shoulders with shawls; weathered from hard labour, the exuberance of their beauty will have long disappeared.

In spite of the sheer silk skirts, blouses and Western dress of the young Uyghur women, they are reserved in their conduct with men — Muslim, Chinese and foreign. Their male counterparts, on the other hand, are very engaging in conversation. They're cleanly shaven in smart-looking cotton or silk shirts, pressed pants and polished black shoes.

One store manned by a well-dressed Uyghur male in his early 30s sold loose-woven multicoloured woollen shoulder bags. But it was a young girl, not more than five, and carrying a yellow bag filled with goods, who caught my attention. These yellow bags were quite popular. Where had I seen them before? Looking closer, I saw the printing on the side of the bag: "The Pet Shop – 992 Pollokshaws Road, Glasgow." Apparently, many market shops in Kashgar used these bright yellow bags to sell their merchandise. It made it appear as though a lot of people had made a group tour trip to the U.K. It was like shopping in Paris and buying something at Versace, only to be handed a bag with an address from Ecuador. Go figure. I heard similar accounts from other travellers, one cyclist being handed a Canadian Tire bag in a sleepy little railway town west of Xi'an.

The Great Game

To understand Kashgar is to appreciate how the various peoples who have inhabited the region have been both pawns and masters as they fought for control of their own territory. A century and a half ago, in what historians called the Great Game, Tsarist Russia and Victorian Britain struggled for control of the Central Asian region known as Chinese Turkestan. If the espionage and spying antics among the superpowers during the Cold War seemed as dramatic as a John le Carré novel, the best cloak and dagger derring-do contest between two nations happened in the 19th century during the Great Game.

For the past two thousand years, Kashgar had been of enormous strategic and historic importance. During this time, the borders of China shrank and expanded. Different dynasties struggled to control invading tribes in the outlying desert areas while some Chinese rulers, either through neglect or naïveté, thought the northern wastelands unimportant or militarily indefensible. The Chinese had only 8,000 troops in Xinjiang province, who were said to be better at gardening than fighting.

Napoleon, the little dictator who could, envisioned conquering India with the help of Tsarist Russia. He wanted to send 50,000 troops across Persia and Afghanistan. The Russians, not letting a bad idea go to waste, mulled the idea over for a few decades and then started advancing east through the Caucasus, making their way past the old Silk Road trading towns of Tashkent and Samarkand. They progressed for 400 years at a rate of 51,000 square kilometres per year. By the mid-1800s they were at the Chinese border.

The British quickly made plans to advance their Indian Empire north through the Karakoram Mountains into China after they underestimated Russian ambitions. The British used Afghanistan as a buffer state. It had been set up in 1891 in the midst of Kashmir to the south, China to the east and Russia to the north.

Oases had to be marked and alliances forged with local tribes. Meanwhile, Cossacks, Bolsheviks and British explorers set out to map the largely forgotten terrain of Chinese Turkestan. Chinese tribal chiefs tried to appease each side to hold their ground without surrendering and granted permits to surveyors, cartographers and explorers.

Evil empires were again conquering the old decrepit Silk Road as Russia and Britain sought to expand their borders. Politics as usual, you say? Well, not if you sent your local Indian hillmen disguised as Muslim pilgrims to hide surveillance gear as Britain did. To curry the favour of local leaders, spies were sent to gather firsthand intelligence used in negotiations. Like all empire builders engaged in a turf war, they all wanted more and were never satisfied with what they had.

The British soldier and explorer Francis Younghusband once encountered his Cossack rivals camped on the frontier between Afghanistan and the Russian border. Younghusband's mission, guided by a Balti mountaineering guide from Kashmir, was to close the no-man's gap in the Pamirs between China and Russia. The fearful Chinese had accused Cossack troops of marching around out of control. If caught by the opposition or its tribal allies, punishment could be ruthless. Two compatriots of Younghusband met their fate before the Emir of Bukhara, a local warlord. The Emir deprived the prisoners of food for days, forcing them to dig their own graves and kneel to the ground. After Younghusband's colleagues passed up an offer to convert to Islam, the executioner went to work. Two heads rolled into the streets before a large crowd, revenge having been meted out.

In his travels, Younghusband pioneered a route connecting Kashgar with Kashmir — the same route I would ride — and helped open up Tibet to the West. In the end, both Britain and Russia representatives were thrown out of Kashgar when anti-foreigner resentment reached a peak in the 1920s. Kashgar to this day retains a mystique from the warlords, camel caravans and secret agents that have shaped its history.

All these spies and explorers led Rudyard Kipling to write about a young orphan boy's recruitment into the Indian secret service in *Kim*, recounting the tales of the Grand Trunk Road that runs from Calcutta in eastern India to Peshawar at the Khyber Pass. The book immortalizes the geopolitics of the Russo-British tête-à-tête where mountain and desert kingdoms like Kashgar were mere pawns in a Central Asian chess game. "Now I shall go far and far into the North, playing the 'Great Game'," wrote Kipling.

Some argue that the Great Game never ceased. The Cold War of the 20th century was simply an extension of similar fears and suspicions. Superpowers jostled for closer access to ports for oil — witness the Soviet invasion of Afghanistan in 1979.

Markets and Bazaars

Throughout Kashgar, interspersed with the markets are rows and rows of stands selling pirated cassettes and CDs. Everything from The Bangles to Ace of Base can be purchased for a few kuai. The best of Abba and all the retro '70s and '80s hits blasting out of Toshiba and Panasonic stereos, re-mixed Asian-style, gave the bazaars the energy of a rave party on steroids. Cassettes were repackaged with brawny muscular Asian warrior men (Jackie Chan meets Shogun) or large-breasted cleavage-popping Barbarella-esque women for cover art. Sex sells everywhere, even here in the desert.

I flipped through some of the tapes as "Boom Shake the Room" and "La Macarena" pounded out of the stereos. If the disco hits in the early 1980s had died a glorious death on the pop charts of the West, they still seemed to be the most popular music here in the Far East.

I bumped into three Danish girls picking their way through Boy George and Michael Jackson CDs. The girls were on their way to New Zealand travelling with the Exodus Group, a British adventure tour organization. I had seen their Mercedes-Benz truck, a behemoth orange vehicle only the Germans could have invented for tour-hungry operators, outside John's Café. It was longer than a Greyhound bus, wider than a Boeing 737 and had 20 sleeping beds stretching across it.

The diesel-powered feat of engineering would undoubtedly be more comfortable than the hard leather seat on my Rocky Mountain. But one look at the hotel on wheels and the thought of all that pampered luxury made me think about what they were missing. When you forsake the speed and convenience of the combustion engine, you see things that go unnoticed at 60 km/h. Donkey carts hauling hay, kids playing in the fields, smoke curling out of yurt chimneys — all seem different at a slower pace.

Taking a shortcut to the side of town where the hotels were, I started to cut back through the market alleys with the three Danes. Suddenly we heard shouts of "posh, posh, posh" echoing off the walls.

As we rounded a corner there it was again.

"Posh, posh."

The firm commands could be heard coming from the donkey cart drivers weaving their way through the streets like drunken teenagers on go-karts. Behind them, Uyghur and Kazakh men walked with two or three black-and-white sheep held by ropes. The sheep would soon be sent to others to barter them away again before being slaughtered. Full-grown horses the size of ponies stood parked like waiting New York taxicabs. The horses were attached by leather harnesses to wooden carts, their heads immersed in plastic feed bags. Behind the horses, tomatoes, watermelons, cotton and corn lay piled on wooden carts.

For the first time, I realized this was the heart of Muslim China, a desert town that had been here well before Christ. Kashgar had seen Marco Polo come and go and still operated at its own sedentary pace, divorced from the reality of the industrialized smog-filled centres in the east. The 6-m-high clay and mud wall that once surrounded the city now stood in sections.

For me, Kashgar with its wretched toilet conditions and food that looked like baby salamanders or the hindquarters of cute furry puppy dogs was the genuine Chinese desert outpost. This was why

I had really come to China. I wanted to know what it was like to sleep in the desert alone in the cold of night and to eat warm slop for breakfast, hoping my stomach wouldn't revolt by noon.

Bazaars, bazaars, bazaars. Kashgar's centrally located markets are the Muslim version of delis and convenience stores for the city's 200,000 inhabitants. The Muslim Uyghurs, Kazakhs and Kyrgyz sell most of the local handicrafts and products in the bare earth markets, separate from the famous weekly Sunday bazaar on the outskirts of town. The Han have different homes and operate their stores and restaurants out of concrete building fronts.

Kashgar was an integral part in the development of commerce among the Western empires as branches of the Silk Road grew and expanded eastward. Being at the juncture of Mongolia, Kashmir and the Pamir Mountains turned Kashgar into a major refuelling stop for camel caravans throughout most of the first millennium. Back then, as now, merchants sold multicoloured geometric-patterned carpets while jewellers and others hawked books, knives, daggers, teapots, spices and dowry chests. Anything, you name it — Kashgar's got it.

Pushing my Rocky Mountain along the winding alleys of the market area while I shopped for Chinese inner tubes and spare parts for my bike, I noticed an Asian woman standing across the street fumbling with her camera as she tried to load film. Wanting to help and find out more about her, I walked over and introduced myself in that awkward way when two people don't speak each other's language.

"Ni hao (hello). Are you from Japan?" I asked.

"No," she said in stilted English. "Beijing," as she laughed nervously, shaking her head.

Our conversation began rather clumsily as we outlined each other's travel plans. Her English was very poor and my *Lonely Planet* Mandarin phrasebook became the sole means of communication. Her name was Wu Shuei and she was travelling alone, something I thought odd but interesting. We talked about getting together for dinner, although I was sure she would decline because of the taboo of Han women mixing with Caucasian men. To my surprise, she agreed and a dinner date was set at the dorm hotel where she was staying. The basics of human bonding and communication were inaugurated.

I later found out that she was trying to support herself as an artist in Beijing where she lived with her brother. After parting ways with Wu in the market that afternoon, I had a better opportunity to scour the markets for bike parts. I had promised to meet Tony and Tim at one of the supply shops. Eager to tell them of my new acquaintance, I finally found Tony at a shop that sold thick orange inner tubes, brake callipers, nuts and bolts, oil and fenders.

Tony was trying to retrofit a clamp to his bike pump so it would work on the Chinese Dunlop valves — a different type of inner tube valve than used on North American and European bikes. The Dunlop valves were incompatible with our Western pumps, but the thicker Chinese tubes were ideal to prevent the flats that had plagued me in the desert. Since our pumps couldn't inflate the Chinese tubes, we would have to hitch a ride on a truck to the nearest town if we flatted out on a highway. Then we would have to track down a Chinese floor pump. In a town like Kashgar, this was no problem. Every street had several old men fixing bicycles.

While we were browsing for bike parts, Tim had been searching for the ultimate Uyghur wool cap. He had annoyed Tony with his eccentric shopping habits when the two were in the markets together. Now I listened once more to Tony's ramblings about Tim's stubbornness. Although Tony and Tim had travelled together extensively and got along quite well in general, the strain of being in close quarters began to take its toll. In many cases, when the three of us went searching for basic staples to eat on our rides or for unique souvenirs, Tony would accuse Tim of not being courteous enough to stop and wait while we looked through shops. Tim, however, expected Tony and I to wait while he browsed the sidewalk stalls of bootlegged CDs and cassettes. Tim wasn't that bad. He just liked to wander off without telling us.

This lack of shopping etiquette and Tim's other habits led to brief spats between the two, especially when it came to sorting out accommodation arrangements. Would we need two rooms, one for Tim and his smoking or put up with one bedroom? These were the insignificant matters — minutiae almost — that we had to contend with as fellow travellers.

Hassan's Haircut Emporium

Tony had been telling me about three teenage Uyghur boys who spoke a little English and ran their parents' barbershop. More interesting than a simple haircut would be the opportunity to talk to some locals at length. He needed his hair trimmed and so did I. We rode to a shop not much larger than a giant walk-in closet. We left our bikes out front, leaning them against the curb. A black-and-white television sat in one corner on a small shelf; a painting of dandelions and poplar trees hung on the wall alongside an excerpt from the Koran. In the centre of the room was a large swivel barber chair circa 1950s bolted to the floor, complete with head and footrest. One of the boys, Hassan, was smartly dressed in a blue cotton button-down shirt.

"Your friend. You bring him today!" Hassan said excitedly, smiling to Tony as he pointed to me.

"See, I bring my friend from Canada," Tony said in halting English.

It seemed that whenever Tony and I would try to converse with someone whose English wasn't all that great, we would start to talk in the present tense and drop articles and adjectives. We would become almost childlike in our phrases — simple and truncated in our words. Our English became almost as minute as the person we were speaking to. I don't know why we did this, but subconsciously we must have thought that talking down at "their level" would somehow help them improve their language skills.

"Leave your bikes. They will be safe with my friend," Hassan said as he entrusted his boyhood pals to guard our principal means of transportation. If they took off on the bikes, we were screwed. Our whole mountain bike trip would be over.

Hassan's friends, excited by the fact we had brought our expensive flashy Western bikes, stood outside drinking Coca-Colas, clicking the shifters on my bike while Hassan started giving Tony the once-over with some long metal shears. He wouldn't make it as a hairdresser in Hollywood, but he did the basic trim quickly and efficiently without lopping off an ear or two.

Tony, curious about how often they worked, asked if the money that they kept in a drawer was split with their parents. They offered us some drinks from the cooler outside the shop as I bought my favourite orange-flavoured Chinese pop drink — Jian Li Bao — a sweet imitation Orange Crush concoction. When it was my turn to let Hassan experiment with my hair, he draped a plastic sheet over my legs and shoulders. Then some of his friends tried out my mountain bike on the street. Not being too tall, most of them had difficulty reaching the pedals, even with the seatpost lowered.

Neither of us spoke the other's language very well but we became friends nevertheless. Over the next few weeks, we would pass by the shop to say hello on our way to the market for food. No Michael Jordan T-shirts, just clean-cut hard-working kids who would pour you tea, park your bike or clean your can of Coca-Cola before you drank it.

After my haircut with the Uyghur boys, I knew that it was the young rambunctious kids who would make my trip memorable. The exuberance of the children made me feel at home in a strange land. I barely knew the history, didn't understand the language and was just beginning to discover new foods and faiths. The kids, however, made me laugh.

Children, with their smiles, giggles and hand signals, were reason enough to travel across the sea to this remote Asian paradise. Their incessant fascination with my bike and camera was never annoying. Dressed in the shiniest red or blue sandals, light pink dresses for the girls, overalls for the boys, the children in Kashgar were oblivious to the "relative poverty" that permeated their lives.

They knew only splashing in fast-running irrigation ditches and jumping or walking down poplar-lined roads. One time I saw two kids wearing gold-embroidered collars with suspenders on backwards. They looked like little Napoleons. Another day, I spotted a little boy with his head shaved who was holding onto a wooden counter as his mother bought some onions and turnips. Dressed in black-and-white striped pants, he reached up to grab his mother's hands revealing an Asian peculiarity — a rear entry opening in his pants for easy toilet training.

Like most people, I had read about and seen film documentaries on far-off destinations in remote poverty-infested locales. Not until complete strangers who didn't speak my language invited me into their mud and brick adobe houses in the middle of the desert, did I come to fully appreciate others. I had only assumed that courtesy, respect and friendship were universally practised values. Now I knew that the size of your wallet or the number of VCRs, PalmPilots or other possessions were meaningless in determining happiness. Everyone from the nomadic Tajiks to the Kyrgyz herders and Han restaurant owners was just struggling to survive.

A bit of the past, a bit of the present — that's Kashgar, that's the kids.

Chicken Feet and John's Café

With the breeze blowing through our stylish crewcuts, we pedalled back from the barber kids to our rooms. I suggested to Tony that we eat brunch together with Tim and Wu at the Oasis Café, a cosy little place located just up the street from our hotel. Wu and the café's waitress ordered for us, chatting amiably with each other in Mandarin. This must have been the first time that we didn't take 20 minutes to order using a combination of phrasebook, menu and hand signals. We had long ago given up trying to use my *Lonely Planet* book to phonetically pronounce Pinyin, China's officially Romanized alphabet of sounds.

Wu knew what to order and more importantly how to bargain and get a good price. The *wai bin*, or foreigner price as it's known in China, is at least double what the locals pay. Bus tickets, food, souvenirs, biscuits, clothes, film — everything. The tradition of tourists and travellers paying a premium is universal, but in China it's an art.

The Oasis Café's half-dozen chairs by the road, nestled beneath a corrugated plastic overhang, became our preferred wakeup grub spot when we tired of the high prices at John's Café. John's, located across from our hotel, was where everyone went to meet and get travel info. It was *the* place to have a beer.

John, the Chinese businessman who ran the place, was the only man in Kashgar, maybe China, who understood the peculiarities of Westerners. His waitress Li Shiang and his family, who helped run the café, understood prompt friendly service. As a result, Mr. John as we called him, made good money catering to all our niggling requests and complaints, from supplying me with a computer to getting others cheap plane tickets. His place had turned into the central meeting place and eatery for all foreigners who wandered into Kashgar.

If you needed to make an overseas call or organize a Jeep ride to Kyrgyzstan via the Torugart Pass, John arranged it. John's Café served french fries and pizza without cheese — Kashgar-style. The billiard tables and noodles with spicy beef were all you needed if you wanted a taste of home — apple pie, too.

At first, John's high prices were too much and we would congregate at a new dive for a few days before the lure of french fries and good customer service beckoned us back. John had a mountain bike that he bought from some traveller a few years earlier and that now made him the coolest Chinese cyclist in Kashgar. The bike came complete with clipless pedals and front shocks. Every time we brought our bikes by, John would pay extra attention to us, giving us a break on prices or some extra food if we tuned his gears. For the rest of our stay in Kashgar, we had that rare prized status — local prices at John's. After that, we quickly forgot about the high prices he charged the rest.

One day at John's, Tony met a German woman cyclist in her late 50s who had just finished travelling the 1,300 km up from Islamabad in Pakistan. This was her second trip along the

Karakoram Highway (KKH) by bike, turning the adventure into a photographic essay with her heavy, but very high-quality medium format Hasselblad camera.

Another traveller that I met at the café was from Wyoming. His name was Jonathan and he worked for Motorola in Beijing. Housed in Beijing University with his fellow workers, Jonathan promoted cellular phone service products. Nevertheless, the most enticing thing he told me was about the taboo of Chinese women dating Caucasian men.

A Korean girl he knew who went through a bad breakup with a Caucasian co-worker of his, sent some of her burly male friends over to the ex-boyfriend's apartment. They proceeded to throw his possessions out the 25-storey window — television set, couches, bed frame, clothes and microwave. Message received. Jonathan's friend now only dates other Westerners working in or visiting Asia.

As Tim and I listened to various culinary stories around the cafés, we strove to try new food, the spicier the better. As usual, we were dismayed that Tony preferred meat and vegetables to noodles and broth, called *lamian*. Before arriving in Kashgar I hadn't had much of a chance to sample the Muslim diet in Urumqi, let alone Beijing, beyond bread and *pilaf* (fried rice and meat). Muslim food is cheaper than traditional Chinese, though the hygiene standards were next to non-existent.

Uyghurs and Uzbeks ran kebab stands in the markets, selling mutton and chicken similar to Greek shish kebabs. If you don't want to know the source of what passed through your lips, don't ask. At least that's what I told anyone who asked me what I ate. Meat pies rolled in bread were the most common and inexpensive Muslim food. These samosa-like creations called *gush nan* were served up in the streets on long narrow metal trays with coals burning underneath. They cost as little as ¥10 ($1.60) for three. Deep-fried fish, also on the outdoor menu, although a little bony, was perfect for grabbing when going for a quick walk to the markets or post office.

The Guang Ming Café Bar, like the Oasis Café, had an assortment of rattan chairs and plastic flowers in odd-coloured vases. A large overhead fan combatted the humidity in the evenings. Renaissance prints, probably ripped out of calendars, depicting voluptuous ladies spilling out of their corsets adorned the back part of this vine-covered Muslim restaurant. Here, the male cooks could stare at the pictures and sample the forbidden fruit of the opposite sex, something their Islamic faith didn't particularly condone.

You name it, I ate it in Kashgar — especially during the night markets where you could find real delicacies. The markets, usually set up after 10 p.m. on temporary wooden tables, were divided into Chinese and Muslim sections — the Han tables on one side, the Muslim tables on the other. I would head out to spend the warm evenings in the streets. Lamps illuminated boiling pots of deep-fried chicken feet or steamed dumplings with onion and olives. Turfan red wine was sold beside yoghurt and honey mixtures spread on giant bagel-like loaves.

The dough used to make noodles was bounced up and down in the air like pizza dough in an Italian restaurant. The elastic-like substance was stretched ever outward with each successive twirl. Eventually, the dough would separate into long thin strands, be doubled over to make more strands, before being dipped into boiling water. That very same water was then used to make tea, offered free to unwitting customers.

My strolls in the warm humid evenings gave me a peek into the life of the Muslims and Han co-operating in economic equanimity. For two nights, I visited the evening food court with Wu, the Beijing woman I had met in the market. She persuaded me to swallow some things I had only seen in biology class, and I obliged knowing that to hesitate would deny my palate a delectable treat. Every part of an animal or bird, from chicken to sheep to the indeterminate, was up for sale to be downed with a cold bottle of water or Coke. I had long ago learned that to enjoy something new, I had to first put aside my impressions and bite the bullet so to speak.

Eating in Kashgar has not always been so lively and safe. On the bus ride from hell into Kashgar, I had read Peter Fleming's 1930s-era *News from Tartary*. In it he described ceremonial beheadings at dinner parties as part of the culinary adventure of this roaming desert outback.

> *You may never know what may happen at a banquet in Kashgar, and each of our official hosts had prudently brought his own bodyguard. Turki and Chinese soldiers lounged every-where; automatic rifles and executioners' swords were much in evidence, and the Mauser pistols of the waiters knocked omi-nously against the back of your chair as they leant over you with the dishes. ... Nobody was assassinated.*
>
> PETER FLEMING, *News from Tartary*, 1936

Going back as far as the 9th century, Urumqi and Kashgar have had a long history of spirited dinner parties and banquets where not all the guests left alive. One governor, hosting a large dinner party but fearful for his life, stepped behind a seated companion and ordered a soldier to decapitate the traitor. While the guests screamed at the blood gushing out of the dead dinner guest's neck, the governor insisted everyone commence eating as though noth-ing excessive had happened.

Drinking and Credit Card Hassles

Although Kashgar might be considered a backwater wasteland trapped in time, it still adapts to the modern-day nomads who pass through it. The town residents make a living from the staples and services they provide for those on bikes and tour buses. Though it may be as barren as a run-down desert service station in Nevada, Kashgar still likes to party on the weekends as long as it involves alcohol. At night, most of the restaurants like the Oasis turn into bars where the famous Chinese "wine" and white light-ning are consumed in astonishing quantities. Although alcohol isn't officially sold in Muslim restaurants, Chinese wine (hard liquor) and sweet sherry are widely available. All alcohol specifications are highly suspect — many bottles claim over 50-proof content. Most Westerners drink the Beijing or local Xinjiang beer, which tastes like a light Mexican Dos Equis.

Across from the traffic circle in front of our hotel was the Seman Hotel (pronounced Si-maan), a low-slung dorm-style building with blue domes where a wing of beds once served as the Russian consulate. Every weekend night around three in the morning, several Pakistani men who loved to drink and dance would stumble out of the Seman's Peacock Dancing Hall. Some would proceed to argue with the curb or the trash bins in front of our rooms; some would get into fistfights — again, usually with the garbage cans. This Friday night ritual kept many people awake including those in our building at the Overseas Hotel across from the Seman.

A lot of Pakistani traders who make the drive up the KKH from Pakistan, look to escape the stringent attitudes on alcohol and women from their more conservative Islamic country. Some are heavy drinkers by Pakistani standards; others just don't have a lot of experience with liquor. Most of the men, however, look at the opportunity to come to Kashgar to drool over Western women, particularly curvaceous blue-eyed blonde women — a rarity in Pakistan. They do this very overtly as they pass by in the halls or streets. Others seek the services of Han prostitutes. This is a flourishing business that provides supplementary income for some local women, both Chinese and Muslim. The lecherous looks at Western women had become so bad when we were there that there were occasional reports of rape by Pakistani men. Thankfully, fights and yelling matches between incensed Western males and the traders are more common at the Chini Bagh Hotel than the Seman or Overseas hotels.

The Chini Bagh, meaning "Chinese gardens," was a pivotal landmark during the Great Game, and was once the site of the British consulate. Beautiful English country gardens maintained by Diana Shipton, the wife of British diplomat Eric Shipton, made the consulate a frequent spot on the Kashgar dinner circuit. More an accomplished mountaineer than ambassador, Eric Shipton later pioneered the assault up Everest that Sir Edmund Hillary would follow.

Now the hotel with its two towers is a watering hole for visiting Pakistani traders, a separate wing perpetually reserved for their partying. More frequent is the grabbing of breasts, a rumour so widespread that some Western females stay away from the Chini Bagh. I was told the pit toilets at the back of the hotel are also a favourite spot for some of the Pakistanis to spy on the buxom foreign women. A lot of Pakistani traders do, however, keep to themselves and respect women.

Passing the Chini Bagh the next day, I exchanged some Chinese currency for Pakistani rupees with the moneychangers that stood outside the hotel, calculators in hand. I thought I could get a better rate from them than from the Bank of China for my trip down the KKH in a few weeks. I had taken my friend Wu along with me, balancing her on the back of my bike rack. We wanted to go to a bookstore I had seen and browse for some Urdu phrasebooks (the national language of Pakistan).

After looking through the various children's books, educational texts and phrasebooks, Wu explained in Mandarin to the clerk about another curiosity of mine. Over her three-day visit in Kashgar, we had become used to hand signals and drawings on scraps of paper to communicate — two strangers who really didn't have a clue about each other's country or customs. I hadn't seen any books on the Tiananmen Square massacre except for the occasional official history book published by the government, so we asked.

"Mei you (we don't have any)," the clerk replied, explaining that store owners risked jail time by state censors if unauthorized publications were sold on such sensitive topics.

Wu had to take a bus back to Urumqi and catch a connecting flight to Beijing later that afternoon. So we paid for the few books that interested us and left the shop. When I unlocked my bike, I noticed someone had taken my valve cap off and deflated my rear tire. We hailed a motorcycle with a sidecar, and with Wu on the side

I sat in the passenger seat carrying the bike on my shoulder back to my hotel. Each time we went over a bump, the front wheel would bang into my back. Wu and I had our last lunch together with Tony and Tim at John's Café where a young Danish couple was celebrating their honeymoon — a backpacking holiday along the Silk Road. Just the sort of trip I would like to take to celebrate the same occasion.

After the flat at the bookstore, I wanted to unload some gear I was carrying around and mail it back to Canada. This might prevent any further flats like the ones I had experienced in the desert once I left Kashgar and got back on the highway. I was apprehensive about the efficiency of China's postal system. I was pleasantly surprised to hear from others that it was amazingly prompt and quick. Just make sure to frank (date your letters) in front of the desk clerk to prevent theft, that is, if you can catch a clerk working.

Chinese mail may be more efficient than Canada Post, but the workers are big on long lunch breaks. You don't need unions in China to slowly jade workers into abusing the system. Most government jobs are "iron rice," meaning you have your job for life. Your job is more rock solid than the rising sun.

Now, glue is another matter. Don't expect your stamp to stick if you lick it. Glue must still be a technological secret coveted by the West because Chinese glue doesn't work. Thick glue like molasses sits ready for your use, plopped in jars at designated counters. Gluesticks? Forget it. The Chinese — at least those in Xinjiang province — have never even heard of them. My own little tube of gluestick was about the only thing I did bring on my trip that was absolutely invaluable.

The previous day in the market I had bought a cheap brass chest about two and a half feet long, the perfect sturdy box in which to send my things back. I had learned that the Khunjerab Pass that straddles the China-Pakistan border was not as cold in late August as I thought. It required little more than cycling tights and a warm top and windbreaker.

I triple-strapped the chest with bungy cords on the rear rack of my bike, glad to soon get rid of unwanted clothes, maps, books and bike parts. The additional rear derailleur, cassette wheel wrench and blown inner tubes were all packaged up in the chest and wrapped in a white cloth as necessitated by the postal staff. In all, I sent off 15 kg of gear and clothing back to Vancouver via the slow route — by boat.

After mailing my gear and clothing, I checked the *poste restante* desk to see if Visa had sent me a replacement card for the one I lost in Beijing. The *poste restante* system (a holding system for mail forwarded to towns in advance of your arrival) was a great idea for travellers who needed a safe place to have letters and packages sent.

A sign written in large block letters at the counter warned of the dangers of mailing anti-proletarian material back to the decadent West:

**All reactionary books, magazines and propaganda material, obscene or immoral articles are forbid to send.
Beware!**

I wasn't going to send back any braised duck brain or treatise on toppling the People's Liberation Army. All I wanted was to send some things home safely and pick up my replacement Visa card. After giving a week's grace period for a new Visa card to arrive from Toronto, I would routinely visit the post office.

Today, nothing.

Day after day, there was no sign of any mail from the credit card company. I had a second Visa card with me from another bank, but the validation date didn't commence until mid-September when I would be in India. Visa police headquarters in Toronto insisted they could replace a lost or stolen card anywhere in the world by FedEx in 10 days.

The brochure that came with my credit card account said they could be contacted 24 hours a day every day of the week. Like the postal system, China's local phone system is remarkably good and easy to use with plenty of public and privately run phone booths in every city. What the customer service representative at Visa didn't realize was that China Telecom's phone system in Xinjiang province didn't permit 1-800 calls on their exchanges. That meant calling an International Direct Dialing (IDD) operator to reach Toronto (13 hours ahead) and running up $166 in calls. All this despite Visa's claims of a toll-free worldwide 1-800 service.

Furthermore, I don't think Visa appreciated where on Earth I was. As for FedEx, they probably never heard of Kashgar. Couriers didn't operate under normal Western business standards, especially in the middle of the desert. After five weeks, Visa's two attempts to courier replacement cards failed, most likely ending up on some yak herder's doorstep.

I left the post office without a valid credit card. I then realized, of the $1,500 I had initially brought to China with me, I was down to my last $50. Another $40 was quickly spent calling my family for a financial aid package.

To stretch my few remaining dollars as far as possible, I dropped by what must have been the kitschiest department store in China. The dingy state-run store, located near the markets, was crammed with every trinket imaginable, from fluorescent hoola hoops and majiang sets to alarm clocks that spoke the time — all for a few hundred yuan. If you ever wondered where all the leftover K-Tel Hits of the Seventies on eight-track cassettes were, or plastic Buddhas with glowing lights, red digital LED Seiko watches and skin-tight Jordache jeans — they landed here. This is where you shopped if you had to have the latest stuffed panda bear, pink rotary telephone or electronic gadgets of questionable quality. It seemed everything the Western world felt ashamed of designing or inventing 25 years ago, Kashgar had adopted as avant-garde. If those in the West once owned it, it must be trendy and cool — right? Wrong. Even the People's Stores as I called them, in the more cosmopolitan cities like Beijing and Shanghai, knew what went out of style two decades ago.

On the more practical side, I stocked up on sweets and boxed cookies. I picked my way through the wide assortment of Chinese candies wrapped in cellophane, treats Tony and I had come to relish when on the road. If the department store wasn't weird enough, the uncanny amusement device outside was. Out on the sidewalk, a white coin-operated weigh scale squawking away had attracted the attention of a dozen Han, mostly young couples. The robotic-like machine, 2 m high, had a built-in speaker that announced a person's weight aloud in English for all to hear. Half a dozen Han stood around watching their girlfriends and wives being sized up and measured. Apparently, this is a favourite pastime and source of amusement for the men. Jenny Craig watch out!

If getting your girth announced to the whole street threatens your self-esteem, then going to the dentist is a true horror story in Kashgar. Among the Byzantine streets where tailor shops nestle amidst tea parlours, the dentist stores loom. In several of these molar hellholes throughout town, pedal-operated drills ground away inside some poor victim's mouth. Outside the dentist's lair, large green chalkboard signs hung above the doors. Anatomical profiles of male and female heads with gaping mouths, bulbous eyes and decaying teeth were drawn in several colours. Pictures of gums, dentures and ruby red lips served to lure prospective customers to the pliers-wielding dentist within. Depending on the location, some of the shops showed crude metal instruments on display in the window. The use of anaesthetics is a rarity in this outermost part of China. If you need an incisor yanked, be prepared. It's going to hurt.

As I pedalled back to the Overseas Hotel, I picked up speed, accelerating along the main avenue. I had been in Kashgar for a week and knew most of the back alleys and main thoroughfares. With my panniers free of gear on my Rocky Mountain Fusion, the bike was light and manoeuvrable. I pedalled away in my top gear, passing cars on the wide road like a Tour de France cyclist barrelling down the Champs Elysées. I must have been going 45 km/h when out of the corner of my left eye I saw her. A young Uyghur girl not more than seven or eight years old was running diagonally across the street in front of me. Our paths were rapidly converging as the gap between us closed in a matter of seconds.

She never saw me.

I hit her from the side with my front wheel first, her hip and ribcage colliding with my handlebars. She screamed in horror as her legs buckled, falling underneath the bike. I cart-wheeled over the handlebars, hit the pavement and landed in the bushes alongside the sidewalk. Luckily, my head didn't contact the curb (I had just mailed my helmet back home).

Ten to twelve people, Han and Uyghur, came running from the nearby shops. They quickly gathered around the girl while I dragged my bike out of the way of traffic. The girl was on the ground, her leg bleeding and dress ripped. Her shrill cries of pain penetrated the air above the shops.

"I'm sorry, I wasn't looking. Are you okay?" I asked in futility, but my apologies fell on deaf ears.

As the others gathered around, no attempt was made to converse with me. Just the look from a few that I had done wrong. The chance of my English being understood by the others was slim. Even if someone spoke a little English, no response was forthcoming. I was the arrogant *lao wai*, the foreigner who recklessly sped along their streets on my big expensive mountain bike. The language barrier was restrictive enough when shopping in the markets or ordering food, but this paled in comparison.

I felt like shit. Absolute shit.

I waited around for several minutes, not knowing whether I should leave in shame or offer moral encouragement. Then I gathered my bike and belongings and left the scene. My right knee and thigh were bleeding from several scrapes; my shoulder was bruised from taking the brunt of the fall that had ripped my shirt at the shoulder.

Like a schoolyard kid who had just batted a baseball through the neighbour's window, I slunk away on my bike with that feeling of piercing eyes in the back of my head. One of the worst feelings in the world is when you want to help someone but you can't. I felt powerless and inept. But it was done. Over. I couldn't correct my mistake.

The Red Army Comes to Town

Putting the bike incident behind me, I focused on solving my money problems. I had called home the prior day to finalize the Parental Bank of Canada loan. In two days, I was promised, funds would arrive at the local Bank of China to last me until I reached India, or so I hoped. Unlike Tony, I had a penchant for spending more money than was absolutely necessary. When the money arrived a few days later, Tony and I walked down to the bank to withdraw the funds.

In Canada, there is a perception — occasionally a reality — that government employees lead a cushy work life with plenty of coffee breaks, holiday pay and generous overtime. In China, customer service in a government building is non-existent. If you work for the Bank of China (there are no other banks), your lunch break is effectively two and a half hours.

The banks close at 1:30 p.m. in the afternoon, reopening at four o'clock until 7 p.m. This little midday recess is a common custom, except that the Bank of China operates on Beijing time (two hours ahead). So when Tony and I walked to the bank around noon, while the other shops were busy selling their goods underneath large corrugated metal doors, the Bank of China remained closed. It was two o'clock in Beijing (their lunchtime) but only noon in Kashgar. The bank ran at its own mysterious pace. Why accommodate those who used its services?

After figuring out that confusion, returning later in the day, we paid our 4 per cent commission as I took out ¥12,060 ($2,000), enough money to last me forever. As I was sorting out how to stash more than ¥12,000 in my money belt, Tony came running over, all excited, telling me that there were People's Liberation Army (PLA) troops coming down the street. We hurried outside where crowds had gathered in front of the shops. Everyone watched silently as a convoy of military vehicles approached from 10 blocks away.

The Kashgar police include Han and Uyghur officers. They are usually chatting about in groups of three with their khaki green shirts hanging outside their pants, collars undone. Now they were suddenly displaying amazingly effective crowd control. Several dark-green Jeep Cherokees matching the forest-green outfits of the PLA soldiers were strategically placed at intersections to prevent traffic from entering the streets. The talking with the locals and cigarette smoking stopped. It was law and order time.

Part of maintaining both political and psychological control over the ethnic Muslims in Xinjiang involves sending a chilling reminder by rolling out troops through various rural towns. Beijing has long had problems with separatists in the autonomous provinces, like the Buddhists in Tibet. Stay in line and don't complain. That's the message the Uyghurs, Kyrgyz and Tajiks were being sent as armoured personnel vehicles with water cannons and gun turrets paraded by.

"Get your camera out, Brady," Tony commanded hurriedly. "Do you have enough film?"

"Hold on, I'll be right back," I replied, as I rushed into the store next to the bank. I bought some Fuji film and quickly loaded it into my Canon, dashing back outside. A blue-and-white Volkswagen led the convoy, followed by an armoured vehicle very similar to a Loomis security truck with a red siren on top. A lone Chinese soldier stood up through a hatch in the roof, hands on an AK-47 submachine gun. The procession rolled by in a rather stately manner. The army vehicles were all freshly painted; one Jeep outfitted with whitewall tires was hauling rolls of barbed wire.

All the soldiers, even those with the Plexiglas face shields and riot gear, stood absolutely straight, their crisp white gloves clasping their bayoneted rifles. Their left hands held on to the sides of the transport trucks. It was as much a show of force as a display of military precision. This wasn't just the Red Army passing through for noodles and beer. This was suppression by intimidation — Chinese-style.

As the Chinese learned after the Tiananmen Square massacre, troops brought in from other provinces, particularly those from different ethnic groups, have the advantage of emotionally detaching themselves when having to participate in their fellow citizen's bloodshed. These Han soldiers were most likely from the outlying areas of Xinjiang or another province.

Not one soldier in the convoy was Muslim.

Id Kah Mosque

If one thing defines Kashgar as the Muslim heartland of Xinjiang province, it's the Id Kah Mosque. The enormous mosque has been a symbol of the region's Islamic identity since it was built in 1442. Complete with Doctrine Teaching Hall, veranda, court-yard and elaborate minarets, the mosque stands across from the central market area. It is supported by over 100 hand-carved green wooden pillars and decorated by multicoloured flower and plant tiles.

Several times a year, up to 20,000 people gather inside the 15th- century monument to worship during special religious occasions. Others use it as a respite from the hectic bartering of the nearby bazaars. The wailing seduction of the muezzin at 3:30 a.m., sending out the call to morning prayer, is what truly gives Kashgar its character. When the sound of an Arab-Turkic dialect wafts through your hotel window in the morning via loudspeak-ers scattered throughout town, you know you're somewhere fasci-nating, somewhere in another world.

The *imam* (the officiating priest in a mosque), as in all other houses of prayer in Xinjiang, is a Beijing-mandated position. The Communist government dictates who fills these positions to pre-vent the preaching of a separate Islamic state. Chinese border offi-cials now actively discourage Pakistani *imams* or *mullahs*, who only years ago came up the Karakoram Highway from Pakistan to preach the faith.

Activist groups, like the United National Revolutionary Front of East Turkestan, operate across the border in Kazakhstan and Kyrgyzstan. They work in unison with the Muslim Uyghurs to advance secession efforts. The Uyghurs claim since China only conquered Eastern Turkestan 300 years ago, a region with similar boundaries to Central Asia, the area belongs in Islamic hands. Either way, it would take a massive armed revolution and reoccupation to defeat the People's Liberation Army.

Across from the beige-yellow mosque is the Id Kah Square, home to the city's sprawling bicycle parking lot. What nipple rings are to Marilyn Manson and skateboards are to suburban teenagers in the West, bicycles are to the Chinese. Everybody has one, complete with lock and horn. Although the keys are probably cut to fit the locks on every third bike, there is relatively little theft in Kashgar. Everyone needs a bike to get around so no one takes one. These bicycles (I had a hard time calling them bikes in the modern sense of the word) were straight out of *Ozzie and Harriet*, similar to the Schwinn cruisers used by paperboys in the 1940s.

If you want to get a loaf of bread, a watermelon or some racy dark brown nylons, you use your bike. Throw the goods in the front basket and you're all set for a quick ride home. I would frequently see women in three-inch red pumps with long flowing dresses draped over their one-speed clunkers. They would ride along holding two or three very confused live chickens upside down.

The Great Sunday Bazaar

"There's some Canadians from Calgary who just came into Kashgar, Brady. I think they're over at John's Café," Tony said, coming into our room.

As with all new arrivals in any foreign town, those who had been there the longest were sought out for tips on accommodations and restaurants. Tony, Tim and I had been in Kashgar for nine days and most of the other travellers we met had come and gone. We were now the most knowledgeable bunch hanging around the cafés and markets.

Meeting some more Canadians was an exciting proposition. I wanted to know what they had experienced, if they were on mountain bikes and if they could help me with any information for my trip ahead. Ten minutes after Tony's announcement about the people from Calgary, the maid — the one we thought moonlighted as a prostitute — knocked on our door and the three Canadians walked in. Two women in their early 20s and a skinny guy with a goatee and Tilley hat wanted to know about the hot water situation in the building. Did we have toilets that flushed properly? Could the girls have a bath without freezing to death? I gave my spiel about how nice the place was, convincing them to take the room next door — No. 605.

Brad introduced us to his cousins Leanne and Medeana. Medeana, a 22-year-old marketing major at the University of Calgary with long curly blonde hair, was travelling with her older sister Leanne, the headstrong one of the three. The three were planning to see some of the Buddhist ruins in the desert towns like Dunhuang after their stopover in Kashgar. They were all lugging around huge backpacks towering over their heads. It looked as if the lean and wiry Brad, who couldn't have weighed more than 135 pounds, might flip over backwards. What could possibly be inside, I wondered? They didn't have a tent or camping equipment to pack around. If Tony thought I stuffed too much gear into my panniers, at least I had two wheels to roll the weight around.

Brad had been living for two years in Hunan province in eastern China where he taught English to students. He was the perfect chaperone and guide for us all. He spoke fluent Mandarin. He would become an invaluable resource in getting to know the dining and shopping customs of Kashgar. Medeana and I hit it off immediately as we traded stories of each other's visits to Calgary and Vancouver. This was the first time any of them had been to Kashgar. They were very interested in checking out the Sunday market that I had missed during my first few days in town. The prospect of bazaars run by European-looking red-haired men complete with funny wool caps intrigued them. We would go the next day.

Kashgar's Sunday Market, the lifeblood of the town, is Asia's largest. It attracts 100,000 people every week. Women in pillbox hats and girls adorned in yellow silk blouses gave us a look of curiosity when passing by. Greeting us with "ni hao" or "yashimu siz" (Mandarin and Uyghur for "hello"), the Uyghur men dressed in embroidered caps and cotton vests nodded their heads politely. The collars on their button-down shirts were bigger than Don Cherry's. It was a sight to see, like Valu Village meets K-Mart.

The market was largely a Muslim affair of organized anarchy. Everything you could think of was up for barter. No price point signs. Linen, jewellery, scarves, rugs, ungodly lingerie, hats, spices, camels, fruits and vegetables. Half the fun of the market was trying to communicate with the Turkish, Uyghur, Mandarin or Farsi-speaking locals. Between "Ingilizche sozliyelemsiz?" and "Tsumar?" I never really knew if the merchants understood my awkward attempts at their native language. I was miserable at foreign languages and had failed French twice in high school. But it was fun trying to learn whether cardamom seeds cost 10 mao or 200 kuai or if a silk scarf was worth the price.

Inside the bustling Let's-Make-A-Deal enclosure, one area of booths was occupied by blacksmiths and tailors using hand irons the size of boat anchors. Carpenters used another set of booths. Cotton weavers and melon hawkers competed with braziers. Some merchants laid down burlap sacks on the ground to sell their pomegranates, tomatoes or watermelons. Others set up shop using makeshift steel girders to demarcate their cubicles that had been dormant for the week but were thriving on Sundays selling some of Asia's finest rugs and carpets.

The market area and side streets were packed with people. Everywhere you went you had to fend off kids selling packs of cigarettes for 60 cents. One inventive garlic salesman draped long beads of fresh garlic over his donkey, leading it through the bustling streets. While watching this one-man mobile store, Medeana and I lost Brad and Leanne in the crowds.

Seeing some silk and felt carpets, the two of us headed to see what you could get for your money. Buying carpets in Kashgar, as in New Delhi or Nepal, is like asking your mother to negotiate a heroin transaction with a Medellin drug dealer — she's going to get ripped off. Many naïve tourists shell out up to $3,000 US for what are surely beautiful carpets. However, the "claimed" history and quality of the weave pattern for these enormous carpets is often questionable. Whether your carpet gets mailed successfully to Boise, Idaho, or Thunder Bay, Ontario, rather than Outer Mongolia is a matter of chance. The best thing is to hire someone you trust who speaks a local dialect when browsing the bazaars. Doing your research back home (not always an easy thing) helps in buying the best-quality carpet for your money. Even Brad (whom we eventually found holding a sheep) didn't know enough about carpets or the customs of the local merchants to warrant spending a few thousand dollars.

Back in the markets, Brad and I meandered through the side streets to the donkey parking lots. Over 200 wooden pull-carts were parked on a huge tract of land. These portable rolling trucks were used by the Kyrgyz, Uzbeks, Tajiks, Kazakhs, Uyghurs and Hui to bring their goods to market. Brad was trying to get a photo of a woman dressed in a vibrant purple dress. She was keeping an eye on the animals and carts until Brad shoved his camera in her face. Unaccustomed to having her photo taken or shy, she waved her hands in front of her face for several minutes before Brad gave up.

On our walk back from the market, the four of us stopped in at the old Chini Bagh Hotel. While Leanne went inside to get some water, we met an Australian couple in the parking lot. They had just driven in on a Land Rover topped to the gills with supplies and equipment. The roof of the Rover was wrapped in canvas ready for all weather conditions. The truck even had a funnel running up alongside the passenger's window. It was connected to a giant plastic tub that encased the engine. The tub prevented water from deluging the engine when the vehicle crossed a river. With the height of the Rover, I figured they could go through at least four feet of water.

The couple in their early 50s were travelling the world in their mobile tank. After leaving Australia, they shipped the vehicle to South Africa, and then drove up through the African continent to Egypt. They had then traversed through Iran, Iraq and Pakistan, finally coming up the Karakoram Highway to Kashgar in China. What a road trip.

Split with the Brits

When Brad and I returned with the girls to our hotel, I realized this was going to be my last evening with Tony and Tim. The Brits had to leave town the next day. They were on a tighter time schedule than I was and had to fly out of Pakistan on September 7. Their travel visa for China expired in a few days, stipulating they had to be across the Chinese border into Pakistan by the end of the first week in August. It was August 4.

I was torn. Either I continue the trip with Tony and Tim but no credit card, or take the opportunity and stay awhile in Kashgar, letting them go on alone. I wanted to go with them, yet didn't want to leave. I wanted to make every effort to get a replacement for my lost credit card, even though I thought it was futile. Maybe I was just using the financial excuse to go off on my own and be independent. I now had enough money to go anywhere.

I decided to stay. Given the 50-odd days left in my trip, I had plenty of time to ride through the Pamir Mountains and into Pakistan alone. Then it would be on to Afghanistan (if I could get in) and lastly Lahore and New Delhi. My trip to Afghanistan and India had always been a separate part of my itinerary. The main trip (crossing the Chinese desert and cycling the Karakoram Highway in Pakistan) was a co-operative effort.

In a small way, I was glad I had lost my Visa card. I liked Kashgar, but solitude was beckoning. Tony had invited me on this trip and I felt badly about splitting up with him. We had been together a long three weeks. Maybe I felt I wasn't totally independent in my life and this was a way to prove myself. I don't know.

At the break of dawn the following day, Tony and Tim left for Pakistan. Outside, in the traffic circle in front of our hotel, Red Army soldiers were practising t'ai chi. Tony and Tim rode southbound past the army officers, disappearing into the poplar-lined horizon.

It was the last time I would see them on the trip. The next few weeks would rush by for me as I scurried to do a thousand things, see a thousand places. Save for a few notes left in Pakistani villages, I wouldn't talk to Tony until he returned to England. Tim and I would never become good friends, but we had got along when we had to. Too much friction.

I was on my own now. Or rather I was looking forward to doubling as tour guide for the Albertan girls and Brad. But then, they were leaving soon as well.

Mohammed's Music and Tombs

Medeana, Brad and Leanne figured out their flight arrangements to go back east and I settled down to write some postcards. My stomach felt sick for the first time on my trip. No sooner had I relaxed when Leanne came into my room. She was flustered and out of breath. She explained that Medeana had locked herself out of their room. Again. The staff at the front desk didn't have an extra key. Could I help?

To get into their room, two doors down from mine, I had to walk out onto my window ledge, inching my way along the outside of the building, six floors up. All I had to hold on to were thin aluminum beams (not counting the good sense that should have been protecting me).

Down on the sidewalk, Medeana stood watching. I could faintly hear her yell something about how crazy or stupid I was to be walking along a six-storey hotel ledge in China.

"You're crazy, you're craaazzy," Medeana's voice drifted away 70 feet below.

Finally, I was in. After that, the sisters reminded each other to put the key in a pocket, lest I had to make another tightrope-walking trip.

Leanne had first come into my room on the way to a musical instrument shop in the markets. Brad had befriended Mohammed, a 29-year-old Uyghur luthier (a stringed instrument maker), who ran the shop and invited him for tea. The next day we decided to inspect some of the instruments Brad was so excited about.

The store, nestled among the Uyghur and Kazakh market shops, displayed intricate instruments similar to violins and guitars. A variety of wood-making tools and half-finished instruments lay on a workbench. Two-string *tutors*, long-necked lizard skin *ravaps* and *tamburs* (guitars with elaborate inlaid wood) were some of the handmade creations sculpted by Mohammed's staff of seven. Many of the tambourines, guitars and horns made in the Kashgar region produced the reedy sound particular to Islamic music.

Some instruments, like the *ravap*, took over 40 days to make. Brad and I each bought one. Ivory, interspersed in black-and-white diamond patterns, made up the small salad bowl–shaped base. I couldn't resist the instrument's long-fretted, shellacked wooden neck.

Brad's fluency in Mandarin, spoken by one of Mohammed's workers, helped him barter down our final cost over two days of tea visits to the music shop. I paid ¥1,150 ($190) for my *ravap*, an exorbitant sum by Chinese standards. Mohammed had rarely had a foreign customer with whom he could have a conversation. He came to like us so much that he invited us to dinner with his wife and three-year-old son. The little boy smiled as he jumped over the table all evening long. The food wasn't particularly great — the usual greasy meat and bread fare.

The price of packaging and shipping our instruments home ran to another $175. Mohammed supplied each of us with a custom-made case to protect the *ravaps*. I had great confidence, despite my credit card hassles, that the instrument would safely make its way home. It was just a matter of how long. We learned that Mohammed fed his family on ¥16,800 a year — or $2,786. Brad, on the other hand, made ¥1,200 a month ($200), almost the same income as Mohammed, but he had no family obligations. By the end of my first five weeks in China I had spent over $2,300 — $65 a day. Most of it went for airline tickets, luggage fees, police fines, long distance phone calls and postage charges. This had to stop. Pakistan was four times cheaper, about the only consolation to my fiscal woes.

Our greatest treat came two days later at noon. As Mohammed's two newest customers, Brad and I were invited out with Leanne and Medeana to lunch at his parents' home. To be invited into a Chinese home, even by a Muslim Chinese, was an honour. Everyone had to take off their shoes and sit cross-legged on large carpets.

The general eating room had a raised wooden floor for entertaining and eating meals. The only women who came into the room were Mohammed's mother and a young girl. Both served us food, quickly retreating to a nearby doorway where they watched us in fascination. The dishes were passed around in a circle, each person taking what they could eat. *Poshkal*, a wonderful crepe-like treat filled with a yoghurt-relish mixture tasted as sweet as icing sugar.

Brad had told us in advance to eat everything they gave us. To do otherwise would be a sign of disrespect. Medeana and I, however, weren't keen on one dish. This caused a problem. Because we ate everything, even the dishes we didn't like, Mohammed thought we wanted more. If you finish your plate, apparently it means you like the food. Since we were eating everything to be considerate guests, it seemed to him that we couldn't get enough. And so the plates came. Dishes and more dishes. Finally, Mohammed was full and the eating stopped. Thank goodness.

Following our meeting with Mohammed's family, we befriended one of the city's young entrepreneurs, Ablimit Ghopor. Ablimit was an enterprising self-anointed tour guide who had been hanging around the cafés and restaurants for a few weeks. I recognized him with his Atlanta Falcons baseball cap. I had never spoken to him, until one day I noticed he was selling a little English-Uyghur phrasebook. He hawked it from restaurant to restaurant for ¥50, trying to hustle additional fees for guiding people around the outskirts of Kashgar. On the inside cover of the phrasebook, a strict warning was typed: "Please do not borrow or show the book to any local good English speakers." The meaning was lost on me. He had needed Mr. John's typewriter and photocopier to make the 45-page booklet, but the truth was, Ablimit hated Mr. John and his profitable café.

During dinner, Ablimit told us about the Abakh Hoja Mausoleum, a domed tomb with four minarets covered in green glazed tiles. It had been built in the 17th century and contained 72 bodies, mostly descendants of an ancient missionary. Ablimit suggested we hire him to go to the tombs.

Having bartered Ablimit's price down to include a half-day in the burial grounds, a donkey cart and lunch, we decided to visit the tomb a few days later. I rode slowly behind the others on my bike. An hour later, after the donkey finally trotted its way through the dry hardpack earthen roads of the tomb sites, we stopped for lunch at an adobe house.

The home was burrowed away in the poplar trees on one side of the tombs and mausoleums. A cat with a rock tied to its neck sat underneath the front porch. The cart's knitted wool cover kept the blistering heat off Brad, Ablimit and the sisters as they headed back out to the tombs. After lunch, we made our way through the labyrinth of mud and straw resting places as the noon sun quickly reached its peak in the sky.

Most tombs were no more than a metre high. Unlike the granite tombstones in the West, most of these had small domes over rectangular-shaped graves. According to the myth of the Tomb of the Fragrant Concubine, a young concubine had killed herself instead of giving up her virginity to an emperor. One hundred and twenty guards had escorted her body before laying her to rest here with her family. A large tomb on the far side of the burial grounds was erected in her honour and sealed up 200 years ago.

After several hours out in the dry burial grounds, it was getting too hot. We had seen enough. I didn't want to cycle alongside the donkey cart at a snail's pace, so I returned separately to the city. Back at John's Café, while having some more french fries, I met an American professor from Columbia University named Ray. He had recently been on the Pakistan-Afghanistan border and warned me about my planned trip through the Khyber Pass.

Ray said he had heard that some United Nations (UN) workers had been shot. The UN armoured personnel carrier had been pulled over by the Taliban rebels and everyone had been asked to step out. Without provocation, they had been asked to kneel, heads to the ground, and a bullet was put in the back of each one's head. He cautioned me to take a guide and translator. I told him that I would be letting the Canadian consulate in Pakistan know when I was planning to enter Afghanistan and would inform them when I got out.

The rest of the Calgary crew and Ablimit eventually returned from the land of the tombs. They were rushing to get to the air-port to catch a plane east, back across the desert. Leanne told us they had been delayed at a fruit stand by a melon fight. Medeana had stopped to buy a watermelon near Pan Tho City, a set of gran-ite carved Chinese warriors and lions on the south side of Kashgar. A dispute among the Kyrgyz merchant, some Hungarians and a Norwegian developed when the Norwegian couldn't agree on a price. Someone spat on someone and the haggling deteriorated into a food fight. Medeana was caught in the middle as a police officer tried to break up the altercation. This was Kashgar. Expect the unexpected.

Bye Bye Kashgar, Hello KKH

My time, too, was coming to an end in Kashgar. Before leaving this home away from home, I needed to get a permit to camp in a restricted area between Kashgar and the Pakistan border. The Public Security Bureau frequently monitors restricted areas on the highway, a route many tourist buses travel. With the help of two female tour guides, I had gone to the PSB office and obtained an Alien's Travel Permit. An alien, I guess, was someone like me from another country — another one of those foreigners.

I had met the two Uyghur guides at the Chini Bagh Hotel earlier in the week when changing money. The two women, Gulmire and a friend, worked for the China International Travel

Service (CITS). They specialized as Japanese and Russian translators, chaperoning Chinese and Western tourists to various tourist destinations outside Kashgar. Gulmire spoke Mandarin, Uyghur, Japanese and a little English. Her friend's forte was Russian.

With Gulmire's work connections at the CITS, she helped me obtain the Alien's Permit in less than two days. The permit would allow me to camp near a lake in a restricted area halfway between Kashgar and the China-Pakistan border. However, I had heard of people who, despite the proper paperwork, were not allowed to access the regions for which they had approval.

I had heard rumours from other travellers that additional licences and paperwork had to be applied for in person in Beijing. The guidebooks were even more inconsistent in their accounts. Despite the assurances to the contrary by the PSB staff, I still wasn't certain of anything. But I refused to take another bus on the highway against my own will. I wanted to start cycling again. Three weeks in Kashgar seemed like too long to be in one place. Discoing with Pakistani men Arab-style, feasting on steamed dumplings and drinking *chai* at the old Soviet consulate: these were the things that made my stay in Kashgar an eye-opening experience. For me, that's what this town had been about.

As I loaded my gear onto my bike, I hoped my old inner tubes would suffice as soon as I hit the highway. I had taken the thicker Chinese inner tubes and cut them down the middle. I lined my wheels with the tubes, placing my own Western-style Schraeder inner tubes inside. The two layers of rubber were protection from sharp objects and internal flaws in the wheel.

I tested the weight on my rear tire. Everything seemed okay. I hoped the punctures that had given me so many problems in the desert were over. Back to John's Café for one last meal as I gorged on shish kebabs and french fries for the 40th time. I said goodbye to John and his wife and then I was off, headed out in the searing heat.

Now it was time to begin the longest part of my journey — the Karakoram Highway. The highway, or KKH as everyone calls it, loosely retraces part of an old Silk Road route through the mountains and valleys of northern Pakistan. Pakistan was unsophisticated and poor, its tranquil north divorced from the bustling cities of the hot south. The next few weeks would be a trip into one of the poorest, most corrupt and fiscally bankrupt nations in the world.

For the first time in five and a half weeks, I was on my own. The mountains would define my course and dictate the weather. Then the politics of Afghanistan and Kashmir (two of the region's most volatile political powder kegs) would take over, imposing their own set of rules.

Karakoram Highway

From China to Pakistan

The Great Wall of China was built to keep people out. Conversely, the Karakoram Highway was constructed to bring two nations together — China and Pakistan. Construction of the wall began at the dawn of the Silk Road; the highway rejuvenated an old trading route centuries later. Tens of thousands gave their lives to complete both engineering marvels.

Named after the Karakoram Mountains in Pakistan, the 1,300-km-long highway winds it way from Muslim China to Muslim Pakistan. The highway starts in Kashgar and passes through Tajik and Kyrgyz villages and the desert plateaus of China's Pamir range. This first section, where yaks graze amid marshes and sand dunes, was where I would spend my first week riding after leaving Kashgar. I was headed toward the China-Pakistan border where I would cross over the Khunjerab Pass at 16,000 feet, the highest paved roadway in the world.

It was August 18 and I had spent three weeks in the bustling markets of Kashgar. I needed to finish riding the Karakoram Highway in two to three weeks. I had a plane flight out of Delhi 2,000 km away at the end of September. If I was going to have time to go to either Srinagar in Indian-held Kashmir or to Afghanistan it meant cycling 60 to 90 km per day. I had to choose one place or the other. I opted to go into the midst of Central Asia's longest

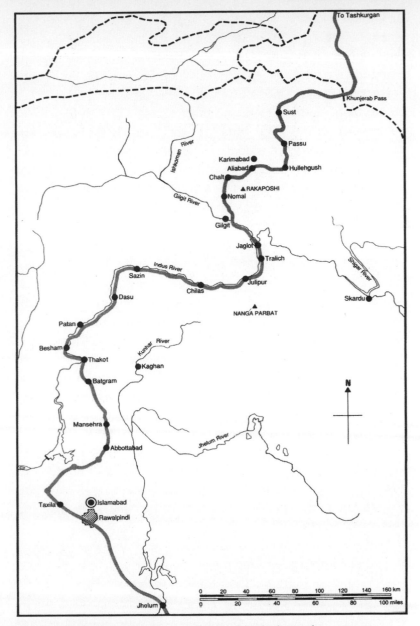

Karakoram Highway (KKH) — 1,300-km long highway that connects northwest China with northern Pakistan. The KKH starts in Kashgar, China and ends in Islamabad, Pakistan.

protracted Islamic holy war in Afghanistan. My immediate goal was to cover the 420 km to the Pakistan border in four to five days. I'd make this by pedalling eight-hour days and camping alongside the road. Once I got over the border and down into the villages of northern Pakistan, I would rest for a day or two.

No more searing deserts, no more British mates to turn to for advice — I set out alone from Kashgar. Two-wheeled mule carts carrying sacks of grain plodded down roads past tall poplar trees and lush green cornfields. Women in brightly coloured dresses and beige sandals balanced wooden poles across their shoulders, tin buckets of water on each edge.

I was glad to be putting the miles behind me again on my fully loaded Rocky Mountain Fusion. Solitude became my friend. When you're spinning your legs hour after hour, passing Chinese trucks and peasant farmers in the fields, you get into a rhythm that numbs your brain of the pain your body is going through. Limbs turned in circles effortlessly like a metronome dutifully ticking away. Psychologically, I set myself goals — getting to the next village, covering 50 km in a given afternoon or getting to the top of the next ridge or switchback. Focus, focus, focus. Without these small goals, the trip blurs and vanishes into tedious indifference.

Part of that discipline meant brief stops. During a rest period to get some cookies and meat pies out of my panniers, two boys climbed up from the fields below to greet me. With their broad faces, I didn't know if they were Kyrgyz or Uzbek. All sorts of groups lived out here in the desert plains, even the odd White Russian family that had settled in the Pamir Mountains after the Russian Revolution.

One of the boys, who couldn't have been more than 10 years old, climbed up a telephone pole to pose for a picture. He wore a wool cap customary for most Muslim males. His blue-and-yellow T-shirt had "Welcome to Hong Kong" emblazoned on it. These kids probably didn't even know where Hong Kong was on a map, let alone understand that China now possessed the former British colony. It was probably just a souvenir handed down from a relative who went to Urumqi or another large city in the east. Children in these parts of China would probably never leave their province in their entire lives, let alone travel like me. My picture-taking attracted the attention of an older man who came over to inspect why some foreign guy with a beard was poking a fancy camera in the face of two of his neighbours. A third kid with a red-and-black Reebok baseball cap, who had been watching from several metres away, ran off into the field.

"Had you be to Pakistan?" the older man enquired.

His basic understanding of English surprised me. I wasn't sure if he was asking if I was going to or coming from Pakistan. So I pointed to the 7,719-m (25,326-ft.) snow-capped desert peak in the distance.

"I will sleep by Mt. Kongur, by the *tagh*," I said using the word for mountain.

No response.

"*Kul*. I go to the *kul*," I said referring to the Uyghur word for lake. Still no response.

Our conversation was at a standstill. Every time I got used to conversing with one ethnic group and understanding their level of English comprehension, things would change. Rural people knew less English and Mandarin than those in Kashgar or Urumqi. The Uyghurs seemed the most educated. It was confusing.

I had to part ways with the kids and get back on the road. So far, since entering the desert three weeks ago, I hadn't had any flats or tire problems. I was confident that the lighter load in my panniers would put less pressure on my spokes and rims. I didn't want the rubber tubes to expand again in the desert heat and pop.

A few hours after leaving the surrounding area of Kashgar, I came across a group of red sandstone homes nestled in farmland. This was Upal (pronounced Wupair), a one-street town inhabited by Kyrgyz settlers. The town is famous for an 11th-century Muslim scholar who wrote the first Uyghur dictionary. It was the last chance to restock water and food before my 170-km leg through the desert canyon and dry river ahead.

A long dusty road led uphill to a small group of stores and teashops. My expensive mountain bike attracted the attention of some of the Upal kids who brought me water and sat on the table beside me, staring at me while I ate. I hate to admit it's odd to be so fascinating as to be worth staring at. As I spread cheese on my bread with my Leatherman knife, the kids all wanted to play with the serrated blade, cutting up my watermelon in little pieces. Others wanted to try on my prescription sunglasses or click the shifters on my bike and watch as the chain got tangled up in the gears. This amused them to no end, especially one little boy with a shaved head.

In the 38 days since arriving in China, I had lost 30 pounds. I went from a healthy weight of 185 pounds down to 155. I was eating all I wanted, felt full after every meal, but the weight still kept dropping, largely a result of the intense heat. Factoring in my prolonged stay in Kashgar, I had been on the road two out of every four days. I felt good and lean, very fit for a six-foot-two 33 year old.

I spent the better part of the day cycling on the highway, leaving the small teashops and drink stalls behind. All along the KKH or Big China-Pak Friendship Highway, as the Chinese referred to it, long thin telephone poles dotted the road like candles on the edge of a birthday cake. Several sections of highway were washed out by flooded streams that had eaten away at the parched soil and undercut the poorly built roads. The occasional tour bus passing through would usually leave the tarmac and detour around the road, driving onto the rocky desert.

I was still riding at the same elevation as Kashgar (1,300 m), but knew from my maps that the days ahead would reveal barren dusty canyons. Finding water would prove difficult. By the end of my first day on the Karakoram Highway, the irrigation ditches and fertile farmlands slowly gave way to dried-up riverbeds alongside Tajik and Kyrgyz villages. No more Mandarin-speaking Chinese or Uyghur-speaking Muslims — just new dialects, customs and food.

When a dumptruck loaded with people pulled up beside a Kyrgyz home where I had camped for the evening, I went over to observe. The highway had built-in prayer stops — semicircular concrete rest areas complete with carpets. I had never seen anyone pray outside of the mosques in Kashgar. There were 11 men and 3 women in the truck, but only the men got out to pray. The men knelt on the ground and said their prayers to Allah for 20 minutes, and then, as abruptly as they had hopped off the truck, they got back on and drove off. For some of them, seeing a foreigner with camping gear and a modern mountain bike was a rarity, especially since the highway had only opened to the outside world in 1986. Most were accustomed to Westerners on tour buses.

Several hours after I settled into my sleeping bag, as the full moon shone above, I heard the sound of steps outside my bivouac sac. I had pitched the bivy sac (a one-person cocoon-like tent), around the side of a house for privacy. The last thing I expected was some midnight company. I opened the fly zipper and looked up at the face of a Kyrgyz man, haggard and missing teeth, who shone a flashlight. He had come out from his home and was gesturing for me to come inside. He started to wheel my bike, dragging its locked wheels to the house. After a few minutes of "No" and "Thank you, I'm okay" (all useless words to him), he went back inside and left me to try to fall back to sleep — or so I thought. Out he came again a few minutes later with some tea, staring at me while I sipped what tasted like recycled dishwater. I smiled appreciatively as though it was the best Earl Grey tea from India, wishing I had a few packets of NutraSweet to add flavour.

When the alarm went off on my electronic daytimer at 3:30 a.m., I fell back into slumber mode. The warm night helped me sleep, even on the hard ground. I couldn't get up, not after only an hour's sleep. I was tired from burning up so many calories the previous day. Getting up early to cover a few dozen kilometres before the heat began at noon was a task I didn't relish. When I eventually woke again, it took me another hour to pack my stuff into my panniers as I stumbled around in the dark with a fading flashlight. When riding alone and camping outdoors, sleeping becomes a luxury. I couldn't lounge around as I had in the hotels of Kashgar. Meal rations became the source to gain energy, water to stay hydrated and sleep to balance everything. It all becomes a daily ritual. Without discipline, you can't cover long distances day after day.

The Ghez Canyon

The moon was still out as the sun rose over the horizon at six o'clock, painting the tip of the Pamir Mountains crimson purple. I stopped, took a few deep breaths and savoured the fresh smell of the air. Even if Tony and Tim had been there, I'm not sure either could have convinced me that this solitary experience amidst the beauty of the cornfields and blue sky would be better shared with them.

Getting back on the road, I vowed to ride long and hard and find a pace that would cover good ground each day. The canyon area where I was headed was prone to strong westerly winds that would make riding at a fast pace difficult. Ideally, I wanted to put 100 km a day behind me but that was probably too ambitious a goal in this heat. I wouldn't know if my legs and lungs were up to the challenge until after a few days of cycling through the Ghez River canyon. My diet, healthy and full of a variety of Muslim and Chinese delicacies over the past weeks, was now cheese, bread, crumbling cookies, warm water and more bread. The bagel-like breads I had packed in Upal were too dry to be considered nourishing. When I ran out of bottled water, I drank water from small streams, filtered through a purifier. At one point, my filter seized up and I had to fill my water bottle straight from the source. Most of the streams were full of bacteria from goats, sheep and yaks higher up in the hills. Usually, I didn't bother to put iodine tablets in my water bottles because of the bitter aftertaste. I risked diarrhea, giardia and hepatitis A by doing this, but my health had been perfect throughout the trip so far. I was counting on a strong immune system to get me through the dubious food and water I ate and drank.

One of the last pools of water I passed that day was a small dirty pond beside the highway. Six boys were cooling off and playing in the muddy water to escape the heat; their clothes and sandals were at the side of the road. The water was a beige sandy colour. A few trees stuck out of the centre of the ditch-turned-swimming-pool. The boys splashed each other in the water, oblivious of their nudity in front of a stranger. They stood at attention for me like cadets at training school when I brought out my Canon and shouted, "Picture, picture."

After giving the kids some bread, I began cycling 140 km through the Ghez River canyon over the next two days with its maroon red sandstone walls. In some parts, the paved highway turned to rough gravelly rock-strewn stretches. The soil became dry and flaky, void of most greenery as the water table became lower. In order to prevent my tires from flatting in this dusty off-road section, I put more air in so the sharp rocks wouldn't penetrate through to my rims. Like most sections on my trip, whenever the terrain changed, I changed the tire pressure accordingly to accommodate for the safest ride with all my gear (higher for paved roads, lower for rocky portions and always more air in the back). Other vehicles weren't so lucky in navigating the canyon fault-free. One truck carrying a bulldozer flipped over when it ran off the road, turning into a twisted hunk of crushed metal.

I thought the ride would be cooler as I cycled beside the Ghez River. It was anything but as the midmorning heat soon reached a searing 35°C. The early morning temperatures had been nippy, but now I needed to stop and change out of my long tights. With the water level low, many gravel embankments stood higher than the river. The canyon rose sharply a few hundred metres on either side of the wide river, its multicoloured brown-and-orange strands revealing layers of uplifted rock.

At a small power station above the river, I changed into my cotton walking shorts to be as inoffensive as possible to the Muslims living along the highway. Underneath I wore my Lycra cycling pants. I put on my sandals, and tied my hiking shoes to the back of my bike, letting them dangle off the edge. I climbed up a metal ladder to the concrete office structure above the station, curious as to who or what might be inside. Deteriorating cement blocks with peeling white paint held the building together. Down below, a set of floodgates controlled the small dam on the river.

I tiptoed around to an open window and noticed a man wrapped in blankets on the concrete floor. He was sleeping away from the sun that streaked through the glassless window frames. The dam's control room consisted of a bare light bulb burning in the corner, a brown wooden desk and radio. I wasn't sure how busy this guy was but it might be awhile, maybe months, before the river rose necessitating the opening of the floodgates. It was hard to determine how much power could be delivered to the nearby villages, as the river was so low.

The canyon continued to rise as I left the dam and river; the heat bore down on my arms and face. I had started to wear a bandanna wrapped around my forehead and soaked in water. After a few days, this resulted in unusual tan lines across my face. When travelling by bike where the temperatures reach the 45°C range, knowing the distance to the next village is essential. I had cycled on the outskirts of the Sahara desert in Morocco and although never quite used to the heat, had endured it nevertheless.

A two-litre plastic Evian bottle was attached to the downtube of my bike frame and wrapped in a wet sock to keep it cold. Three or four additional one-litre bottles lay in the top quarter of my panniers where they could keep cool. Another three additional water bottles were strapped to the side of my bike wherever I could fit them. Part of the problem with keeping hydrated was that I often downed several cans of Jian Li Bao, the sweet orange pop drink that made my mouth dry, rather than quenching my thirst.

My *Lonely Planet* guidebook, on the Karakoram Highway, was usually a cyclist's bible and best friend. But it showed only five food stops between Kashgar and the border, most of them for bread, water and cookies. More importantly, this meant I could only rely on five places to get bottled water. There were probably others, but where? The guidebooks I had read were great for advice on towns over 50,000 people, but map details were not their forte. The large-scale maps stuffed into the side of my pan-niers indicated settlements scattered throughout the area. The maps were surveyed in 1981, but I had no idea how reliable they were now or if I could get extra water if I ran dry.

As the heat sapped my energy, I soon found a new source of water to deal with my dwindling supply — tour buses and 4 x 4 vehicles. Many vehicles with Han and European passengers would slow down, waving bottles of water and pieces of bread out the window. Each time I would wave for them to stop, eager to replen-ish my supplies. I would never suggest heading out on the road with no water, trusting that strangers will want to share their food and water, but this kind of traveller's etiquette was a pleasant, heartening gesture I found in all my travels.

Basically, there are four kinds of vehicles travelling the Karakoram Highway in China: Nissan and Mitsubishi tour buses, the ubiquitous blue Chinese trucks headed to Pakistan to trade goods, army Jeeps and the Mitsubishi Pajeros, Toyota Land Cruisers and Jeep Cherokees rented from hotels or owned by gov-ernment officials. In China, it's nearly impossible to drive your own privately rented vehicle. You have to pay for a driver who acts as a government censor, deciding where the car or Jeep can be driven. This, of course, drives up the cost. The four-hour drive from Kashgar to the Kara Kul Lakes (a popular tourist destination) costs ¥600 ($100) per person.

Of all people travelling on the Karakoram Highway, those in rented cars would always yell out words of encouragement as they zipped past me. At one point, some Brits passed me in a Santana (the Chinese version of a Volkswagen Jetta) and shouted, "Don't stop now. Hammer on mate." When I was cycling alone in remote areas, a very solitary endeavour, it was always a welcome boost especially when I was headed uphill.

Heading into the Pamirs, it seemed as though one needed a car to get to the next town. No one, however, owned one. The dis-tances between settlements seemed inconceivable — often 150 km. Everyone got around by foot or donkey cart (the preferred animal-powered traffic) or hitched a ride. Life was slow-paced and mellow. Locals may not travel beyond the confines of the hamlet they live in for years. I thought of my own life in the West, driving from town to town, province to province and state to state, bringing me closer to the town next and the town next closer to me. Here in the butt end of China, was one of those few remaining places on earth at the opposite end of both the Automobile and Jet Ages.

As I thought about the differences in cultures, I remembered that Gulmire, the young tour guide I met in Kashgar, would be chaperoning a busload of tourists to the lakes up ahead. I was keeping my eye out for the charter bus she toured in, until one afternoon I saw a familiar red shirt flash by in the window of a Mitsubishi. The small bus pulled over and Gulmire, dressed in her green khaki pants, a Nike baseball cap and red T-shirt, jumped out of the vehicle and ran over to me. She was excited to have caught me on my trek through the canyon and introduced me to the group in the van.

Gulmire's ability to speak several languages allowed her the privilege of a much-coveted travel visa as part of her work with the government travel bureau, the CITS. She had travelled to parts of Asia otherwise off limits to other Chinese nationals. Most Chinese, whether they be Han, Muslim or from some other ethnic group, will never leave their own region. Of all the places the Chinese do travel to within their large country, the far western corner where I was cycling was one of the least visited, despite the accessibility provided by the highway.

The Pamirs

Marco Polo once described the Pamir Mountains as a place where "a lean beast grows fat in 10 days." The Pamirs (meaning "pasturage") were rounded by glaciers tens of thousands of years ago and are almost completely void of all vegetation, even at lower elevations. Unlike Nepal, Pakistan or Canada, where mountains are tucked in between valleys or hidden behind other peaks, the

Pamirs and the accompanying Kunlun range in China are virtually unobstructed because they rise straight out of the desert.

> *The place is called Pamir, and you ride across it for twelve days together, finding nothing but a desert without habitations or any green thing, so that travellers are obliged to carry with them whatever they have need of. The region is so lofty and cold that you do not even see any birds flying. [The people are] Savage Idolaters, living only by the chase, and clothing themselves in the skins of beasts. They are in truth an evil race.*
>
> MARCO POLO, *The Travels of Marco Polo*, 13th century

Camels, yaks, donkeys, sheep, goats, mules and occasionally a sun-dried brick adobe house or yurt (home to the Tajiks and Kyrgyz) were the only signs of life among the marshy pastures. Most of the poplar trees at the base of the mountains were uprooted by the Kyrgyz and replanted near villages to provide wind protection. Through the last remnants of the river canyon, I slowly neared the Pamir plains where Kyrgyz workers with scythes amassed piles of wheat. Several kilometres off the highway — 3,300 m above sea level — marvellous grey sand dunes furled over each other like billowing fabrics. This stretch of the KKH through the wide-open desert was lonely and bleak. The climate was cooler as the highway rose away from the canyon where the road dipped gently up and down following the river.

Hour after hour I churned my legs around and around as the road went in a straight line, unwavering in forgiveness. The road was flat as a billiard table and began to climb ever so gradually. White mileage markers passed one after the other like endless dominoes. In the desert, this is what you do. Hammer onward, driving the chain and gear teeth around, one revolution after another. This endless unfurling of tarmac and desert made me long for something to spice up the ride. Everything looked the same. Mountains on my right, marshy sections on my left.

It was repetitive, but I had to keep going. The desert can mess with your psychological resolve when hours of spinning the pedals doesn't yield any discernible difference in your surroundings. A clever but cruel trick played by geography on travellers of plains, deserts and oceans alike. Sadly, I confess that the blue skies and the faint grey moon over the horizon were pushed far from my half-cooked brain. The lunar landscape environment yielded the fear, "Oh please don't let me get stuck in this desolate land!"

In the midst of this dune and desert stretch of the Karakoram Highway, two Kyrgyz construction workers in orange plastic vests and baseball caps were painting mileage markings on the road. They were using large sheet-metal stencils to paint red numbers every few kilometres. One of the construction workers, Sawat, lived in a nearby Kyrgyz yurt settlement, Bulun Kul, just off the highway. Their lone means of transportation was a rickety bicycle.

Like all of the Kyrgyz who lived in yurts along the KKH, their hospitality could be counted upon if I needed some water or bread. Because of the proximity to the Kyrgyzstan and Tajikistan borders (in some places 10 km), the region was considered a restricted zone by the Chinese police. Foreigners were not allowed to wander from the highway without permission. One family allowed me into their yurt, letting me stretch my legs and drink some warm *cha* (tea). Dozens of carpets were piled on one side of the 5-m-wide yurt for sleeping use, its chimney rising an equal distance to the roof. An iron coal stove, an integral component in all yurts, served as the kitchen in the centre. We all sat on a raised seating area, standard in Muslim homes for entertaining guests and eating meals. While I sipped boiling hot tea and ate some soup cooked from a giant wok-like pan, one of the Kyrgyz kids tried on my cycling gloves and jumped around like Muhammad Ali. He danced a little boxing routine on the carpet as his mother and younger sister clapped in amusement.

Full with whatever local animal gave its life to end in my soup, I started to cycle the final few hours toward the Kara Kul Lakes. The Kyrgyz boy followed me on horseback, where he alternated between chasing jackrabbits and trying to catch up with me on my bike. As I pedalled away, he yelled something aloud (hopefully goodbye).

Kara Kul Lakes

The "Black Lakes," as the Uyghurs call the Kara Kuls, are a set of lakes between two enormous mountains, Mt. Kongur and Muztagh Ata. The three lakes, Besekh Kul, Shor Kul and Kara Kul, are the only place south of Kashgar that tourists regularly visit unless they're taking a bus across the border to Pakistan. The lakes had been turned into a quick stopover for tour bus operators who would dump their customers off at the diner, let them eat for a while and then send them for a few hours of hiking. If staying for the evening, they would sleep in steel-framed yurts that didn't do justice to the real thing. For an outrageous fee, you could experience an evening in a North Face sleeping bag and "pretend" this was how the Kyrgyz lived.

At the construction trailer turned restaurant, I had dinner with a young British couple, Dave and Michelle. They were busing their way south to Pakistan and planned to fly out of Gilgit, the main town in northern Pakistan. By the time it was dark, Dave and Michelle decided to retire to their padlocked steel yurts. I left the two of them and wheeled my bike to the nearby sandy beach, pitching my bivy sac and secured my bike gear.

Each night along the highway, I had begun the habit of taking my cable lock and winding it around my bike frame. I looped it through the wheels, pannier straps and finally a tiny eyelet at the end of my cocoon-shaped quarters. If anyone wanted to snag my bike at night, I would feel a pull on the bivy sac. Of all the things that happened on the KKH, I never had to fend off bike thieves. My handlebar bag that hung from the front of my bike always came inside with me at night. It acted as a kind of pillow underneath the end of my sleeping bag. In it were my camera, passport, money and tape recorder, as well as my trusty flashlight. With this setup, I was safe, zipped up against the outside elements, all my belongings secure. Alone in the warmth of my down sleeping bag,

I watched the reflection of the snowy white peaks of nearby Muztagh Ata off the lake's sapphire blue waters. Muztagh Ata, meaning "Father of Ice Mountains," stands at 7,546 m (24,750 ft.) and is a popular trekking destination for mountaineering expedition groups. If the tourists in their bright white buses thought these lakes were beautiful in the daytime, they were missing the best of the mountain-desert scenery — the snow-capped peaks under a full moon.

As the sun came up over the mountains the next morning, a large foot stepped on my tent-like sac and rudely awakened me. The red nylon material wall jutted towards me, narrowly missing my head. At first, I thought some drunken tourist had had a little too much fun the previous night. But when the grunts and moans seemed more like cows being herded to pasture, I quickly squirmed around, unzipping the flap.

I poked my head out and stared out at the hairy hind legs of a huge black wild yak. It was taking a shortcut through the beach over my body. Suddenly, a dog ran up behind the yak and stopped to urinate on my tent. What a way to start the morning. It turns out that a Kyrgyz herder was taking his herd of yaks for a stroll around the lakes. Yaks, similar to the Tibetan ox, dominate a lot of the valleys and plains near the foothills in this part of Central Asia. Along with *dzos* (a hybrid of cow and yak), yaks are as big as moose and hardly as charming.

Tashkurghan

Safe from my encounter with the yak, I wound my way upward to the Subash Plateau, a 4,100-m-high expanse of flat arid plains. Wherever I stopped to get some food from my panniers, a dozen or more boys and girls and their parents would rush to meet me at the road. It took some patience and bartering skills to dissuade those who wanted to sell me a hat or bag. The last thing I needed was to start collecting more weighty trinkets and souvenirs to bag me down.

At a marsh field, I stopped to buy a handbag from some Kyrgyz settlers who were hustling agate and camel bone carvings. Such casual encounters with the Kyrgyz were becoming commonplace throughout the Pamirs. I was the wealthy foreigner in their eyes. I became accustomed to their invitations for tea, only to get the full sales pitch afterward. It was tempting to buy something of interest from each family in return for their hospitality. Sometimes I traded things I no longer needed or gave them spices I had brought from Vancouver. Extra parts from my repair kit that I deemed useless seemed beneficial to fixing things on the Kyrgyz tractors or stoves.

The desert plain headwinds that I had slogged through for the past two days finally ended with a screaming 68-km descent that I covered in less than 45 minutes. The downhill dipped over the other side of the plateau after a brief detour through a rocky gorge. The highway went through a tiny depression area called the Sarikol Valley where the desert suddenly came to life, changing from the drab dry desert to a lush fertile valley. Unlike the Kyrgyz who lived in the canvas teepee-like yurts, the Tajiks, who occupied the Sarikol Valley, lived in adobe houses constructed from clay, brick and straw.

A few kilometres outside Tashkurghan, a town of 20,000-strong Tajiks, I came upon a German tour group camped out in a wheatfield. Curious, I turned off the road and went to explore, only to be invited to join them for dinner. Amidst a half-dozen large green safari mess tents, 20 people were getting ready to eat. Their guide, who spoke German and Mandarin, was preparing a meal of veggies, french fries, tea and fresh bread. I did not hesitate to stuff myself with something other than the rock hard bread that I had been eating for the past few days. This was no tour expedition for the pampered. While the guide would drive one of the two vans from destination to destination, the rest of the group was expected to do their share of hiking, setting up camp and cleaning up.

The Germans had been up to the base camp of Muztagh Ata on camels the week prior. Over 140 people from eight climbing expeditions were trying to get to the top. One of the climbers on the mountain had to be flown back to a hospital in Europe to save his fingers from frostbite. The guide said the mountain was too smelly and polluted because of all the garbage and feces left behind by hikers and high altitude climbers. The German's organized tour had led them on treks on the Kyrgyzstan side of the border with additional Russian guides, all very non-touristy. My perception that all tour groups were over-organized, tightly controlled nightmares inside unsightly buses was beginning to change. Travelling up a mountainside on camel, hiking into the foothills and valleys of the former Soviet Union — this sounded like fun. Definitely, it was much more adventurous than being shuffled through bazaars and Buddhist ruins along predetermined desert stopovers.

Tashkurghan was the only city with any stores, shops or buildings in the Western sense of the word along the entire Chinese portion of the Karakoram Highway. The city (whose name means "stone fortress") has been a citadel for over 2,300 years along the Silk Road. An immense 600-year-old Masada-like mud brick fortress now crumbling with age sat on the edge of town. Sprawling wheatfields, small creeks and rows of poplar trees marked the entrance to town.

Being the largest town along the Chinese half of the KKH, Tashkurghan has a sizeable number of non-Muslim visitors, both Westerners and Han Chinese. For me, that meant official accommodation. Real beds, the only ones since Kashgar. After dinner I went into town, determined to find a place to sleep. I checked into a hotel, the first substantial expenditure I had made in the four days since leaving Kashgar (I had only spent ¥88 or $14). In the lobby, I met up with the two British backpackers from the lakes, Dave and Michelle. After checking into my room, I joined the two Brits along with an American woman, Sandy, for a late night chat. We had been talking for hours in Sandy's room about her English tutoring in South Korea when I realized that I had left my bike outside unattended. I ran out of the lobby to the front steps and was relieved to find the bike leaning up against the building. Upon further examination, I saw that my Walkman, which had been in one of the outside pouches on my handlebar bag, was gone.

I had barely used the Sony tape recorder. I was angry for chatting away inside but knew things could have been worse. My bike could have been stolen, forfeiting my trip. I had become used to gauging where I could leave my bike unattended in China and didn't consider the likelihood of it being stolen. In Vancouver, someone could just ride off around the corner and disappear into a large urban setting. A thief would stick out in this part of the world. More importantly, the Tajiks or Chinese would never steal my bike. No one would believe they had bought it themselves. It would look out of place.

My trip required that I pay complete attention to my bike's whereabouts. For some people, having to be physically on a bike, in sight of it or have it locked up, would seem like a hindrance. Back in Canada, I was used to sipping coffee at cafés and keeping an eye on one of my two expensive mountain bikes. I can only explain that watching over a bike isn't an inconvenience. It's like a mother and her child. She always knows how far her little boy or girl can stray in the supermarket without having to double-check on the kid. It's the same with a bike. It was my baby. You get to know when you can leave it alone and when it should be locked up. In Kashgar, I had routinely left my bike unlocked beneath the stairs of my hotel. Maybe I was lucky or maybe I had good judgment.

The next morning, I went with Sandy to the PSB office where she helped translate a stolen goods complaint. The officer concluded that the thief was most likely a Westerner. It would be too difficult to sell such a valuable electronics item in this area. I would not be getting it back. I took the loss as a reasonable tax on my stupidity. Luckily, if I needed a cheap Taiwanese tape recorder, I could probably get one in Pakistan.

Camels and Border Police

Since the KKH followed the Tashkurghan River, I could sense I was closing in on the Pakistan border because the road began to climb again. The highway had been flat from Kashgar to the Kara Kul Lakes with the hot arid canyon in between. Then it climbed up to the Subash Plateau that led down into Tashkurghan. Now it made the final climb to the Khunjerab Pass. Another hundred or so kilometres to go and I would be at the border. Unless the winds died down, I would have to spend another night in China before dipping over into the Karakoram Mountains. At this point, the highway passed a thin sliver of Afghanistan called the Wakhan Corridor. This narrow valley was originally designed as a buffer zone between Russia and Britain during their quest for control of Central Asia a hundred years ago. Before that, before Afghanistan existed, it was used during the Silk Road years to access Kashmir (now northern Pakistan and India).

I started to stretch my hamstrings each afternoon along this border dividing China and Afghanistan, given the ascending elevation. I developed a routine designed to keep a good pace. Since leaving Kashgar, I would stop the bike by the roadside, unpack a little bread and eat whatever else I had picked up from the last village.

Today, however, was one of the more interesting meal stops. Not because the food was any better, but because of the company. Camels absolutely stink. Sixteen of these long-legged creatures sat just off the highway, relaxing on the dirt. Some slept while others ate what little grassy vegetation sprouted from the ground. One of these ruffle-haired beasts, an albino, scratched its neck against a telephone pole.

I wasn't content to sit on a boulder as I usually did, so I walked over as close as I could get and sat down — downwind, of course. Despite my strategic positioning — about 5 m away — the odour was dreadful. I have no idea how these two-humped Bactrian camels bathe, but then again who has to smell them except their mates? If possible, camels, the animals, smell worse than Camels, the cigarettes.

My camel-watching over, I cycled to the tiny Tajik village of Dabdar that evening to eat a late dinner of tea and *pita manta kawaps* (shish kebabs). The restaurant, more like a mud and brick shack, was similar to many run by Tajik and Kyrgyz families. Benches were covered with flowered plastic tablecloths. Watercolours of sparkling Brie cheese, French wine and waterfalls decorated the walls. In the corner, a portable stereo system incessantly blared thin reedy Islamic music. A little Tajik girl, not more than seven, wearing a green scarf around her head, came out periodically to check on my meal. She spoke Persian, like most of her Indo-European-looking counterparts. Out here she was called Wakhi — not Tajik — a tribe whose homeland stretched from eastern Afghanistan into northern Pakistan.

Ordering came down to recognizing key words on the blackboard up on the wall, words like *nan, kawaps* and *samsas*. I could see straight through to the mud-thatch roof, the makeshift ceiling covered with glued-on strips of gold cross-weaved ribbons. You don't pay for your meals at counters or cash registers at Muslim eateries in China. Everything is done manually. The cooking is performed in an open corner of the room. As usual, the floors and walls are made from hardened mud. Some had red faux French doors (like this place) along with the standard blue metal bench chairs with small rugs for cushions.

After riding 385 km over the past five days, I was utterly spent. The boiled noodles with vegetables and meat I had eaten in Dabdar didn't make me feel any stronger. My lips were cracked from the long days in the sun. The hemp-based chapstick from Wyoming I had brought along proved useless. On top of that, a storm front was moving in and I was developing a cold. The garlic that I was putting in my bread each lunchtime wasn't having the holistic effect I had hoped.

At 4,100 m (13,520 ft.), the air was thin and definitely starting to affect me. I was cycling in slow motion. The effects of riding at that altitude began to wear down my strength. Riding in the desert along flat stretches was one thing, but heaving a bike in these conditions was another challenge. I had brought along altitude sickness pills and read everything about cerebral edema — an abnormal collection of fluid in the brain. The problem of edema usually only occurred among mountaineers, which can be fatal at high altitudes.

When I didn't think it would get worse, it began to pour, making everything more miserable. Out came the windbreaker, but it was useless. When you cycle in the rain, you always get wet. It doesn't matter if you have tights, booties and three layers of clothes. The water always gets in. So I plodded along in my shorts and jacket, hood over my head, miserable, cold, wet and breathless. I craved for the flat, mundane expanses to end and the steep downhills of the Karakorams to begin.

A half-day later, I reached the Pirali checkpoint, 40 km from the border. This tiny stop consisted of abandoned concrete work camps left over from the construction of the Karakoram Highway. Dilapidated buildings occupied one side of the road. On the other side, a newer building stood clean and proper with a satellite dish and all the windows and doors intact. Twenty PLA soldiers outfitted in camouflaged uniforms and Chicago Bulls caps were temporarily based at the former customs facility. They were blasting ditches to lay telephone lines a few kilometres away.

As the skies cleared and the clouds left for a few hours, I chatted in the noon sun with a Lieutenant Lung. His English was remarkably good. We talked about the brain drain that would happen if everyone in China were issued visas and allowed to travel abroad. The lieutenant had many friends from university in the engineering and medical fields whose services were in high demand in Hong Kong and the West. He talked a bit about Tibet and Beijing's propaganda that was disseminated in the Chinese media and schools. For Lt. Lung, a three-month stay was the usual stint out here on the edge of the Pamirs. All he and the other soldiers had was each other for companionship. Their sleeping quarters were sparse. Thick cotton cushions were stretched out on the cement floor, lying side to side. Blankets were neatly rolled up on one end. The windowsill inside the old work camp had rows of paper cups with toothbrushes and toothpaste tubes. It looked like a big summer camp.

That night, as it rained outside, Lt. Lung allowed me to sleep inside the entrance to the old customs building. I was thoroughly exhausted. At dawn, I got up with the Chinese soldiers and brushed my teeth, using the water tap at the side of the building. As the soldiers got ready for a day's work of blasting and digging ditches, I found out that the lieutenant had left early. So I told the others in my best hybrid of Mandarin and English to say thank you for his hospitality.

Shortly up the highway, I took refuge under a tower and cycled to the east of the road. A strong headwind had begun and so had the miserable rain. Hidden beneath a gully, off to the side, was an army barracks that seemed largely deserted. I propped my bike up under the white tower with red trim and tried to dry off. Then, a soldier who had seen me from the basketball courts and officers' quarters below walked up, Chinese Kalashnikov assault rifle in hand. He unlocked the door and let me inside, away from the rain.

Using hand signals and my Mandarin phrasebook, we managed to communicate in rudimentary terms as we shared my bread, onion and garlic lunch. The soldier flipped through the book's pages and stopped at the word *prostitute*. He pointed to it saying "Jianada?" inquisitively, mimicking the word for *Canada*. After nodding my head that we do have ladies of the night in our placid nation, I gestured that I wanted to take a photograph of him. He nodded and I quickly shot a picture of him. But as suddenly as he had agreed to the innocent gesture, he shook his head and waved his hands. Too late.

The soldier got up with his gun and went outside, back down the steel steps to the barracks. I began to eat my lunch on some two-by-fours, glad to be dry. As I waited for the rain to cease, I noticed four People's Liberation Army soldiers ascend the steps towards the tower. One had a camera, the others, semi-automatic rifles. I now realized that without my soldier friend to oversee me, I was a lone foreigner in their watchtower.

Soon after entering, one of the four soldiers pointed to the keyhole in the open door as though he were asking how I got inside.

One of the soldiers hurried up the tower's spiral staircase to see what, if anything, I had stolen from the office above. Since neither of us spoke the other's language, I brought out the phrasebook to help with the questioning. One soldier, however, was more interested in what was inside my jacket as he pointed to my chest pocket. I opened the zipper on the pocket and showed him there was nothing there. Then I suddenly realized what he wanted — my camera.

When the first soldier left me unescorted at the tower, I went outside to my bike to get my camera. After taking some photos, I returned and packed the camera away. Someone must have seen me with my camera but didn't know that I had returned it to my panniers. Ultimately, they let me gather my things and leave, confused about not finding the camera. I was relieved that my camera and film weren't detected and considered myself lucky.

Taking pictures around military checkpoints, barracks and depots is something of a calculated risk. It is illegal in most countries and can land you in jail or saddle you with a heavy fine. The last time I photographed an army site was in Morocco near the Algerian border. I had stood on my bike and clambered up over a barracks wall to see what was on the other side. I leaned on the sun-baked clay wall and snapped some shots of tanks and armoured personnel carriers. They say curiosity killed the cat. Well, whoever said that was right. I was caught by an army base staff member and then carted off to a day in jail.

Had I learned my lesson? Of course not. There's a difference between acting prudent when called for and travelling safe for safety's sake. China was a different country with different opportunities. I always thought if you're going to fully experience a country, you had to take advantage of the situations you find yourself in. I refused to become another Samsonite ecotourist. The one thing I wasn't willing to gamble was my film. That was irreplaceable.

After the rain subsided, I cycled back to the highway, snapping a few more photos of the bunkers and soldiers digging ditches. No sooner had I ridden 15 km down the road than a

Author sitting in window ledge on
Great Wall of China outside Beijing

German woman,
Ruth Kaiser
with statue of
gold Chinese
unicorn,
Forbidden City
in Beijing

A young boy in Beijing waits
outside a McDonald's, largely the
preserve of the middle class

Weighing my bike in the foothills of
the Tian Shan Mountains. My initial
luggage load came to 57 kg (125 lbs)

Worker fixing the Great Wall of China

With Tony camping on mountainside on our 2nd night in Tian Shan Mountains, China

At the top of Tiger Pass (summit of the Tian Shans) with Chinese tourists from a passing tour bus

The pollution of coal factories in Hoaxia, our first stop in the Tian Shans

Kyrgyz herdsmen riding home on the desert hills just south of the Tian Shan Mountains, where I had the first of many flat tires

100,000 strong bartering away in the weekly Kashgar Sunday market – Asia's largest

Uyghur man selling garlic from back of
his bike at Kashgar Sunday Market

Irons for sale in the bustling
Kashgar Sunday Market

Two Uyghur boys in their
finest in Kashgar

Muslim spires on top
of a mosque in Kashgar

Goat in back of truck ready to be auctioned
off in Kashgar's Sunday Market

A yurt – a canvas teepee-like home fortified
with lattice wooden panels supporting a
domed roof – is used by many of the
nomadic Muslim tribes in China

Uyghur boys posing for photos
on Karakoram Highway outside
Kashgar, China

Id Kah Mosque – Kashgar's
main attraction and religious
centre where the muezzin calls
out each morning over the
speakers, beckoning the
faithful to prayer

Highway workers in the Pamir Mountains (China side) with author's Canadian flag

Kyrgyz children at Ghez checkpoint on Karakoram Highway near China-Kyrgyzstan border

Author riding the Karakoram Highway through the Ghez Canyon, China

Kids in puddle cooling off from the desert heat of the Takla Makan in China. The midday heat often reached 40°C

25,000-foot Karakoram Mountains in Hunza, northern Pakistan, at sunset – the real Shangri-La

Camping out in the Ghez Canyon on the outskirts of the Chinese desert with my trusty *Lonely Planet* guidebook

Taliban soldier outside Kabul, Afghanistan, wearing perfume and charcoal eyeliner to ward off evil spirits

Taliban rebel tank (with author in middle) on the frontlines near Kabul

Taliban tank quartermaster, Hosain Abdul Qoud in front of his tank at Mir Bacheh Kowt, Afghanistan, a small village north of Kabul, where the fighting was sporadic

Author foolishly holding unexploded ordinance in Kabul

Author holding Kalashnikov AK-47 submachine gun in Darra, Pakistan, a town in the Tribal Areas that manufactures weapons for the war in neighbouring Afghanistan

400,000 people have been killed by landmines since fighting broke out in 1979 in Afghanistan. 60% of victims are children. I met this man – who lost his leg – travelling by bus

Kids outside Lee Rosey private
school in Gulmit, Pakistan

Sikh guards at the Golden Temple, Amritsar, India

Marvellous trucks in Pakistan, painted to stir
up business and tickle the imagination. The
driving habits of these young Pakistanis leave
much to be desired as the diesel behemoths
twist their way through the mountains with
little regard for passenger safety

The Golden Temple in
Amritsar, the religious
epicentre for the Sikh
religion. The temple was
being replated in solid gold
during the author's 3 day stay

To see additional photos from this trip, visit
www.greymattermedia.com/BradyFotheringham

checkpoint with a gated barrier came into view. Finally the Khunjerab Pass, what would turn out to be at 16,000 feet the highest point of elevation in my trip.

A border officer in pressed green pants and army uniform stood beside a construction trailer waving for me stop. The lone green-and-yellow trailer with "Frontier Defence of China" painted on the side was the last barrier between Pakistan and me. I expected nothing more than the usual hello or goodbye. However, as my life with the Chinese police had been going lately, nothing went smoothly.

"Please can have your passport," he said as I got off my bike. "Step in box please."

With his crisp white gloves, he motioned me to step into the trailer. The cubicle on wheels had eight bunk beds built into the walls. As we squeezed into the crammed quarters, I noticed a relic of the 1970s playing on the VCR. Three soldiers lay on tiny cots watching a videotape of the *Poseidon Adventure* translated into Mandarin. As with so much of Chinese culture in these parts, I wasn't at all surprised to watch Gene Hackman, Shelley Winters and Ernest Borgnine struggling in the epic disaster movie of my youth. Maybe in 20 years they would be watching *Pretty Woman*.

"*Cha*. Would you like have *cha*?" he asked.

I gladly accepted the warm liquid. That was the last of the niceties. Then came the interrogation.

"What picture you take?" "How many photo?" the officer asked in quick succession.

As the officer made a phone call on his rotary telephone, it became obvious that I wasn't going anytime soon.

Communicating without speaking Mandarin was hard enough. Convincing the border officer that the photographs I took back at the watchtower were with the consent of an army soldier was even harder. They wanted the film out of my camera but I stalled, hoping they would lose interest. I pretended I was another dumb tourist who didn't understand their language, hoping they would get frustrated and let me leave.

I was getting nervous. For 20 minutes I sat while he talked to his superiors or whoever was on the phone. Then they wanted to see my bike. We went back outside and examined my handlebar where I kept my camera. Minutes later, a northbound van drove up to the checkpoint and stopped outside the gate. The Pakistani driver thought I was lost. Thinking I needed help with directions and a little translation, he joined the conversation. Luckily for the Chinese officer, the driver spoke both his native Urdu and a bit of Mandarin and English. This enabled the driver to relate to me the border official's instructions.

"They want your film. They want to see what's inside your camera. They say you took forbidden pictures," the driver said. "You must give it to them or you won't get through."

With that interpretation, out came the film exposed to the daylight, of China's finest men in uniform. Goodbye film. I was slowly and painfully learning my lesson. Throughout this ordeal, the officer was very gracious in stark contrast to the Public Security Bureau jerks back in the desert who were out to gouge me. Saving face is important to the Chinese. This border officer followed that tradition to the letter, instead of being confrontational. The officer apologized for any inconveniences the little delay had caused my trip. In his best English, he said he was sorry and then I was off.

All bundled up in my cycling tights and windbreaker and long-fingered gloves, I rolled forward through the grassy knoll and then across the plateau to the border. Pakistan was 10 minutes away. The chilly wind whistled in my ears, turning them red. My eyes watered as I wiped my nose with the back of my glove. I was leaving China, the most populous and ancient civilization in the world, and heading to one of Asia's poorest nations — Pakistan, a mere baby at 50 years. Over the 16,000-ft.-high pass I went, and down the other side.

Pakistan

Mile upon mile a white thread of road stretches across stone-strewn plains, bordered by the bones of the innumerable victims to the long fatigue of a burdensome and ill-fed existence — the ghastly debris of former caravans.

JOHN KEAY, *Explorers of the Western Himalayas*, 1977

The KKH and the Roof of the World

The altimeter on my handlebars registered 16,120 ft. A little off, but close enough. I had arrived at the Khunjerab Pass, a windswept plateau on the China-Pakistan border. This bleak and lonely flat expanse of land at 4,730 m is the world's highest paved roadway. It is the equivalent of 11 World Trade Centers stacked end upon end. The pass not only divided two nations, but also the desert and mountains. The sight was worth the entire trip alone.

On either side of the highway, massive angular mountains crowded the horizon. Snow-capped pinnacles pierced through white misty clouds amidst a kaleidoscopic purple sunset. The Karakorams distinguish a region of feudal princedoms, valley kingdoms and city states many call Little Tibet. The region is home to more tall mountains than in Nepal and Tibet combined. This was "The Roof of the World," where four of the greatest mountain ranges in the world converged — the Himalaya, Pamirs, Karakorams and Hindu Kush.

The rounded Pamir Mountains of China were behind me; in front were the sharp jagged peaks of the Karakorams. The mountains were silent sentinels of Earth's highest peaks, celestial giants thrusting towards the heavens. A sign said "Keep Left." It took me a minute to realize I had to switch to the left side of the highway (Pakistan takes after Britain for rules of the road).

I plunged down into Pakistan swooshing along at speeds in excess of 70 km/h. I negotiated my bike around 45-degree switchbacks, velo-shussing down the highway. My Rocky Mountain shuddered so violently whenever I applied the brakes that the front wheel started to shimmer and the back end skipped laterally over the road. The aluminum rims were getting so hot that my rubber brake pads wore halfway through. My bike was so heavy with gear I couldn't manoeuvre well enough around corners. It handled with the grace of a bulldozer. I had to line up for a turn in advance, lean my body to the left or right and gently persuade the bike to change course.

Treacherous cliffs dropped 500 m away into the meandering greenish-blue Hunza River below. The occasional grapefruit-size rock hurled down from the mountains, bouncing across the road into the river below. If I suddenly leaned too much into a turn, I would career off the edge and join Allah in the great afterlife. This was definitely a killer highway. I could have ridden more slowly, but the downhill was too tempting. It's not every day that I got a chance to cycle over a pass akin in height to a 1,265-storey building. Back in Canada, ripping descents were few and far between. I navigated the scree-covered and broken asphalt road, wind in my hair, like a pro-elite downhill mountain bike racer. My riding buddies back home would be envious of my descent on this contemporary version of the Silk Road. In just under 90 minutes, I had covered 117 km.

Hunza

"Salaam aleikum (peace be with you)," the Frontier Constabulary guard said as he greeted me with the traditional Muslim welcome.

"Aleikum salaam," I said in response.

The customs checkpoint of Sust was my first official stop in northern Pakistan. Everyone passing through on the way to China or back had to show papers and sign a logbook. The guard had a magnificent black beard and stately uniform modelled on the outfits of the British military. He addressed me at length in basic English. This was a first — a remarkable change from China. No more *Lonely Planet* phrasebook fumbling for the right word. I exchanged a few words in Urdu, Pakistan's principal language, and gave the guard some lapel pins from Canada.

Then came the inevitable questions about my bike and country. "How much did it cost?" he asked.

I was used to this question and said $500. This was a lie, but still a lot by Pakistani standards. It was worth three times that. The guard couldn't comprehend that I had cycled from Kashgar (420 km away) and was now headed another 880 km all the way to Islamabad and Lahore on the Pakistan-India border and beyond to Delhi. Then came the most peculiar comment of my whole trip.

"You are strong strong bicycle man. But tell me, are you actor who cut off heads and walk with limp?" the guard said.

What the hell? Puzzled, I asked what he meant, sure that it would all make sense.

"You know, the Hollywood actor. Are you brother?"

"Oh, yes. *Seven*, the movie *Seven*. Kevin Spacey," as I recalled my Hollywood trivia. "He's a great actor, but no, I am not his brother."

The customs guard had been referring to two movies starring Kevin Spacey — the thriller *Seven*, where actress Gwyneth Paltrow's character was dismembered, and the *Usual Suspects,* where a mobster faked a bad leg. I guess I looked like him with my oval-shaped face and bald spot, despite my growing beard. Welcome to Pakistan, the world's ninth most populous country and apparently home to a couple of VCRs and cineplexes.

The Karakoram Highway was originally a precipitous mule and horse trail used as a trading route to connect the valley kingdom of Kashmir to Chinese Central Asia. This branch of the Silk Road was used by caravans as far back as the 4th century. Ivory, spices, silk and jade were hauled through rocky river gorges and grassy valleys. As recently as the 1950s when the Chinese and Pakistan governments began to design the highway, many villagers were still using the paths. Up above the highway, remnants of old mule tracks from the Silk Road days were still evident, etched along mountainsides.

China and Pakistan commenced work on this Friendship Highway in 1966. The impetus was to improve trade between the two countries so that trucks, not horses, could make safe, quick trips through the Karakorams into China. Over 23 million cu. m of earth and rock were carved through to build the highway, using 812 tonnes of explosives. The Karakoram Highway, from Islamabad in the south to Kashgar in the north, was opened to foreigners in 1986 after 20 years of blasting, digging and bridge building. The 1,300-km-long highway has since been dubbed the eighth wonder of the world.

On a human level, the highway cost an average of 12 workers for every 10 km paved. That's 1,560 people buried under rock-slides. The enormity of the construction project struck me, as I realized how difficult it must have been to carve a major highway through two mountain ranges. Such a monumental engineering feat in such a geologically active region was not lost on the military elite of each country, especially China. During the superpower rivalry of the Cold War, China was never on good terms with India and didn't want to lose access to Pakistan. Beijing insisted that the highway be wide enough to accommodate two tanks riding abreast, just in case they wanted to invade.

The highway's reinvigoration of the old Silk Road has kick-started the economies of northern Pakistan and the desert plain settlements of China. Pakistani traders drive north to the markets of Kashgar returning with silk stockings, melons and cheap stereos and radios. The Silk Road has become the Silk Stocking Highway. Now the route between the two countries is a twisty two-lane test of driving skills and steely nerves. Swift-flowing rivers and heavy rains subject the road to frequently falling rocks, boulders and landslides in this mountain and glacial paradise. Aside from these natural highway hazards, the trucks travelling the Karakoram Highway make the journey twice as treacherous. Many locals aptly called the KKH the killer highway.

Pakistani drivers are god's gift from driving school hell. If you were ever to combine the flair of an Italian Grand Prix driver, the speed of an autobahn-bound German, the wildness of a French-Canadian and the Asian disregard for mirrors and turn signals, you would get a Pakistani motorist. I found it difficult to avoid the erratic driving habits of these teenage truck drivers on the twisty Karakoram Highway. The last thing I wanted was to become an integral part of someone's front bumper. Brightly painted diesel Bedford trucks belched black smoke, lurching up hills. Once at the top, however, the clutches started to burn. The trucks would roar around corners, one wheel precariously off the edge, the other on the shoulder. Terrified passengers clung to their seats.

Flamboyant exoticism. That's what Pakistan's trucks, buses and vans are with their brightly coloured flower motifs. They are a painter's dream — moving shrines with tinkling chains and dozens of gaudy red reflectors stuck on the front, and swathed in every colour imaginable. Even the motor rickshaws and tiny Suzukis in the big cities to the south have some part of their exterior detailed with stylized pictures. Prayer and inscriptions from the Koran invoke Allah's name to protect against misfortune. The more colourful the vehicle, the thinking goes, the more passengers and cargo business. The moving murals testify to the driver's pride in his vehicle.

The drivers spend enormous sums of money to have their vehicles painted by cadres of specialists. Everything from rivets, hubcaps and bumpers are covered with paintings of mosques, mountains and the *burraq* (a half-woman half-winged horse). Inside these kitschy vehicles, inlaid wood decorates many dashboards. In some buses, up to two-dozen toggle switches for different sounds are hooked to the driver's horn. With all the funds poured into these rolling billboards, it's no wonder there's no money left over to repair the rusty hulks and decrepit engines. Pakistan's poverty and crumbling social and education systems, however, contrast markedly with this glittering pop-art decoration.

The trucks were just one thing that made me addicted to this mountainous northern getaway. If one route beckons adventure cyclists to explore and discover new mountain ranges, this was it, the most exotic touring destination in the world. After six days of cycling through the gentle rounded giants of the Pamirs, I had been accustomed to the barren desert in Xinjiang province. Now I was faced with real mountains — a climber's utopia with enormous peaks, some 8,000 m high. It's here in the Karakorams and tranquil setting of Hunza, that James Hilton was inspired to write about a mythical Shangri-La in his 1933 book *Lost Horizons*. This was a land where groovy old men with funky white beards ate dried apricots and lived to be more than 110 years old. All this in a country where the life expectancy is only 59 years.

This section of the Karakoram Highway, a nirvana of majestic spires and snowy pinnacles, became indelibly etched in my mind. This surely must be the most beautiful place in the world, I thought. Of the 14 peaks in the world over 8,000 m high, four of these (K2, Gasherbrum, Broad Peak and Nanga Parbat) are speckled throughout the glacier ranges of Pakistan's Northern Areas — an amalgam of valley fiefdoms called Hunza, Gilgit and Chitral. A half-century ago, the British partitioned this land into Indian and Pakistan, henceforth dividing Kashmir of which Hunza is a part. Until then, Hunza was cut off from the rest of the world and was a remote paradise visited by few outsiders.

The only signs of civilization in this mountain region were the odd broken Coke, Sprite and Pepsi bottles scattered beside the road. Graffiti markings sprayed on large Volkswagen-size rocks every few kilometres advertised the "exklusiv clene akommaday-tions" of the Asia Star Hotel. It seemed every time I turned a corner, the first large boulder would have a phone number spray-painted in large neon letters. I started to careen through the first of several small village settlements interlaced with terraced fields and stonewalls. I quickly appreciated the beauty and isolation of this mountain paradise with its precipitous drops into the river below. My Canadian flag flapped in the wind at the back of my bike as Himalayan marmots whistled from above the highway.

The Karakoram National Park, which straddles the border area, is home to some of the rarest animals on Earth. Snow leopards, living at altitudes above 5,400 m (18,000 ft.), are one of several endangered species in the Karakorams. The Marco Polo sheep, which stand over 1.2 m tall, are one of the most magnificent breeds of animals in the world. Standing proud and fierce, the Marco Polos' precarious existence is shared by ibexes, caracals and the Persian wild goat — all native to the north.

Unfortunately, poaching is growing in popularity. Operators take willing adventurers with deep pockets into the Pamirs for a little shoot and kill fun. For $20,000 US, you can depart Moscow fully escorted by a guide, complete with gun import permit and international veterinary certificate. The prospective hunter is promised (according to the latest ads on the Internet) 11 days in the freezing cold and one successful trophy kill. The package includes return airfare to Moscow and the 10-hour Jeep drive in from Osh, Kyrgyzstan. Additional sheep run another $14,000 US per head. If that doesn't fill your wall space at home you can add a wolf for a mere $450.

Far below the confines of the Marco Polo sheep, I had overshot the nearest village that had an inn. I ended up between settlements, searching for a suitable place to camp as darkness fell. As I slowly rode along in the dark, I noticed a flicker of light coming from a cave off to the side of the road. I pulled over and wheeled my bike to a group of men huddled around a fire and boiling tea. Sure enough, I was invited to join the Burushuski-speaking men. The eldest of the Pakistani men offered me tea and passed around a half-smoked sample of the region's homegrown Mary Jane, rolled into a long withering joint. This generosity became a trademark feature of the people of Hunza (both the tea and drugs). They were the friendliest group I had ever met in my travels. Few regions could match the splendour of the Karakorams and fewer people were as kind as those in Hunza. And to think that these tribesmen were descended centuries ago from the Huns, the kings of Silk Road invaders, slave traders, pillagers and rapists.

Three hours later, I left on the bike, my stomach full of tea and with a few more addresses scrawled in my notebook. I rode a couple kilometres in the dark, gingerly making my way to Galapan, a one-street stop where I had a late night meal at a greasy spoon eatery. The words *restaurant* and *hotel* don't hold the same meaning in Pakistan as they do in the West. The motel, hotels and inns offer rope beds or single cots in one-storey buildings built from mud, stone and straw. The vegetables, *chapattis* (bread) and drinks are served on bare tables of linoleum or wood. The floors are mud. The kitchen, well, don't go there if you have a hang-up about cleanliness. This is, after all, Pakistan — land of the adventurous. Roughing it is a must in the north and there's no rougher place than a Pakistani kitchen.

Upper Hunza is a land of endless hiking trails and sheer valley walls that drop straight into the Hunza River. For generations, the only means for many people to visit friends and relatives on the other side of the river was to construct long spindly wooden bridges. Where the width of the Hunza and embankments warranted, narrow planks were attached to a birch cable. Two other cables suspended the rest of the structure in a triangular shape, and the whole bridge hovered precariously above the river. Most bridges had decayed and fallen apart over the last few centuries, so that some families had been separated from their relatives for generations. Now the Karakoram Highway, which crosses the river in several places, has served to reunite many long-lost relatives.

Just down from Galapan in Passu, I ate lunch with a group of Germans who were spending a few days exploring the riverfront orchards. They told me that the highway was susceptible to glacier movement and frequent flooding. The KKH is constantly being upgraded and fixed by road crews as glaciers creep up to the roadside like slow-moving lava. The immaculate fields, lush with maize, apricot and walnut crops, are all vulnerable to mudslides and floods.

Lunch with the Germans was sparse; your basic *chapatti* and *chai* (bread and tea). The menu didn't have the selection of meat dishes, rice and yoghurt sauces that I would relish in other towns. I stocked up on candies at the inn (20 for a rupee) and hit the road for the next 56 km, passing low-level homes on riverbank settlements. Down below the highway, alluvial fans formed along the Hunza River from streams dumping sediment deposits.

Sure enough, I ended up cycling past one of the glacial areas where large deposits of soil and rock, mixed with dirty snow, edged slowly onto the highway. Just as the Germans had said, these monolithic soil and ice slabs extended 60 km (as in the case of the Batura Glacier) back through the valleys. I could hear the creaking of rocks as the highway dropped 400 m in 10 minutes in a swooping hill. The villages of Khalbar blurred into Hussaini which blurred into Abdegar which blurred into Gulmit. Each melded with the next, 20 to 30 km apart. I had never seen so many close settlements in a mountain range.

China's deserts were big expanses of soil dotted with the occasional yurt and adobe home hundreds of kilometres apart. In Pakistan, everything was compressed — the mountains, the villages and the valleys. An intricate system of irrigation channels fed each group of homes, etched as they were into the sides of the valleys. Water flowed from glaciers to streams to crops and finally into the river. Through hours of labour, men and women built fields and tilled the soil, carving out a peaceful but strenuous existence where nothing existed before.

As in much of rural Pakistan, one village had a small hospital (mainly for maternity care), another village had the post office and a third the library. I rode into Gulmit (pronounced Gool-mit), a small town whose schools and agricultural projects are funded by the Aga Khan, the wealthy Karachi-born *imam* of the Ismaili sect.

Gulmit had a hospital and a museum near the Marco Polo Inn that housed a stuffed snow leopard and other exotic items from the days of the British. A small 200-year-old palace still stands above the town where the Mir of Hunza used to visit in the summer.

Schools in Pakistan are divided into the Aga Khan–funded and the public and private schools — like Gulmit's Lee Rosey private elementary school. A British teacher trainer, Camilla Marland, was ending two years on a Volunteer Services Overseas program at Lee Rosey where I visited. She invited me for lunch after I stopped to change out of my shoes into my sandals. Camilla had been living with a Pakistani family and was eager to get back to her fiancé in Manchester. She had been instructing the head teacher, Mukhdar Karim, in English lessons. They were using antiquated books printed in the 1940s. One described "African Negroes" as "tribal people who were cannibals." Our knowledge of the world has changed substantially since these British textbooks were printed, and the outdated texts were another example of Pakistan's poverty, even here in a private school.

Camilla and Mukhdar introduced me to the two fifth-grade classes. The students stood up out of their seats and those who didn't have desks (most students shared) sat on the floor along the side of the room. The boys were dressed like British schoolchildren in trousers and ties. The girls had on long flowing purple robes.

"This man is from Canada. Do you remember when we talked about all the pink parts on the map last month?" Camilla asked the class, referring to the British Commonwealth.

"His name is Brady and I want you to say hello," she said.

"Hello Mr. Brady bicycle man," the class replied in unison like a well-trained marine unit.

"Do you have any questions for Mr. Brady?" Mukhdar asked.

"When are we going to get our F-16s?" a little girl asked.

This was not the first question I envisioned a nine year old asking me. The girl was referring to the pending sale of fighter jets initiated seven years earlier by the United States, a promise the American government hadn't made good on. The children were taught that a strong military is necessary to fight the Hindus next door in India. Unfortunately, 50 years of fighting over Kashmir has strained both countries' economies and left Pakistan $60 billion in debt. Pakistan's entire economy, despite being rich in natural resources, is largely administered by the World Bank. Loans from the International Monetary Fund literally decide the fate of countless educational, agricultural and industrial programs.

As I prepared to leave outside the school, four kids ran up to my bike, and then nervously stepped away. The two boys and two girls held out their hands and giggled.

"Pen, pen," the shorter boy with flappy ears and red hair said, in a pleading voice.

I gave the last of my Canadian stickers and pins and a couple of pens that I had picked up in Kashgar to the four school kids. When taking pictures, I would often get stilted poses from people, whether they were adults or children. To capture the laughter on these kids' faces was an opportunity I couldn't pass up. I had to put them at ease. After I gave them some sweet Chinese candies, the children allowed me to photograph them uninhibited. I knew if I were patient, the photos would turn out great. In the nearby fields, a few women craned their necks and watched. The kids were exuberant and energetic. One girl held up her candies while the other sucked on her pen.

Each was wearing a lavender *shalwar qamiz*. The *qamiz* is a long baggy tunic; the *shalwar* is a loose pair of pyjama-like trouser bottoms with a drawstring. The boys had on jeans and button-down cotton shirts. Men and women both wear the *shalwar qamiz* in hot weather; it is also worn in India by Sikh and Kashmiri women. On colder days, the men wear their woollen *chogas*.

Women

Many Western feminists, both male and female, incorrectly equate the Islamic faith with a lack of rights for women. Unlike Christianity, Judaism and Hinduism, Islam embodies a woman's right to education and to her own property separate from her husband's. The reality, of course, is that only 1 per cent of Pakistani women can read and only 14 per cent have any formal education. Most women are married by their early teens and have no rights in their marriage. Divorce is out of the question under any circumstance.

To make matters worse, honour killing has allowed men to murder their wives or girlfriends, usually at the slightest hint of an illicit affair. *Karo–kari*, as the ritual is known, refers to the male (*karo*) and the female (*kari*). Hundreds of women and a few men are murdered each year because of this perverted practice that is accepted on the Indian subcontinent. Under Pakistani law, an honour killing is classified as murder, but a legal loophole permits killings under grave or sudden provocation.

As in many parts of the world, women are forced into subservient roles. More importantly, a lack of education limits a woman's ability to be independent, to learn about feminist movements and to choose a life outside the home. As in China and the Indian subcontinent, Pakistani girl babies are more likely to be abandoned at birth than boys. Poverty in India, Pakistan and China forces families to put the young males of the family to work, thus the preference for boys. It has little to do with Buddhism, Hinduism or Islam.

Pakistanis, however, proudly proclaim that their country had the first female prime minister in the Muslim world — Benazir Bhutto. Female editors, lawyers, doctors, financial advisors, managers and businesspeople are integral parts of the urban workforce. In education, there are more female university professors in Pakistan than in all of Great Britain.

The custom of *purdah* defines the role of women vis-à-vis their male counterparts. *Purdah* decrees that a woman's decisions must be made after consulting with a male, diminishing the very independence her faith supposedly provides. Sexual segregation is a large part of this custom, dictating that a woman should avoid contact with males not closely related to her. A woman must keep conversations brief when encountering other men and her eyes must be averted to the ground. Modesty is best. In northern Pakistan, social attitudes have changed little over the centuries.

Nomadic and poor women in rural areas, however, do not practise *purdah* because they have to work outside. The *chador*, a one-piece cloak wrapped around the head, is impractical in the fields and is not worn. In place of the *chador* in Hunza, an Ismaili Muslim region, is the long *dupatta* or scarf draped modestly by women on their shoulders. Many rural women envy the middle-class women who keep *purdah* and can afford to stay home.

In Baluchistan and the North West Frontier Province towns, women are more conservative and *purdah* is a way of life. There, women wear the *burqah*, a full-length veil over their head and shoulders that reveals only the eyes. This tent-like outfit (its true meaning in Farsi) is worn in many Middle Eastern Muslim countries, such as Iran and Iraq. In those countries, the *chador* is traditionally black or dark blue. It's not unusual for women in Iran to wear jeans underneath a long coat. In Pakistan, however, the only denim you'll see will be in big cities, such as Islamabad, Lahore and Karachi. There, the women view the stricter Islamic conventions as constraining their mobility. Again, tradition is the governing factor.

Despite the chaperoning in public by male relatives, at home the Pakistani woman is queen. Special areas called *baithaks* (sitting rooms) are built in every house for men to entertain visitors. The rest of the home is forbidden to males other than the husband. The Islamic faith as decreed by Sharia law, or holy law, asserts that a true Muslim is an enlightened person before the eyes of God. This means that pictures of graven images (people and animals) should not be displayed in the home. A house is a holy place. Women aren't supposed to show themselves before a stranger's camera or to men who are not relatives, hence the *dupatta, chador* and *burqah*.

In Hunza, I rarely saw women shopping in the streets. They worked in the fields or taught in the schools. When I climbed the highway from Gulmit to Karimabad, the first steep hill since the border, I saw more women outside the home for the first time since Kashgar.

Karimabad

A thunderstorm was moving up the valley as I cranked my way up the winding highway that climbed and then dipped around a bend. I could hear the thunder in the distance. Then the rain came, sprinkling at first before turning into a downpour.

I had on my brand new North Face Gore-Tex windbreaker that I had shelled out $450 for back home. Now I put it to the test. It kept my upper body warm, but not my legs and bum. I had eaten a vegetable and *chapatti* dinner in one of the small villages that dotted the highway after Gulmit, but had dallied too long at the private school. I was now facing a dark and forbidding ride through the deluge of rain. Finally, I arrived in Karimabad late at night. It was not what I had planned.

One foot after another, I pushed my bike around the hairpin turns of the main road. The only light coming from Karimabad was from the inns and restaurants built on precarious mountainsides. All the souvenir and handicraft shops were closed. The homes below were sealed shut. Karimabad was slowly coming apart — the rain eating away into mud-and-brick retaining walls. Water rushed down the steep gravel roads and overflowed the interlocking system of irrigation channels that fed the various fields. Bricks were washing out into the middle of roads as Jeeps became stuck in the mud. Sides of buildings were crumbling like flaky piecrusts. There was nothing anybody could do but wait.

Inn after inn was full up for the night. I wheeled my bike to the Hunza Motel, New Hunza Tourist Hotel, Karimabad Hotel, Hunza Inn, Karim Hotel and Serena Lodge. At 30 rupees ($1 per night), all were full. I pitched my bike up against another dorm-style rope-bed guesthouse and walked inside, soaked to the bones. Nothing. Nothing again. No rooms. They'd been booked for five hours. I was too late. Even the Mountain View Hotel, a modern place by Pakistani standards, with television and phone at $10 a night was full.

As I stood outside, frustrated and dripping wet, I contemplated riding back down the steep road to the highway. Maybe I could make it to the next town. However, I hated the cold, especially when it was miserable out. I didn't want to pitch my bivouac sac in the rain. It wouldn't be worth the hassle. At the bottom of the road, I saw a vehicle begin to make its way up the hazardous road, its headlights shining through the darkness as a torrent of water rushed down the paved side of the road.

The old Land Rover stopped beside me and seven Italians piled out. They had been driving around and needed a place to stay. Their Pakistani driver wanted to take the rental Jeep back before midnight. Nene Tessarolo, an Italian from Vicenza, came back from an inn and said there were vacancies in nearby Altit, an offshoot village three kilometres east of Karimabad. I rode ahead of the Jeep, so that its headlights shone in front of me, paving a path of light through the rutted Jeep track road. We wound our way back down the mountain to the Kisar Inn. The inn, with its cots and outdoor toilet, had several dozen pails scattered around the building perimeter to minimize the rain damage to the property.

The next morning when the rain had subsided, I went into Karimabad with four of the Italians — Nene, Paolo, Angelico and Tessa. We wanted to see the damage done to this town that attracts many travellers and tourists on their way north.

Karimabad, with its accompanying Baltit and Altit villages, was bigger than most of the terraced riverside settlements along the Hunza River. It turned out that the three towns had never had so much rain in over 30 years. The summer monsoons had drifted north, causing landslides and mudslides throughout many northern villages. Villagers were caught unprepared as their mud houses and retaining walls washed away or collapsed. In four days, 160 people were killed throughout the valleys. The highway itself was blocked in numerous places by rocks or completely washed out. Many foreigners in Karimabad, including the Italians and me, were stuck until road crews could repair the highway. We didn't know how many days it would take to get out, but being stranded in this town turned out to be a godsend.

The view from this hillside town was absolutely stunning, something not evident the night before in the darkness. Directly opposite the highway and river, Rakaposhi, the most visible of all snow-capped peaks in Pakistan, loomed above the far valley wall, 7,788 m (25,550 ft.) above sea level. A sweeping panorama of the Hunza River with the KKH snaking through the middle could easily be viewed from all around the town.

The Italians and I went for breakfast on top of one of the inns. Because the views were so spectacular, most of the restaurants and inns had seating facilities on top of their mud roofs. The five of us sipped *chai* and read some of the English Pakistani newspapers while we looked out over the valley. The restaurant owner brought up orders of minced lamb and other spicy dishes flavoured with chilies and peppers, with Orange Fanta to wash it down. This was the life I thought, stuck in a town with great views, excellent hiking opportunities and ghee-drenched rice with saffron and raisins.

Not only did every inn have a world-class view, but every eatery also had its own earthenware oven to make *chapattis*. The upright ovens were essentially hollowed-out holes in large clay blocks, about the size of electric ovens, set into the ground. These were the standard appliance of every restaurant and teashop. Large, thick unleavened breads, the size of small pizzas or Mexican tortillas, were slapped by hand inside these raging hot ovens — no oven mitts, just lots of courage and thick calluses. The heat was so intense from the charcoal fires at the bottom that sparks of coal spat out the small hole at the top. Because of the heat, the bread stuck to the curved oven walls. Several minutes later, a metal prong (similar to a fire poker), was used to extract the fresh bread. When it had risen, the baker would crimp the edges and stack the *chapattis* or *paratha* bread in a pile. From there, they would quickly be snapped up and eaten — hot and tasty.

The shops in Karimabad were full of more goods than I had seen elsewhere in Pakistan. Flavoured yoghurts, breads, candies, cheeses and a wide assortment of raspberry- and chocolate-filled

Nabisco cookies could be found in almost any grocery store. Rugs, bed linens, pots, pans and woven cotton-net bags were all sold along the main cobblestone drag. Metalwork inlaid with geometric patterns and camel-skin lampshades designed by skilled artisans sat in open window fronts. Most handicrafts in Hunza were made locally, unlike in the larger cities in the south where china and glassware were churned out by factories.

This town, with its grandeur views, seemed unspoiled by the tourist goods sold in its stores. The storefronts didn't look any different save for a few with shelving units and modern glass windows. The town had integrated parts of Western pop culture into its quaint surroundings. Pakistani versions of the movie *Jurassic Park*, translated in Urdu, were on all the grocers' shelves for nightly viewing. Uyghur- and Persian-influenced music was available on tapes and CDs.

Trekking was very popular in Karimabad, which tied right into the village's marketing strategy. Bookstores sold mountaineering coffee-table books, postcards with Pakistani peaks and T-shirts with climbing logos. The town's merchants clearly knew where their bread and butter came from. Come and spend your money, but spend it on the mountains.

As I was browsing with Nene and Paolo, I met a local tailor, Ikramullah Baig, who ran a small garment shop. After much discussion over price and plenty of *chai* (a tradition when making an expensive purchase), I bought a thick *shalwar qamiz* for 2240 rupees ($76). For three days I proudly wore the traditional outfit with a V-neck and embroidered sleeves, until I found out that its design was meant for a woman.

During our conversations, Ikramullah told me about the large, white-roofed stone palace on the edge of town with a satellite dish, arched gateway and armed guards. He suggested that if I was interested he could arrange a meeting with the wife of the Mir — from the ruling family of Hunza. Ikramullah told me that the Mir's wife, the Rani of Hunza, had a daughter-in-law born in Texas who had been educated at an American university. She spoke perfect

English and would likely be amenable to arranging a meeting with her mother-in-law. I looked forward to this meeting. It might give me some insight into the female side of this male-dominated culture.

Mirs are like royalty in northern Pakistan. They rule with iron fists. The Mir has the privilege of deciding who can marry whom and whether Mohammed or Abdul gets that prime grazing land for his goats. Although the powers of the Mirs diminished a little when Hunza joined Pakistan in 1974, this ancient custom is still in practice today. In the age when Mirs of rival valley kingdoms battled for supremacy hundreds of years ago, two brothers bitterly fought to rule Hunza. The people of Baltit and Karimabad favoured the elder son, while the subjects of neighbouring Altit sided with the younger male. Finally, the older brother had his sibling killed and went on to rule all of Hunza, making the Baltit Fort his home.

Most of the people I had talked to on my trip, whether shopkeepers, truck drivers or border guards, were male. I wanted to learn about the other half (the half that had sewn the woman's *shalwar qamiz* I was wearing). Ikramullah would let me know the next day if he could arrange something. I thanked him and went back to the inn.

During the next hour, it poured again and poured and poured all afternoon long into the night. It was like living in Vancouver again. I couldn't ride out of here. There was never enough time for the roads to clear.

The Italians and I got word that the highway crews were slowly making their way up to Karimabad, clearing one landslide after another. The telephone lines were only functioning a few hours a day, so we had no way of knowing when the roads would be open. The only telephones in Karimabad were at the three expensive hotels in town that had Western bath facilities and television sets. However, these places were running at the same level of intermittent service as the cheaper inns up the hill. No TV, no reliable phones and lots of leaky roofs.

The seven Italians and I hunkered down in our inn to play cards and talk about our trips and lives back home. We sat at a long table in the middle of the common room. We would flip a coin to decide who would have to walk from our rooms in Altit up the hill to Karimabad to get cigarettes or cookies. Occasionally, one of the hotel owners would come by with a Jeep and drive us to the village.

Sleeping, reading, eating and smoking pot. For two days straight, it seemed like we did nothing else as the rain came down outside. Joints were passed around the table hour after hour in the dark smoke-filled room. The only light came from two kerosene lanterns in the corner. I tried to inhale a few times but failed miserably, choking and coughing. Tessa and Nene would laugh every time I tried, offering me their "Ten Hints To Better Weed Smoking." I was a bitter failure at smoking some of the best pot in Central Asia. I couldn't whistle or blow bubble gum and now I couldn't inhale. Just like good ol' Bill Clinton.

As the rain poured relentlessly that night, the inn's mud roof and walls began to give way. In the midst of a deep sleep, a chunk of water-saturated mud fell on my head. I thought a rat had jumped on my face until I realized that it was slimy dirt from the wall. It was all over my hair, up my nose and on the pillow. That was it. I could rough it anywhere, but I treasured my sleep. After washing myself in the bathroom, I moved to the other side of the room for the rest of the night. In the morning, I moved to the New Hunza Tourist Hotel up in Karimabad. The owner of the Kisar Inn argued with me over my decision to move to a drier place and refused to refund my deposit.

When the rain relinquished after my third night in town, I began to make plans to hike up to the Ultar Glacier situated behind the village. The 7,388 m-high glacier was one of the more popular trekking and climbing destinations around Karimabad. Guides weren't necessary for most of the hikes around Karimabad, but I split the cost with a Dutch man and his son anyway. We hired a Baltit guide and former porter who had climbed K2 in

1970 with the legendary Austrian mountaineer Reinhold Messner. Messner would later go on to solo climb Everest and Nanga Parbat in the same year.

Our four-hour trek to the meadows at the base of the glacier began just above Karimabad. We walked slowly in order to acclimatize ourselves to the increasing altitude. Since I had come down from the Khunjerab Pass a week earlier, I was fine. The others weren't as anxious as I to get to the glacier. The porter and I marched ahead as the rest took their time through the rocky gorge and glacial scree. Aside from a few small rock faces where we had to pull ourselves up, most of the climb was on narrow singletrack trail that wound its way up the valley.

I couldn't see Karimabad or Baltit, but the towering peaks across the valley of Rakaposhi and Diran Peak looked more impressive, now that we were much higher up. Two Baltit men carrying huge backpacks of canned goods passed us without breaking stride. They weren't even breathing heavily. The men were headed for a small canvas tent on the meadow above — a kind of mountaintop convenience store. For a price, you could have a meal and a shoulder rub. Our guide said they walked up to the glacier twice a day seven days a week. These guys were fit.

Scattered along our route to the meadow were small memorial cairns to climbers who had perished on the mountain. When we reached the top of the valley, 4,000 m above sea level, we saw two graves set in cement. The green-and-blue memorials commemorated the lives of Japanese climbers who had fallen off the icefalls at the base of the glacier. After lunch at the makeshift tent-store, we hiked around the meadow for a few hours before heading down.

Hiking away from the glacier, we opted to climb along footwide trails, laid into the side of the sheer valley walls on our way down. To my left, the boulder-strewn floor lay 800 m below. The four of us used the irrigation channels built into the sides of the cliffs as footpaths. The cliff protruded over our heads at such a sharp angle that we couldn't walk upright. In some places, we were forced to crouch on our knees and cling precariously to the muddy irrigation channel bottoms. Far below, I could see the valley where we had started seven hours earlier. The complex engineering of this set of irrigation channels had built-in reservoirs to collect water during run-off season. Other spots had valves to control the water flow. All channels fed directly to the three towns below. There were even short irrigation tunnels cut through the corners of the mountain to assist in directing water downhill.

Exhausted from the climb down, the Dutch father took a shortcut with his son around a stony outcrop. The two headed into an intricate system of trails that wound its way through a steep village walk into Karimabad. I continued along the irrigation route with the porter and ended on top of a cliff overlooking the town. Below, the Karakoram Highway paralleled the Hunza River. The two highways of life, one for people, the other for crops, slithered their way through the fertile mountain valley.

I could see women and children scampering along the sun-baked roofs of flat-topped houses. They were sorting out baskets of dried apricots, wet from the previous day's rain. I had been talking with the porter about his guiding expeditions up some of Pakistan's most forbidding peaks, when he put the now familiar relationship question to me.

"Why you no married?" he asked. "You have woman problems?"

Well, not really. He didn't understand why I was happier travelling thousands of kilometres away from home when I could be raising a family. I wasn't about to explain the dating particulars of the average Canadian male, nor was I willing to convert to Islam and abide by the holy Koran. The esoteric topic of mating in Western society, as he put it, had always puzzled him. I was assured I could have up to seven wives if I was not happy. I was very happy right here in Pakistan, I told him, single and alone with my mountain bike.

He found it hard to understand how a Westerner could earn enough money to buy a fancy bike and take a trip overseas. He told me he made a meagre 300 rupees ($10) per trip as a porter when he guided expeditions up K2 and Rakaposhi. The two

Dutch hikers and I had paid him slightly less than that for a day's work. As our conversation regressed again into a debate over Islamic versus Christian marital vows, we hit the entrance path to the Baltit Fort, a massive whitewashed structure.

The porter told me that the 770-year-old fort, visible from the highway, was not only used as the Mir's residence until 1945, but also as a dungeon. The garrison and militia rooms had recently undergone major renovations. One room contained a set of drums that used to signal the alarm when an attack by neighbouring villages was imminent. Poplar poles carried most of the fort's load, an architectural style that had its roots in Tibet.

After climbing through the dungeons, reception rooms and living quarters, I made my way up the spiral staircase to the mud roof. Four men in their wool *chogas* were packing down sections of the roof with their bare feet. Up here, far above the town, the monsoon rains had also done their damage. The men were putting lumps of clay over the deteriorating parts of the roof, especially around the edges. They mixed the dry clay with the soggy wet mud, squishing it until a new hard layer formed. This was Pakistan's version of do-it-yourself. Bob Villa, move over. Here comes an episode of "This Old House" Muslim-style.

Back in Karimabad, I stopped at the tailor shop to see about my appointment with the Mir's wife. Ikramullah, the tailor, was out but had left me a note. I was to go to the front gate of the Mir's sprawling compound the next day at 11 a.m. I had learned the previous day from talking to some of the shopkeepers that Saadia and her mother-in-law the Rani of Hunza were greatly disliked in town. They were considered outsiders, since the Rani had been born into a wealthy Shia family in southern Pakistan. Both women were Ismaili converts because the Mir's kingdom (Hunza Valley) was predominantly Ismaili. This intermarriage of people from different Islamic sects had made the Mirship unpopular. His wife's conversion was especially offensive because she was from the educated cosmopolitan world of the south and people there looked disparagingly at the tribesmen of the north. Why couldn't Mir

Ghazanfar have married one of his own — a local Ismaili woman?

When I was finally introduced to Saadia Habib Oberoi at the Mir's *haveli*, a small palace with trellised balconies and Victorian furnishings, I saw the locals' point. In her early 20s, Saadia wore a beautiful *shalwar qamiz*, but it was made of silk, not like anything I had seen in Hunza. Exotic in design, it had intricately woven patterns. With her good looks and striking black hair, she looked like a *Vogue* model, more appropriate to the affluent cities of Islamabad and Karachi. Saadia couldn't have blended in with the other women of Karimabad if she tried. She exuded wealth. The Rani, on the other hand, 40 years Saadia's senior, was dressed in a more traditional red-and-black robe.

For lunch, we were served carrot *murraba* (sugary stew with almonds), brain curry and *paratha* bread (fried *chapattis*). The curry tasted like a mix of tofu and hardened oysters, except a bit spicier. Different but good. The Rani (who only spoke Urdu) told me through Saadia that she hated the commercialization of Karimabad with its "tacky" guesthouses. The town needed more upscale hotels to profit from the tourists, like the Mir's own Rakaposhi View Hotel. I hated to think how much valuable agricultural land more large hotels would take up. By fancy hotel, the Rani meant a modern Pakistani version, something similar to a large cedar ski chalet in Colorado or Whistler — small but opulent.

The Mir's palace, like the few expensive hotels in town, was the only structure I had seen in Hunza with drywall and numerous electrical outlets. The Mir's Rakaposhi View Hotel had beautiful hardwood floors, ventilation ducts and extensive use of glass — very Western, I thought. In keeping with Hunza tradition, the Mir had decreed that television sets were only allowed in the lobby. The Rani thought this was a big compromise in favour of cultural preservation. No mud floors, kerosene lamps or chunks of mud falling on guest's heads!

Saadia lived most of her life far removed from the reality of rural Pakistani women. She was used to the United States where she had met her husband, the Mir's son. He was taking his doctorate at

Harvard and Saadia was completing her master's degree at Texas A &
M University. She flew back and forth regularly from the United
States to Pakistan to visit her family. The Rani had met General Zia
ul-Haq, one of Pakistan's more infamous military dictators from the
1980s. Despite the general's brutal reputation and ban on political
activity, the Rani said he was "a very warm person and could make
you feel wanted and comfortable." General Zia is best known for
sanctioning the hanging of Benazir Bhutto's father when he was
president.

I left the palace with a different impression of Pakistan's royal
family of the north — one of an aristocratic family trying to
mediate the ways of a people still living very much in the days
of the old Silk Road. These two women from wealthy back-
grounds with endless opportunities were battling centuries-old
prejudices about religion and old money. Such deep-rooted societies are slow to change cultural traditions regarding democracy,
the role of women or marriage between different Muslim sects.
To bridge the gap between the rural women of Karimabad and
their more educated counterparts in the south, the Rani had
started an embroidery school called Threadnet Hunza. She had
also co-funded several agricultural projects with the Aga Khan.
As Saadia had told me, a private school existed on the Mir's
property for any family that could afford the 150 to 250 rupees
a month. That was $5 to $8 that most Pakistanis didn't have.

As I left the palace, Saadia informed me that the KKH was open
again. She told me to write the Mir any time if I ever returned to
Pakistan. Come for dinner with Mir Ghazanfar, she said. I wished
her good luck with her degree and set up my bike for the road
again. I knew the 105-km ride from Karimabad to Gilgit would go
quickly as the hills were in my favour, especially since the highway headed west, hugging the river valley.

For the first 40 km, I could see Rakaposhi beside and then
behind me. Several hours later, its peak disappeared behind one
of the many glaciers that ran along the south of the highway. The
KKH crossed over the Hunza River, the third crossing since I left

the school kids at Gulmit. Now the river ran to my right on the north wall of the valley, slowly curving around to the south.

I was halfway between Kashgar and Islamabad. There were 650 km more to go. It seemed as if I had travelled much more than that with all the downhills and majestic scenery. When the KKH was constructed, Chinese workers built most of the 85 bridges and dozens of tunnels along the route. Apparently, they were more skilled at road and bridge building than the Pakistani crews. Lion heads are carved into the entranceways of the Chinese-built bridges, symbols of the Chinese god that protects those in need during storms.

Riding the KKH, even in the cool mountains, meant stopping at small wooden shacks such as the Rakaposhi general store to replenish my water bottles and pick up food. Occasionally, I treated myself to Coca-Cola, Fanta or 7Up in glass bottles. When you aren't drinking out of aluminum cans or one-litre Snapple and Dr. Pepper bottles, you're in some place culturally detached in the best of ways. It was one big time warp. Maybe it was the heat and dust, but pop tastes better in cold, glass bottles. A few rupees and drinks later, I cranked my bike and headed off along the side of the road.

Riding a fully loaded bike was a challenge in itself. If I was on a slight incline, my front wheel would lift up in the air because of the weight of the rear panniers. These mini wheelies made getting up to speed awkward, to say the least. Usually I would head down a hill or across level ground, slowly starting out in my granny gear. Then I would shift up with my derailleur, switching to my middle ring and then to the Big Kahuna — my big chainring. Bikes loaded down for touring handle much like a Hertz rent-a-truck. You're afraid to corner sharply or brake in earnest. However, with practice a good cyclist can navigate his or her bike through anything at speed. I was enjoying just that. My pig-like Rocky Mountain Fusion behemoth was now a graceful Greyhound bus, large yet fast.

Being able to pedal for hours on end in my biggest gear was heaven come true. All bikers search for the elusive never-ending downhill. I had only found it once before in Morocco, during my last trip with Tony. I had come out of the High Atlas Mountains down a 155-km gravel road. Three hours of non-stop exhilaration doesn't come close to describing the feeling. The whirr of the tires would change as my bike went from pavement to gravel to mud. Here on the Karakoram Highway, I had on a cross version of knobby slicks for tires that allowed the bike to grip the off-road dirt when cornering, yet travel fairly quickly on the pavement.

The highway continued to cut through the "black mountains" (the origin of the word *Karakoram*), eventually passing through the small village of Chalt. Up above the town, an abandoned Jeep track was visible. Once an old caravan trail, it was another relic from the Silk Road. A monument in the form of a large yellow pneumatic drill, 5 m high, stood beside the road in memory of the Pakistan and Chinese workers who perished building the Karakoram Highway. Almost in defiance of these workers' efforts, a landslide a few corners later blocked the road. Cars and trucks of all types had been waiting for several hours for the road crews to dig away with shovels and a bulldozer. A small path in the dirt and rocks was enough for me to ride my bike through. The benefits of two wheels over four were obvious.

As the KKH dipped up and down, it would simultaneously weave in and out beside the Hunza River, coming within 100 m in some places and 10 times that in others. Then the valley suddenly opened. Up to now, every corner revealed another view of the peaks ahead. Sometimes I would see a new village planted among the hills. Other times, the river would widen into broad alluvial sediment deposits as it flowed under bright red bridges. This time, however, the mountains changed. I was at the juncture of the three greatest mountain ranges in the world. The Himalaya stretched all the way from Nepal through Kashmiri India. To the west ran the Hindu Kush into Afghanistan. The Karakorams extended north to the Chinese border. I could see all three merging in one spot!

The Karakoram Highway is built on top of some of the most

active tectonic plates in the world. The Indian plate drives underneath the Asian continental plate, uplifting against it in the biggest tectonic train wreck on the continent. Folded backwards and compressed, granite and slate "geological slices," some more than 600 million years old, are constantly moving. They precipitate rock falls and landslides, making highway maintenance a continuous task.

The beauty of this mountainous country, where homes cling precariously to hillsides, made me wish I could spend a year here. I could easily imagine living on a diet of fruit, bread and mineral-rich waters, sometimes sampling the brandy distilled from mulberries. When the British annexed this remote area in the 19th century, the Mir of Hunza said that the valleys were "more precious to us than the strings of our wives pyjamas." I agreed. Hunza is a place I swore I'd return to. Even moving at the relatively slow pace of a bicycle, I knew I was missing a lot.

Gilgit

Eventually all good things come to an end. Gilgit is the dividing line where Hunza ends and cool mountains begin to drop away from the highway, making way for wide, blistering parched valleys. The town of Gilgit is the administrative centre and gateway to northern Pakistan. Until a half century ago, the area was mostly impassable except by horse or mule. Mudslides and tumbling rocks the size of Volkswagens frequently washed out the old gravel roads. Until the Pakistan Army built the first stages of the KKH in 1960, Gilgit wasn't connected to the outside world in the modern sense of the word. In the 19th century, the British used the Gilgit region as a launching post for intelligence expeditions to check on the Russians as they advanced through Central Asia during the Great Game.

Gilgit, at 1,500 m above sea level, is now a bustling supply town, a sleepier version of Kashgar. It is the centre of activity in the Northern Areas. Fall colours livened up the city's drab brown hills, a change from the heavily irrigated green fields of Hunza. More Westerners come into Gilgit than into any other city in northern Pakistan. Gilgit has everything from an airport, library and hospital to dozens of trekking and tour guide offices. Most important, it has a reliable telephone and fax system. High-altitude mountaineers stop to gather climbing supplies and provisions on their way to Skardu and the Concordia glacier. Once in this glacial paradise, the foolhardy and accomplished attempt to conquer Broad Peak, Masherbrum and K2 — the most challenging climb of them all. Most climbers on their way to these 7,000- and 8,000-m wind-whipped peaks fly into Gilgit from Islamabad.

When I arrived in Gilgit, I cycled around town for an hour, checking out the dozens of inns, motels, hotels and flophouses. I booked into the Madina Guesthouse, a shaded campsite. I had heard the Madina, with its canvas tents and plywood shower facilities, was cheap and had good food in large quantities. A single rope bed or mat was 25 rupees ($1.19). In China, I had been paying 80 yuan ($13) for complete rooms with Tony and Tim. Even the dorm beds in China were about $6, a far cry from Pakistan. This place was cheap. Dirt cheap, and I loved it. There were cyclists and backpackers, couples and wanderlust travellers.

At the check-in desk, I was told about two British cyclists who had come through Gilgit the same day I had left Kashgar, a two-week difference. A Dutch guy on an Enfield Bullet motorcycle said that there was a note for me from a British traveller named Tony at the Hunza Tourist House. It turns out that Tony and Tim had stayed in town for three days in case I might catch them, but to no avail. I was too far behind.

The Madina was the hippest hangout in Gilgit. It attracted pothead wannabes and real potheads, tourists pretending to be backpackers whining about the cockroaches and the spicy food and real backpackers whining about how the food was too bland. "Southern India had the best hot peppers," I heard from some. "These Muslims eat too much meat," said another.

Then there were the seasoned travellers who quietly scribbled in their journals and hung their socks and panties on the clotheslines. Others — tourists who had never been outside their own countries — tried to adjust to the ways of the seasoned traveller. It was here I realized the real distinction between tourists and travellers – those who leave their assumptions at home and those who don't. There were the tourists who would peek into your canvas tent (no buildings in this place), trying to find a blow dryer and iron. Then there was the Hash Zone. Purveyors would congregate with the marijuana hawkers, exchanging the best pot stories from their trips through Southeast Asia. Over *dhal* (lentil soup) and *garam marsala* (a mixture of cardamom pods, cumin seeds, cinnamon sticks and cloves or nutmeg), I heard three people trying to impress each other beside the wash basin.

"Dude, you wouldn't believe the price I bought Bangkok Gold for in Phuket," the discussion would go.

"No, you spicy chai head. You've been with the wrong crowd. The most righteous stuff ain't in that German obsessed-with-nine-year-old-little-girls porn city, but in this back alley noodle joint in Almaty," another would say.

"Man that must have been the best. Better than that White Rhino and Mexican Red stuff I did in Calcutta. Too mellow. I got some Zombie Weed. You got a light?"

And so the conversations went. That is, until the fight.

I had only seen a working television set once since leaving Beijing seven weeks earlier. Then I heard the news. It was the talk of the town. It was August 31. Princess Diana had died in a car crash in Paris. I didn't care too much for the British monarchy, but the Pakistanis loved her. They all knew who Princess Di was. One shopowner I met shook her hand in the refugee camps in Peshawar near the Afghanistan border. Sombre over her death, he reminisced about the two-minute encounter, going on and on. He was heartbroken.

At the guesthouse, the news had turned two backpackers from the Queen's commonwealth against each other. The Madina had a 36-inch colour Toshiba set. A repeat of the Belgian Formula One auto race was on. Or was it? As I approached the common area where people were reading and playing cards, the channel flipped back and forth between CNN and the BBC. One station was running non-stop coverage of Princess Diana, the other had the Grand Prix race. Two young men, British and Australian, were in a heated argument over control of the television. They were starting to swear at each other in front of about 20 others. The Aussie, who was sitting on a chair, had the remote control and wanted to watch the F1 race.

"It's just a bloody car race," the Brit yelled to the Aussie. "Princess Di is much more important."

"You stupid islander with lousy dental work, get off my back. I was watching it first. The news will be on about this royal stuff for weeks," the Aussie retorted.

On went the macho argument. The Brit would try to stand in front of the TV set only to frustrate the Australian even more. No one wanted to intervene. After 20 minutes, most were sick of the juvenile routine. Then I left, unable to concentrate on reading the Pakistani daily papers.

In Gilgit, I began to discover the changes in cuisine throughout the various regions. The Tajik and Kyrgyz greasy meat concoctions gave way to Pakistan's Moghul-influenced diet developed in the old Muslim courts of India. Freshly ground peppers and spices were kept in airtight containers to retain the aromas and flavours. Saffron, cardamom and poppy seeds were often used in meat sautés. A cast-iron round pan called a *karahai*, similar to a wok, was used in most places; *bhuna gosht* and *bheja masala* (devilled brains) were some of the more exotic dishes available, again much cheaper than any food in China. Chicken and mutton with lots of onions were the staple foods plus lots of chilies unless you said otherwise.

Chai was a must. Gilgit's shops aren't so much arranged into markets as tea parlours and emporiums. *Chai* is the opiate of the Muslim masses. From the Haidry Tea Shop to the Pamir Tours office, everyone used tea to negotiate sales. Pakistan's green tea was a lot more like what I was used to at home. Sugar was an essential ingredient to a soothing cup of tea, and cream or milk wasn't too hard to find if you wanted it.

Yoghurt seemed to be the most common dairy product. *Raita*, a mint-flavoured yoghurt sauce accompanied rice dishes. You would break off some bread from a *chapatti* and scoop up some rice and dip it in the yoghurt, much like pita bread and hummus or tzatziki. For lunch that day I even tried *khagina,* boiled eggs scrambled in chilies with garlic and ginger. It was too disagreeable a selection to eat again. I was willing to try anything once, but no more eggs for me. Nothing from a chicken except the meat.

The food was great, if not just for the change from the Turkish- and Persian-influenced food on the Chinese side of the Karakoram Highway. Unlike Kashgar, where the nights were alive with Han and Muslim food markets, Gilgit went to sleep early. The only sign of life in the streets were some men sleeping in blankets in shop doorways. A couple nights during my three-day stay in Gilgit, I rode my bike past the alleys and closed shops for a few hours, chatting with armed guards and being chased by a pack of wild dogs. I loved the solitude of the night and the sounds of a sleeping city.

I would return to the guesthouse when the muezzin called out from the mosques in the early morning hours. Even with this Islamic flair, Gilgit didn't have the flavour that had so drawn me to Kashgar. Maybe it was the lack of visibly diverse cultures, but Gilgit quickly bored me. It was just a pit stop on the way south, except for the exuberance of the kids. Every afternoon, I saw kids from a local public school walk by, dressed in orange jump-suits much like those of prisoners awaiting trial in detention centres. The private school kids were dressed in bright blue shirts. The boys wore grey-and-navy striped ties; the girls wore white shawls over their heads. They wanted everything I had. Pens, money and more money. I had given away all my stickers and pins back near Gulmit and had nothing for them that represented Canada. They seemed to value the pens more than anything. Maybe their school was in short supply?

Nevertheless, Gilgit was steeped in Silk Road history, just like China. In China, I had to envision the ancient Silk Road explorers trekking across deserts as they bartered their goods and fended off highway bandits. In Hunza and the Gilgit region, the history of the Silk Road was more apparent. West of the city through pine and juniper forests, a large Buddhist carving, the Kargah Buddha, stood as testimony to the influence of the monks who had brought this new religion to Central Asia.

Television has changed the way Pakistanis have been able to follow their national obsession. Cricket, more than any other sport, defines the spirit of Pakistan. Much the same way that Canada follows hockey, Pakistan craves cricket matches. It's not a sport. It's an obsession. Radio and television have helped bring cricket to more rural communities than anything else. From the dry Panjab hills to the Pathan tribesmen in the Tribal Areas, cricket is a game everyone relates to.

In schoolyards, playing fields and back alleys, young boys and even the occasional girl practise their cricket moves. Wherever there was a piece of level ground, children and adults imitated their favourite batsmen. If a game were on, every shop in town would have a transistor radio tuned in. The whole country is captivated with the game. The newspapers even divide the sections into cricket and other sports. Young and old, male and female, everyone follows their favourite team from Gilgit or the valleys of Chitral or Hunza.

When the national team plays, fans listen in on their radios or watch on beat-up old black-and-white TVs. When Pakistan plays its traditional rival India, both countries are riveted to the news. I saw this happen when Pakistan played India in the Sahara Cup, an international cricket tournament held in Toronto. In 1986, a quarter million people welcomed home the Pakistan team after it beat India for the first time on Indian soil. The Pakistani prime minister even proclaimed a national holiday.

The game that interested me the most was polo — especially the Pakistani version. The polo grounds in Gilgit are lined with towering willow and poplar trees amidst a snowy backdrop. During the summer matches, the grounds are crammed with enthusiastic spectators. Polo originated in Persia and was reborn in Pakistan's Northern Areas. The Pakistanis were never content with the gentlemen's sport that the British had cultivated, so they made it better. The Pakistanis created a hybrid version called *buzkashi* where teams sacrifice goats and sheep, using the headless carcass as the ball. *Buzkashi* matches are played with brutal gamesmanship. Horses often end up as bloody and scarred by the mallets as the players, bashing the sheep's remains back and forth across the field. The horses are on a strict diet of walnuts and mulberries to keep in top form — anything to beat the next team during each seven-minute *chukka*.

The bridge that leaves the polo grounds crosses one of three major rivers in the region. Over time, the juncture of these rivers has turned Gilgit into a trading hub much like Kashgar. The valleys that the Hunza, Gilgit and Indus Rivers flow through have made for favourable trails that link far-off villages and tribes. People have used the river routes for centuries, venturing over mountain passes down into Hunza and Gilgit to barter goods in the markets. These were the routes that linked Central Asia with Kashmir and the Indian subcontinent.

When I left Gilgit, I reached the end of the Hunza River an hour south of the city. The two tributary rivers, the Hunza and its sister river the Gilgit, both feed the mighty Indus River, one of the longest rivers in the world. The Indus, which gave its name to India, carries six billion cubic feet of silt each monsoon season as it winds its way in a snake-like formation through the Karakorams. The Indus starts in the high plateaus of Tibet and flows across Kashmir from India, paralleling the Himalaya range. Then it swoops south through Pakistan, following the Karakoram Highway for 340 km. For the Northern Areas, the river is the lifeblood of the farmers' fields. All along the Hunza and Indus Rivers, apricot orchards and maize grow with birch and poplar trees as windbreaks. In 1841, an entire valley wall gave way after an earthquake, and fell into the Indus. The river backed up all the way to Gilgit, 134 km away, creating a large lake. In time, the mud and rock wall broke. Water rushed down the valley, flooding villages and drowning thousands as far as 500 km downstream.

The Indus would become a familiar sight for me over the next week as I rode alongside into the scorching plains of the south. The oven-like summer of Pakistan was evident as I cycled into Jaglot, a small hamlet stop. This led to a morning tea ritual to cool down. These early hours were my only chance to cover any substantial distances before the afternoon heat set in. It was the Takla Makan desert all over again — hydrate or die.

Nanga Parbat and the Croatians

As I was finishing my *chai* the first morning out of Gilgit, I started to pack up a few fruit-flavoured *lassis*, a nourishing, sweet yoghurt drink. A guy in a white T-shirt on a bike rolled up to the roadside stall beside me. Minutes later, a truck stopped and out jumped another young male dressed in cycling tights. He pulled his bike down from atop the vehicle with the help of some men. Then the two cyclists joined me in the shade of the trees.

Ivan and Dennis were Croatian Army soldiers on leave from the Balkan War back home. They had thrown a dart in a map and it hit Pakistan. Let's go there, Ivan had said. Forget it, Dennis had said resolutely. So the two were here in Pakistan — Ivan on his bike and Dennis with his bike on top of a truck. Dennis had fallen into the habit of riding on vehicles with his bike ever since they left Kashgar 720 km away. His legs and body were too tired to keep up with his army buddy. The two were obviously incompatible on the road. Dennis liked the view from the buses and trucks and found he got to know quite a few locals this way. He was always rested and didn't regret having to shepherd his bike around from town to town.

The three of us decided to travel together to the next stop in Chilas. Dennis, as usual, caught a lift on a rusty old diesel truck. He sat on top of some burlap sacks and was off, the wind rushing through his hair. Ivan and I cranked up the pedals and headed off behind the truck up a hill. Our two bikes and the truck were neck and neck for a while, until we turned a corner and headed down the other side. Down we went, and then up again. It was one giant roller-coaster ride.

Soon the highway's corners became sharper and sharper as the road slowly opened up into a valley. I accelerated down a hill and screamed around corners at 60 to 70 km/h. Unfortunately, when I turned a corner, the brute force of the winds coming up the valley would buffet the bike as my speed was suddenly cut in half. On more than one occasion I was almost knocked off. This sudden change in velocity made it seem like I was thrust into a wind tunnel. My daily mileage was picking up considerably since crossing the Khunjerab Pass and barrelling down through the Karakorams. In many instances, I was riding distances of 105 to 134 km per day.

I was glad to find a new riding companion to pace myself against. For a few hours, we switched leaders back and forth, up and down, left to right. Ivan and I began on an equal footing, but by the late afternoon, he was several kilometres ahead of me. On this blistering hot day, I inevitably began to succumb to the heat after 80 km. He was in better shape than me, particularly on the hills. After slogging it up one climb, I stopped.

Then I saw it.

A 7,000-m sheer granite face rose straight out of the Indus River. Nanga Parbat, the Killer Mountain, was straight in front of me; a giant granite pyramid stood no more than 50 km away. I could almost reach out and touch it. It was immense. Massive. One giant slab of rock, uncluttered by other peaks or valley walls. At 8,125 m (26,685 ft.), Nanga Parbat is the westernmost peak in the Himalaya range. In Karimabad, Rakaposhi had been beautiful, yet so elusive, standing across from the Indus with its narrow peak. Only Everest and Annapurna stand out more than Nanga Parbat.

The granite monstrosity is often called the Killer Mountain in memory of 17 Germans who died during a perilous expedition in the 1930s. Consequently, German high-altitude mountaineers have become obsessed with conquering the mountain. They have essentially claimed it as their own. The Himalaya massif is so steep that snow doesn't stick on one side. During my stay in the area, a Basque climber from Spain died attempting to summit the mountain and another person lost their hands to frostbite. Up near the China-Pakistan border at K2, the world's second highest mountain, an expedition of six Japanese climbers were all killed in an avalanche.

I later found out that Tony and Tim had trekked to the 3,200-m-high base camp called Fairy Meadows, a high plateau near the halfway mark. Wild roses grow on this plateau. It takes 10 hours of climbing to reach the base camp — 6 hours of them on tight twisty switchbacks. Unfortunately, when the two Brits returned to the base of the mountain where they had stashed their bikes in the woods, Tony's gear and clothing were gone. Everything except the bike was stolen. Some idiot had taken his precious film, forever irreplaceable. It was a big disappointment on an otherwise unforgettable trip for Tony.

After passing the majesty of Nanga Parbat and another hamlet stop, Raikot Bridge, I made it out of the Karakorams and into the plains. The up and down hills of the Gilgit region were gradually coming to an end as the highway slowly dropped in elevation. The road was just as treacherous, but the gradients were less severe. Finally, I reached Chilas, a town where the arid soil had leached all the nutrients from the ground. Dennis was lying in bed asleep in a flimsy one-storey whitewashed motel, the Shangri-La. He was well rested from the truck ride. Ivan had arrived a half-hour ahead of me. I was beat.

Chilas is interesting for the petroglyphs near the highway and river — reminders of travellers who preceded those on the Silk Road. Ivan and I walked down to the river to see some of the hieroglyphic images. Icons of long-horned ibexes, drawings of fertility festivals and religious symbols on huge boulders told the story of civilizations dating back to the Bronze Age. For centuries, the Himalaya had acted as a barrier, both physically and culturally. It divided the Indian subcontinent from China. Kashmir (now divided between Pakistan and India) was once a sub-route of the

Silk Road where venturesome Buddhist monks travelled through the Indus Valley over the border into China. The eventual clash between the Buddhist faith and Islam, introduced by the Mongols, led to the desecration of Buddhist artwork in the 9th century. The Chilas region has gone through every faith imaginable. Paganism and fire worshippers were here long before Buddhism, which gave way to Hinduism and Islam.

The nearby Babusar Pass that connects with the KKH at Chilas, was one of only two roads north to Gilgit before the highway was blasted through to the Chinese border. Over the years, everyone from tribesmen to the British hauled supplies over the 4,100-m pass. Consequently, Chilas became the crossroads for those on their way to Hunza and Chitral.

Police were stationed at various checkpoints in Chilas to prevent *dacoits* (thieves) from robbing the villagers. After a good rest, I went out late that night with Dennis and Ivan and chatted with the police at 3 a.m. about guns, the nasties in India and cricket. One of the officers shared some wheat thins with me as he and his co-workers smoked hash. This was an evening ritual, the officer said — every evening, every shift. Most Pakistani men in the surrounding villages considered marijuana and hash as essential as a good diet. Drugs didn't have the stigma that they do in the West. The following morning after Dennis had caught a ride to the next town, Ivan and I left Chilas. The mountains were well below 6,000 m as the Indus Valley neared the final stages of the Karakoram Highway. We ended up riding into the land of the ungoverned — Indus Kohistan.

Kohistan is a region of outlaw tribes and bloody feuds. A 140-km stretch of highway cuts through Kohistan with its dramatic red canyon walls and stone watchtowers. This was where Hunza and Gilgit (regions within the Northern Areas province) ended, and made way for the North West Frontier Province. Outsiders are treated here with suspicion. Even the neighbouring regions and valley tribes are viewed with contempt.

We heard of horror stories about cyclists who were pulled off the road. Kohistanis would line the highway, blocking all who tried to go through. A female cyclist in spandex cycling tights was actually dragged off her bike and raped, ostensibly for exposing too much of her body. This was a rare occurrence. Most people, whether backpacking or cycling, throw their bikes and gear on top of a truck or bus and ride through the area until they're in the next region.

As we stocked up for water one morning, Ivan and I met two European cyclists, a young couple in their 20s. They had just come up the KKH from Islamabad and Rawalpindi and were each loaded up with front and rear panniers. Twenty people had stood across the highway and forcibly removed them from their bikes. All this, despite the fact they were dressed in loose clothing from neck to ankle. The guidebooks recommended hitching a ride through Kohistan, but we wanted to make a dash for it.

We soon learned we were in the heart of Pakistan's Kalashnikov culture. From Shatial where we had stopped, all the way to Dasu, machine guns were widespread. Every Chief of Police and Frontier Constabulary guard carried some sort of automatic weapon. Shatial, a small village with cafés, was run by Pathan tribesmen in their black-and-white checked turbans. Merchants sold M-16 knockoffs and AK-47s at roadside shops along with tea and *chapattis*. The Muslim-gun ethos ruled. You could save some money and buy a Chinese-made weapon or go for accuracy and quality and get the Russian model.

In Dasu, Ivan and I stopped for two days at the C & W Resthouse to escape the heat. Dennis had gone ahead to Islamabad. Ivan would meet with him later. That night, Ivan and I ate *koftas*, some of the best chunks of minced lamb I ever had. The meat was fresh and not too tough. Even the food in the finest restaurants in Vancouver couldn't compare to the tenderness of some of Pakistan's meat dishes. As we walked through Dasu's bazaars, we met Pusli Gummade at Habib's Gun Shop. A pelican was pecking away at a *chapatti* on the floor while Pathan and Kohistani men browsed Avtomat Kalashnikovs. The Pathan looked a little rough with their long flowing turbans and gun shops, but they were warm when we spoke to them. Pusli told me the story of two Norwegians who bought a machine gun from him and tried to smuggle it out of Pakistan. They ended up in prison because they didn't have the proper export permits.

When we left Dasu for Besham several mornings later, we began to encounter groups of rock-throwing kids. Children often ran along the goat paths above the highway. They would take aim at our unprotected heads and bodies, zinging a few rocks at us. Usually we were moving at a fast clip so they missed. When we approached towns pedalling up a hill, the situation was different. We were sitting ducks as we weaved our front wheels back and forth in an effort to avoid the kids, but our speed was too slow to make a difference.

I had heard about the lawlessness of the Kohistani adults, but they had seemed friendly, albeit a bit reserved. Nothing to be afraid of. The kids, on the other hand, were getting to be little shits. The kids viewed any foreigner, especially a slow-moving target like a cyclist, as prime target practice. It was a game to them. At Pattan, just outside Dasu, we decided to fight back. The next kid who thought our spokes were a good place to throw a sharp stick would see what the best of Canada and Croatia had to offer. In order to fend off the enemy we had to be armed. We bought some slingshots with thick brown rubber bands wrapped around two sticks. Sure enough, minutes later, a stone made a familiar ding off Ivan's spokes.

Ivan had had enough of being hit in the head with stones and wood. He cursed something in Croatian and flung his bike down. He had to see who was toying with his mind that day. I quickly pulled over and whipped out my slingshot from my handlebar bag. There, in the middle of the street, was a girl in a purple dress and several boys (probably her brothers). We didn't let the fact that they were only 10 years old distract us. We were on a mission. I bent over and loaded up. Zapp! A rock flew straight towards my knees. I bent sideways rather awkwardly, averting a bloody shin.

The opposition was amassing troops.

Ivan and I geared up for a full frontal assault. We ducked into the side of a shop and peered down the street. Zaapp. Craack. Another one. I fired a few rocks that skipped off the ground, bouncing into the shops. After a few minutes, we were at a stalemate. Then some burly shopkeepers came out and started walking towards us. We cut our losses, jumped on our bikes and pedalled out of town, dogs chasing behind us.

By the time we hit Besham, 78 km down the highway from Dasu, I started to notice an increase in cargo Jeeps and bus traffic on the roads. We were now in the bustling south where settlements gave way to larger towns with bus depots and post offices. Ivan took the next long-distance bus out of town for the 260-km trip to Islamabad. He had to meet up with Dennis who had given up on riding any more sections of the highway. I, too, was trying to cover as much ground as possible to maximize the time I could spend in Afghanistan and India. I had to quicken my pace for the next four days. After that I would be in Islamabad at the end of the Karakoram Highway and fly across the country to Peshawar on the Afghan border.

The trappings of civilization were becoming apparent in Besham, especially when I saw a television set. Much to my surprise, the whole town was transfixed. They were watching Princess Diana's funeral service. Every restaurant that had a TV set was tuned into the SKY-TV network. Man, woman and child — all were captivated by the proceedings. It was unfortunate that the last two times I had seen a TV, in Gilgit and now in Besham, the nation was obsessed with grieving for a British princess and the accompanying tabloid gossip. Mother Teresa's death a few days earlier hardly registered on the "interest scale," despite the fact that the funeral was held in Calcutta, next door in India.

Dodging Water Buffalo in the Kaghan Valley
The roaring Indus River up north was now a meandering, mud-coloured expanse of water irrigating fewer and fewer fields.

The mountains had turned to rolling hills; the yawning ravines gently changed to broad valleys. After I departed Besham early one morning, the Indus finally left the highway, winding its way another 1,500 km to the Arabian Sea. I thought that riding at 4 a.m. in the pitch darkness could have its merits. But I soon realized that it had its pitfalls.

Since parting with Ivan, I was back in the habit of rising before dawn and camping alongside the road again. In the early morning hours, well before dawn, I rolled down the highway outside a town called Batagram. I had been holding my flashlight with my left hand, resting it on the handlebars to help see in the dark. Now the batteries were dead.

I continued along at about 30 km/h, a slow speed under normal conditions. The sound of my tires rolling over the gravel edge of the road turned into a relentless blur. Abruptly, my head hit a hard steel object. I fell flat on the ground, my bare knees cutting into the gravel. My shoulder took the brunt of the hit. Both panniers fell off, rolling to the side of the road. My handlebars t-boned as the bike skidded sideways.

I had hit the gate at a checkpoint stop — a long metal pole stretched across the width of the road at chest level. I pulled myself up and assessed my bleeding knees. My forehead was severely bruised. My joints felt stiff. The bike was fine. Then I heard the murmurs of someone off to my side. Looking over, I saw the faint glimmer of a kerosene lamp through the fabric of canvas tent. An elderly man drew open the flap of the army-issue tent and slowly walked towards me.

"Salaam aleikum," I said.

"Kya hal heh?" he replied, asking how I was.

"I'm fine. A little sore, but okay," I said.

These checkpoints were common along tribal boundaries in Pakistan. Two or three men with guns would be assigned to stop anyone who was unfamiliar, making them show their papers. At this checkpoint, the guard had forgotten to wake up in time to open the gate. He offered me tea, but I declined. If I stayed, I would end up visiting forever, chatting away the morning hours. I needed to press on. I headed off after treating my cuts with Polysporin and cotton swabs from my first aid kit. I pedalled slowly for the first hour until the sun began to rise over the forested hills.

Much of the southern Karakoram Highway after Besham and Batagram dips through basins and pine plantations and terraced rice paddies. Soon the sun was up and I was climbing a hill. Abruptly, two kids buzzed past me. But they weren't on bikes, scooters or a car. The two boys, one carrying a bundle of tree branches, were sitting on what can only best be described as a wooden skateboard à la Flintstones. About a metre wide, the rolling platform had three wheels made out of coaster bearings (one in front, two in back). The axles were carved out of wood, the rest out of 20 or so small branches nailed together. A steel handle, jury-rigged to the front axle, steered the contraption.

The kids were ferrying their small cargo load down the steep side of a 1,670-m-high pass, using nothing more than their rubber sandals for brakes. I tooted the horn on my bike as they careened down the road while I grinded my gears up the hill. When they went around a corner, four tiny feet hit the pavement, bleeding off speed. They negotiated with the skill of a Formula One driver. This was where those bus and truck drivers received their training!

I stopped by a *chapatti* stall for lunch, only to have someone snag my tool kit and Canadian flag. For the past 2,500 km, the flag had proudly flapped behind me. Now it was gone. I began to get impatient riding this last stretch of the KKH. The Karakoram Mountains and Indus River were behind me. Then I bumped into Baber.

Baber Rasheed was a Punjabi businessman I met at a tiny blue three-wheeled *paan* stall in Mansehra, an old Sikh garrison town. Paan is an addictive and popular after-meal digestive — a betel leaf wrapped around an assortment of candy, lime paste, fragrance and spice fillings including a dash of opium if you're willing to pay. As Baber and I let the juices from the *paan* leaves melt in our mouths, he told me about a beautiful wooded valley that might be a refreshing change in scenery from the highway.

The Kaghan Valley, Baber said, deviated from the Karakoram Highway and followed a twisty road northeast paralleling the border of Azad Kashmir. I could take a Suzuki van with him and the two teenage kids he was chaperoning back to their families up the valley. I could stay for a day in a town called Naran, where the hiking was spectacular. From what I had read about the rest of the ride on the KKH into Islamabad, I knew I would be cycling through dusty nondescript market towns. Baber's company would be a nice change from the solitary confines of the valley plains. The largely undeveloped 160-km-long forested valley wound its way through fertile fields, eventually crossing the Babusar Pas back to Chilas.

When we packed into our little red Suzuki van with my bike on top, the women immediately put their *dupatta* scarves over their heads. None sat in the same row as me. Baber told me about how he was saving up for his daughter's wedding in Abbottabad, where he lived. He had to give a large dowry, and the drain on the family's resources had left his business nearly insolvent. Our conversation moved from topic to topic, ending with a brief Islam 101 lesson. Baber explained how Muslims only use their right hands to eat. Their left hands are considered unclean since they are used for bathroom duties and wiping. They can use both hands to break apart a *chapatti*, but only one must touch the mouth. And toilet paper — forget it. It's considered a modern convention used mainly by the urban-educated Muslims. Then Baber proceeded to tell me that he had to keep his underarm hairs a few millimetres long — no more. To do otherwise is to contravene Islamic tradition. He had lost me there.

We passed several inns run by the Pakistan Tourist Development Corporation (PTDC), the main government-run guesthouse operation, as our driver made his way up the road. He swerved through hairpin corners, one after the other, which wound sinuously into the rugged valley. We had to hold onto the handles built into the back of the seats in front of us to keep from sliding back and forth. Himalayan pine and fir trees whizzed past the window until we reached the dusty town of Balakot.

Baber, the two kids and I checked into a PTDC cottage, booking two rooms. The shops around the cottage were a bustling hive of activity with loud music, steaming *chapattis* and greasy meat kebabs. Across the street from our rooms, the side of a hotel was plastered with a large blue-and-red advertisement for Tander cigarettes. The closer I got to the bigger towns and the capital in Islamabad, the more I noticed a proliferation in billboard ads. I never once saw a woman smoke in public or pray by the roadside with the men. Since alcohol is forbidden in Pakistan, smoking may be the only vice left to men.

After unpacking our things and locking up my bike, we had a quick bite to eat in our bedrooms. Then we left our rooms on the latticed second floor balcony and climbed to the roof. Baber had ordered some tea to be brought up so we could chat with a view of the town. When the tea arrived, I insisted on paying, but had forgotten my money belt in the room. Back I went, running quickly down the stairs.

When I went inside, the younger boy was watching a rented Indian video as I grabbed some rupees from my stash. I looked closer inside the three zipped pouches in the money belt and noticed that some American money was missing. I was certain that I had three $100 bills and two $20 bills. Only $220 was in the belt. I was missing $120. I asked the boy if he knew anything about it, but he refused to say. He looked scared. I thought this odd and went to look for Ali, the older teenager. He was the only person who had a key aside from Baber and me.

I found Ali downstairs. He insisted he knew nothing about the money. Had I spent some of it elsewhere? he asked. Not a chance, I said. I took him upstairs to the roof where I explained what happened to Baber. There was something about Ali's eyes (the older boy) that seemed shifty. It wasn't a fair judgment, just a gut feeling. Baber took Ali downstairs and I waited for what seemed an eternity before the two returned. Baber had my money in his hands. Apparently, Ali had forced the younger boy to hide the $120 US in his sandals.

"Do you want me to beat him?" Baber asked. "I do it good with a brick."

"No, that's stupid. That will only cause more problems," I said.

Baber said he was deeply disgraced that this had happened to me. I was a guest he said and more important, as a foreigner, I should never be swindled. It puts a bad name on Pakistan. Ali must be punished if he is to be prevented from repeating his actions.

"You can take him out back. It's done all the time. You not get in trouble. I will make sure," Baber said.

Baber only relented when I told him I would be more disappointed if someone got hurt than if some money was stolen. I suggested we go back and watch the video the kids had rented. Baber refused to stay in the same room as Ali and went to bed in the second room we had rented. I settled down in front of the VCR and TV eating peanuts. The two boys had already started the movie. The tape was scratchy and the sound was out of sync with the actors' voices. The Indian movie was male-oriented with lots of action, guns, kung fu moves, gyrating belly buttons and cleavage cleavage cleavage! India, by volume, has the largest film industry in the world, renowned throughout Asia and called Bollywood. The Pakistani men love the slimmer Hindu women from India. Hindu movies are the best-selling section in the stores. Many Muslim restaurant kitchen walls are adorned with clippings of Hindu actresses from the Delhi newspapers.

Because of the antagonism between India and Pakistan, Indian movies are illegal to show in Pakistani theatres. The only way for Pakistani men to see their favourite Hindu actresses is to rent movies (which are legal). Our flick, with its banner ads running across the top of the screen, hindered proper viewing. A gun-toting martial arts man rescued a helpless busty woman. The movie was interrupted every 20 minutes with trailers for other films — women with rocket launchers, belly dancing their way into rich men's fortunes. It was like watching old

Hollywood movies. The plots were unsophisticated compared to those in the West.

The next day, alone, I headed farther up the valley to Naran. Baber stayed behind in Balakot and shipped off Ali on a separate bus to his parents. I was in the back of a van, trucking along at a fair clip. Black Jeeps with white canvas tops, rented out by guesthouses, were being washed in front of every stream we came upon. Then I realized I was only 10 kilometres from Kashmir.

When people think of Kashmir, they think of India — northern India. Pakistan's third is overlooked, left out of the guidebooks. Everyone has a different idea of where the boundaries lie and who should own it. Many of the Kashmiris — the Muslim, Sikh and Hindu — would like their own separate state, taking a part of Pakistan and India with them. Kashmir itself is separated into Azad or (free) Kashmir, the eastern Pakistani province nestled up against the Indian Army–occupied Jammu and Kashmir. Marco Polo described "Keshimur" (the Switzerland of India), as a province where:

> the men are brown and lean, but the women, taking them as brunettes, are very beautiful. The food is flesh, and milk, and rice. They observe strict chastity, and keep from all sins forbidden in their law, so that they are regarded by their own folk as very holy persons. They live to a very great age.
>
> MARCO POLO, *The Travels of Marco Polo*, 13th century

At Naran, the paved section of the Kaghan Road ended. I spent most of the afternoon hiking up to Lake Saiful Muluk, a crystal blue alpine lake 3,200 m (10,496 ft.) above sea level. Unlike Heaven Lake in China, Lake Saiful hadn't fallen victim to tourism. No horse rides, no gondola lift and no boats. At the wooden food hut at the top of the lake, I met seven university students in dress pants and starched white shirts. They had underestimated the length of the three-hour walk and the requisite clothing.

An hour later as the sky clouded over, I started to walk back down from the lake. I was only wearing shorts and my wind-breaker and my legs were getting chilly. Some of the students started back with me to Naran, but I soon outpaced them and completed the moderate hike down in two hours, jogging part of the way. I was hungry from the climb and felt like gorging myself on bread and lamb. I bought my favourite-flavoured *lassi* drink, some *paratha* bread, and was searching for some mutton or chicken (the most expensive meat in Pakistan) to wrap inside.

Then I saw the electric wire outside one of the street stalls. My eyes followed the yellow-and-red striped wire around the counter, up a metal pole and to a table in back. Out on display at one food stall, was at least 15 kg of ground beef simmering in a deep layer of fat on a metal pan. Above the meat a small model airplane propeller was hooked to an electric motor. The plastic blade slowly spun around in a futile attempt to keep the flies away. Hungry as I was, I piled the greasy meat with a wooden spoon onto my bread, making a clogged-artery-sandwich special.

For the first time during my three weeks in Pakistan, I questioned the sanitary conditions of the food I was eating. So far, I had been able to eat everything on my trip with no upset stomachs or diarrhea. Salads washed with unfiltered water, banana shakes made of rotten bananas. I ate it all. For me it was part of the trip. If my body slept on a rope bed, my stomach took in the spiciest and grubbiest food, as long as it was tasty. I had learned how to prevent my mind from judging the food's appearance. I let my palate be the final arbiter. When you're accustomed to clean plates, spotless glasses and washed fruits and vegetables, it takes a big leap of faith to change your diet and enjoy it at the same time.

I looked forward to cycling the return journey through the valley so that I could see things up close and personal. I headed off from Naran for Mansehra, 134 km away. It was too late in the morning to realistically make the highway before dusk. So I settled into a leisurely pace, riding through the undulating hills south to the village of Kaghan where the Jeep road changed from gravel back to tarmac. The road started to twist alongside sheer drop-offs into the river. One wrong move and I would be off the edge for a brief freefall, then a tumble, crash and splash into the river.

When the road crossed into loamy soil or gravel segments, cars and trucks had to slow down. My bike, however, only needed a narrow strip of hard dirt to ride through the softer muddier sections. At one point, the driver of a Toyota van was leap-frogging with me. This created a catching-up situation where I gained ground on the van on the rough parts, only to lose it on the tarmac. Since driving is done on the left in Pakistan, I needed to pass on the driver's side. Going into a right-hand turn on a gravel stretch where my speed matched that of the van, I tried to pass on the inside. The driver, however, used up the whole road, barrelling into the turns. My bike was between his front and rear wheels, right beside the passenger sliding door. As the van moved ever closer to the right, I would be forced to the edge of the cliff. Only when the Toyota finally completed a turn, could I straighten out again. Eventually, I passed the vehicle lower down the valley as passengers stared out the back in bewilderment.

Then the next obstacle: flocks of sheep. The last section of the valley road was paved, which allowed me to pick up speed during the 84-km descent to the highway. There was minimal traffic until I encountered numerous four-legged animals along the road. I never knew when an animal would climb over the edge of the road and decide to wander across the tarmac. If I did see a sheep in advance, I preferred to dodge the furry little creature rather than stop. Prejudging which way a sheep, horse or water buffalo will run if suddenly approached by a speeding bicycle is a refined art. The water buffalo, well, that was easy. I yield to buses, tanks, diesel trucks and water buffalo. The buffalo weighed more than most Suzukis on the road.

The horses in particular were easily spooked by my Chinese bike horn as they grazed nearby. I often rounded a corner at full speed passing the horse in a split second. Spooked, the horse would gallop down the road, sometimes around a blind corner. Inevitably, a Pakistani farmer would run out of his field and head down the road. I would hear them yelling after their horses and screaming at me for disturbing the livestock. I prayed each time a horse went for a run that a truck didn't turn a corner the same time the animal did.

When I reached the Karakoram Highway where the Kaghan Valley Road intersected with Mansehra, it was time for a hot shower. Except for the occasional cold dip and hand wash, I hadn't had a hot shower since leaving Kashgar 25 days earlier. I did not smell nice at all. My clothes remained intact more or less until I arrived in Rawalpindi late the next day with a little help from a bus. I was at the end of the great Karakoram Highway! After 16 days of riding and 10 rest days scattered among Karimabad, Gilgit, Dasu and Naran, my odometer registered 1,483 km.

Rawalpindi, or 'Pindi, is like night and day compared to Islamabad, the nation's capital. The twin cities (15 km apart) are nestled against the backdrop of the Margalla Hills. 'Pindi is the market town; Islamabad is the sprawling centre. One is crowded with frenetic bazaars, yogis, food vendors, motor rickshaws and dirt everywhere. In Islamabad, there is no pollution, just well laid out malls. And The Mall and The Supermarket aren't concrete mega-plexes to sell clothes and food in the Western sense. They are sectors where people live, with a few shopping, food and handicraft facilities.

In Islamabad, it took me a day to figure out that the markets, or *markazs,* are commercial areas with shops and homes built around them. I rode the streets on my bike looking for a fruit vendor or *chapatti* stall and could only see houses. Each time I pedalled about the wide-open streets with their green rows of flame trees, jacaranda and hibiscus, I thought I was in the wrong place. My guidebook wasn't helping matters either. I asked directions and was told I was in the market. Crowds or traffic jams were rare. The streets were as far apart from each other as runways at an airport.

Built 35 years ago, Islamabad is divided into eight zones: administrative, diplomatic enclave, residential, educational, industrial, commercial, rural, and parks. It's about as overplanned a city as I'd ever seen. Streets didn't have names in the regular sense. The names were letter and number combinations like F-7 or G-6/1. Avenues ran between sectors and numbered streets lay within each sector. The people who lived in Islamabad, mainly bureaucrats and the middle class, call the sectors by the names of the markets, not the street signs. How was I supposed to know that F-8 was the Ayub market?

Notwithstanding the navigational horrors of Islamabad, the architectural beauty of some of the government buildings set the town apart from Rawalpindi. Islamabad may be sterile-looking, but it does appear stately and presidential. The soaring Shah Faisal Mosque with its four 90-m-high minarets looks like a set of space rockets straight out of Buck Rogers. I definitely preferred the labyrinth maze of alleys in Rawalpindi, however, where I could buy a set of cabin trunks and throw them in the back of an ageing Suzuki. Chiffon scarves, whips, copper antiques, junk jewellery and cane juice were all sold alongside the services of teeth pullers and wannabe dentists.

When I left the twin cities for the airport in Islamabad, my taxi driver, Inayut, told me about the despair that Pakistan had fallen into. As we rode in his tiny yellow Japanese import with my bike on top, I listened to him vent his frustrations. As a former Pakistani Air Force pilot of 20 years, Inayut had seen his inept government at work. Then he quit.

Military dictators and generals had ruled Pakistan for 24 of the past 50 years. Inayut said most Pakistani leaders have pandered to the public's fears of the great Hindu nation next door. He thinks Muslims should be smarter than that and get out of the "us versus them" trap. To Inayut, the sabre rattling between Pakistan's leaders and those in India distracted from more important matters. Running water and reliable electricity were more important than fighting a hopeless war in Kashmir.

"Why should I have to save up for a private school for my children because the military is spending half our money?" he said. "Education is not the priority it should be."

Pakistan was mired in its own self-pity, he said. A month earlier, India had celebrated its accomplishments when the two nations observed a half-century of independence. Pakistan, on the other hand, had a few token ceremonies.

"We are more dependent than independent. Our nation is wallowing in misery. India competes on a world market making its own software, airplanes and cars," Inayut said. "We are so reliant on others. It can't all be the Hindus' fault," he said.

"They even kicked Coca-Cola out of the country because they wouldn't give the secret syrup," he said excitedly.

Inayut failed to mention that the government in Delhi eventually allowed the soft drink manufacturer back a few years later. Fed up, Inayut was ready to leave Islamabad with his family. He wanted to emigrate to Canada, but the price of paying for lawyers and bureaucrats cost around 4 lahks (400,000 rupees or $19,050). Factoring in the delays to process the paperwork, he could wait for years.

It was rather disheartening to wake up to the fact that an entire nation isn't eating apricots and sipping tea in view of idyllic snow-capped peaks. There is a real world in Pakistan and I was in the thick of it. My conversation with the taxi driver helped put in perspective the realities of a struggling Pakistan trying to pull itself out of poverty and bankruptcy. When I walked through the Islamabad airport past armed guards, I tried to understand the dichotomy of Pakistan's northern paradise and urban malaise. I was bound for Peshawar near the Afghanistan border, where another world awaited me. Next stop Kabul.

Afghanistan: Of Bullets Not Ballots

CHAPTER TEN

The Khyber Pass

They hooked up jumper cables to his genitals and doused him with water. Then they electrocuted him. I was talking to Majid Qari, a Taliban soldier, who was telling me about his capture by the opposition forces in Afghanistan. He is now unable to father children. He is only 21 years old.

We were heading through the Khyber Pass to the Afghanistan border with a half-dozen other passengers in a Toyota Hi-Ace van. Majid was wearing charcoal eyeliner and perfume to ward off evil spirits. His effeminate looks and shaven head were indicative of many of the Taliban recruits that were headed into battle in the country's northern regions.

Along with me was Papa, an elder Pakistani who would be my mediator, translator and saviour. He spoke Urdu, English and Pashtu, the native language of the Pathan who live along the western border of Pakistan and the hills of Afghanistan. His long white beard, regal beige *shalwar qamiz* and spectacles gave him an air of a graceful old tribesman. We had met in Peshawar (more on that later). I was counting on him to help me gain the trust of the Taliban once we reached Kabul, the Afghan capital.

I wanted to meet with some of the fundamentalist Taliban rebels. This would prove to be a difficult task given that the country was bogged down in a bloody civil war. I wanted to write about the Islamic holy war that was sweeping the country. I had come to see a remote desolate place that not many people have access to — a land ruled by bullets, not ballots.

On we drove through the Khyber as it wound its way up the serpent-like road to its peak of 1,060 m. The Khyber Pass is an engineering feat unrivalled anywhere else in the world. The British built the road through the 56-km-long pass in 1920. The 34 tunnels and 92 bridges are the most amazing part of the Khyber, a never-ending maze of hairpin turns and rocky foothills. If the Khunjerab Pass is the highest paved pass, then the Khyber Pass is the most famous.

For over 2,500 years, the proud and fierce Pathan people have defended the Khyber from foreign aggressors. Ever since Herodotus wrote of the Pathan, they have staved off Alexander the Great, Genghis Khan, Tamerlane, the Moghuls, Sikh and British Empires and most recently the Russians. On the Pakistan side of the Khyber Pass, we had seen the narrow gauge railway that cut through the craggy mountains and dusty hills. The grade is so steep that engines were attached on both ends to haul British troops from Peshawar to Landi Kotal, a village just short of the border with gun-toting Pathans.

At one time 40,000 British soldiers were stationed in and around the pass. In 40 assault raids, the British never once penetrated through to Kabul. Even now, it is forbidden to photograph the military installations used to thwart the British Empire. This included the forts on the strategic hilltops that I was passing. The steam train line lies in pieces today, as the fighting in Afghanistan has led to numerous sabotage raids on the tracks. Occasionally, the railway is repaired for a three-coach train to make a weekly journey but the service is so intermittent that the run is no longer considered reliable.

Out here in the North West Frontier Province (NWFP) next to Afghanistan, the district was originally cobbled together by the British to settle tribal disputes. It was here that the word *khaki* was derived. The splendid crimson red infantry uniforms of the British

Raj (the pre-1947 ruling period) were unsuitable for camouflage in the barren tan-coloured hillsides. The uniforms were too bright to blend in with the dust, or khaki, as the Pathan called it. Thanks to The Gap, the khaki military clothes of former colonial powers live on, now a fixture of today's fashion-conscious.

As we got close to the border, I realized this was it. Getting past the border to Kabul wouldn't be an easy feat. The Khyber Pass straddles the Pakistan-Afghan border. On one side is Pakistan, a world unto itself. On the other side lies Afghanistan, a land where the warring factions have little regard for law and order. We were driving through the Pakistani side of the pass. There were no police to help us and no embassies or consulates (all closed due to the war).

Travelling overland through the Khyber Pass into Afghanistan is one of the most dangerous stunts to pull in all of Asia. I had no idea if securing entry into Afghanistan, a country stuck in civil war, was the stupidest or most calculated thing I had done in my life. Would I step on a landmine or get shot for the slightest Islamic social faux pas? I was very much the foreigner in a land where kidnapping and extortion were a reality; 75 people die each day from landmines. Now we were ready to head through the rest of the Khyber Pass — the Afghan side.

Getting a travel visa in most countries usually means paper-work, a few bureaucratic hurdles and delays and you're through. In Afghanistan, however, the proper papers were only half the bat-tle. If the Taliban didn't like our looks, we wouldn't get through. This was where Papa would be worth his weight in gold. Could he get me in?

When we arrived at the border town of Torkham that separates Pakistan from Afghanistan, we were forced to change vehicles. Everyone had to get out and line up in front of a wooden shack. It was hot and dry out, even for 9 a.m. in the morning. Eyes to the ground, I walked behind Papa to the makeshift customs shed. Outside, a few Taliban conscripts stood with machine guns. In we went. I followed Papa's instructions and let him do the talking while my passport was stamped in triplicate. The real test was yet to come — getting past the fence.

To get this far to the border I had gone native a week earlier. I would be risking my life if I tried to cross into Afghanistan in anything other than disguise. To appear Western would cause enough questions and interrogation at checkpoints. After two and a half months of biking in China and Pakistan, I had started to blend in with the other Muslims, particularly the Pathan — the same ethnic group as the Taliban soldiers. I had a full beard, dark brown tan and wore a black-and-white turban. I was wearing sandals and a *shalwar qamiz*, custom-made in Peshawar.

With the exception of my sunglasses (a luxury Afghans couldn't afford), I looked like any other Muslim male from a distance — maybe even an Egyptian student visiting friends. My dark hair, large nose and chestnut brown eyes also helped. I had come to the Afghan border with a minimum of belongings. All I carried was my camera, some money, a toothbrush, notebook and my passport. My camera was concealed in the pouch of my undershirt, the flowing *qamiz* draped over the bulk of the lens, hiding it from view.

When Papa and I walked up to the barbed-wire fence — the real border — hundreds of people were streaming through an open gateway. A young Taliban soldier waved his AK-47 in our direction at knee level, motioning us to come over to him. We stopped. He had the gun. We were diverted to a smaller opening several metres to the right. His judgment alone would determine if we would go on.

"Charta zi (where are you going)?" the soldier asked in harsh consonant-sounding words.

"Jalalabad and Kabul," Papa replied.

Keep it short and simple, I thought. I'm just your cousin or whatever you want to tell him. Anything to get me through. I hadn't come this far to be turned back. On the other hand, I had never even counted on getting this close to Afghanistan. I prayed.

"Kha, der kha (very good)," the teenage soldier responded.

After two days of tedious preparation I was in.

Peshawar and Papa

If you want to go to Afghanistan and if you can get into Afghanistan, you first go to Peshawar. It was there that I had met Papa. Peshawar (pronounced Pa-shower) is a large frontier city in the Tribal Areas of Pakistan next to the Afghan border — a kind of wild wild west. Until the 1950s, the city, more than 2,500 years old, was enclosed within a giant city wall with 16 gates. It's essentially an old garrison town that was used as a strategic launching post by the British during the Afghan wars of the late 19th century.

Peshawar was conquered by the Greeks, ruled by Buddhists, destroyed by Huns, rebuilt by Brahmins, captured by Mughals, invaded by Sikhs and annexed by the British. Now *Shehr* or The City, as the Pathan call it, is dotted with ancient forts, intricately carved balconies and medieval back alleys. Peshawar even houses precious Gandharan Buddhist art in the city museum.

From the storytellers in the streets to the beggars clutching your clothes and the herbal kiosks with their wooden shutters, the city exudes character. There are potters' bazaars (where the British Royal Family shops), jewellery bazaars and fruit bazaars. There are bazaars for coppersmiths, woollen shops and birds on the Street of Partridge Lovers. Even one for women — the Meena Bazaar. UNICEF workers, camera-toting Japanese tourists, goat herders, German backpackers, arms dealers and spies jostle among the flophouses and haggle with moneychangers. The hippies that once came through Kabul in the '70s on their way to ashrams and Hindu gurus in Delhi are long since gone. The Afghan war changed everything. Because of this transformation in the region's politics, I knew I needed contacts. I would only get into Afghanistan with the help of others.

Through a cabbie contact at the airport, I had been given the name of a reliable source, someone named Papa Raman who could get me into Afghanistan. We had met in a teashop down the street from Green's Hotel where I had booked a room for a few days. The desk clerk had passed on my name from the taxi driver to several people who knew about border crossings and the Taliban. Papa walked me through the dos and don'ts of Afghanistan. Rule #1: Let him do the talking. No one will understand English anyway, he said. Rule #2: Don't take photographs, especially of women. Children were okay. I was to pay Papa $50 US a day, $300 US for six days. In spite of the fact that he was making a fortune (the average annual Pakistani salary is $130), I needed him.

Papa pleaded with me to help him pay for his daughter's wedding. He thought anyone who was a writer was a big-name journalist. Was he in for a surprise. I reminded him that I was funding my own trip and didn't exactly have a CNN expense account. He probably told everyone his daughter was getting married to gain sympathy. I played along with his story. His ability to gain the trust of the Taliban rebels who would be at every checkpoint was the only important thing to me. Although I paid Papa a sizeable sum by Pakistani standards, I was getting a glimpse of Kabul at below the going rate for fixers (a translator and guide in a foreign location).

Papa was Pathan and like the others of this warrior race, wherever you go, greeted everyone with an open smile. The Pathan speak in excited tones and swagger in their *shalwar qamiz* baggy trousers. The Pathan are Muslim, just like the people of Hunza in Pakistan's north or the Uyghurs in China. There is one big difference. The Pathan abide by a much more brutal set of rules.

The Pathan govern their lives through an unofficial code of conduct called *pukhtunwali*. The essence of the code is keeping one's honour. Revenge, hospitality and refuge (even for criminals), is a guiding force in their lives. They will invite you into their home regardless of your social status or where you're from. You will be served a full-course meal and be treated like royalty. You are their guest and fully deserving of the best they can offer.

Because of their generosity, however, they are not good at negotiating. They would rather make you happy than cause a fuss. Whether bartering goods in a market or conducting business, they will usually defer to your price. If the Pathan aren't very astute when it comes to money, their temperament towards relationships is markedly different. The men are very jealous. This is where the revenge comes in. A husband will chase another's wife and take her as a second wife (Muslim custom allows for up to seven wives). Wives have been known to poison their new husbands in an effort to return to their first loves. If a husband beats his wife, she may only leave if he breaks bones. Even then, custom maintains she has to return. These are the ways of the "wily Pathan" as Kipling called them — the biggest tribal group on Earth, all 16 million of them. We were off to meet the other half in Afghanistan.

With Papa's help, the Office of the Khyber Political Agent had approved my permit to travel through the Khyber Pass to Kabul. This stipulated that I was to travel "not before Sunrise and not after Sunset." The quasi-legal agency required me to carry the document on me at all times. As well, I was not allowed to "make photography of the prohibited areas and of Women Folk." The Khyber Political Agent was the unofficial authority when it came to getting into Afghanistan. No embassy or guidebook will tell you about it. You learn through others or by fortuitous planning.

It was an encouraging moment indeed. I finally had the proper documentation. The travel visa that I obtained almost a year earlier from the Afghanistan Embassy in Washington, D.C., had become a mere formality. All those doubts while riding the Silk Road that I would have to go home early were over.

For the first leg of our trip to the Afghan border town of Torkham, we were provided with a bodyguard fresh out of puberty. These were the rules. No one goes in or out of the Tribal Areas in the NWFP without the Political Agent's approval. The armed escort rode in the back seat of our van until we reached a sign: "Attention: Entry of Foreigners is Prohibited Beyond this Point." Then our teenage bodyguard got out. He would go no farther, he said.

The NWFP is a patchwork of tribal- and government-controlled areas, many full of armed bandits smuggling machine guns and black market VCRs. Sectarian violence and car-jackings have turned this arid, agricultural-based area of hamlets into a virtual no-man's land. The Tribal Areas run under a hybrid system of old

British law and Sharia, the Islamic code of legal conduct. Those living in the Tribal Areas are immune from the Pakistan police force and laws of the country. The Political Agent in Peshawar administers law enforcement with his own armed militia or *lashkar*. In this land of fearsome warriors, tribal chiefs and disparate ethnic groups, the Pathan are kings. They settle most of their local issues by a group of elders or *jirga*. If two tribes are fighting over land, the *jirga* mediates.

Punishments are sadistically cruel by Western standards. An eye for an eye is literally how justice is administered. Some would describe it more accurately as the law of the jungle. It has been this way for centuries and is considered custom. Because of this lawless country, tourists, expatriates and even non-Pathan Pakistanis are forbidden from entering many of the Tribal Areas for their own safety.

Off to Kabul

From the bazaars of Peshawar and the Khyber Political Agent to the hills of the Hindu Kush Mountains, Papa and I headed off to the Afghan border and Kabul in our new vehicle. I paid the driver for two seats, pulling out a few Afghani notes. The Afghani is probably the most useless currency in the world. The notes come in denominations of a thousand (500,000 Afghanis = $33). You need about 15,000 to buy a drink and 100,000 for dinner. People walked the streets with bricks of money wrapped in elastic bands stuffed in plastic bags. Wallets and purses are useless.

This time we were packed into a small bus that slowly picked its way through the potholes. Then more potholes. The road conditions were appalling, but not for a war zone. After riding the Karakoram Highway, I was used to gravel roads. But these were far worse. Then I realized what the trouble was.

The road was shelled to pieces. Almost 20 years of fighting had destroyed most of the roads, once considered strategic targets, scarring them with these giant dimples. If you blow up the roads and highways, the enemy can't move its tanks and gain ground, so went the military's thinking. The country was so bankrupt that it couldn't afford to fix the transportation network even if there was a cessation in war activities.

We were travelling between 10 and 25 km/h at best. A short strip before Jalalabad, the only major city between Peshawar and Kabul, was fairly smooth. A few lizards, similar to Gila monsters, dashed across the road causing the driver to swerve. The occasional flock of sheep along with minivans and broken-down diesel trucks dominated the road. The trucks in Afghanistan are not painted as elaborately as in Pakistan and the mountains aren't as high, but the scenery is just as daunting. It's dramatic in a different way; it's more barren and destitute. The Hindu Kush, a mountain system nearly 1,600 km long and 320 km wide, ran alongside the road off in the distance. The mountain's name means Hindu Killer, so-named after the Muslim courts of Central Asia that transported Hindu slaves over from the Indian subcontinent.

As we steered our way around the potholes, I began to learn a little bit more about Papa. He claimed he knew his way through the many checkpoints that we would have to manoeuvre. Although Papa spoke the necessary languages, he hadn't been to Afghanistan for seven years, something I wouldn't learn for two days. Afghanistan was different seven years ago — much more stable. The Taliban rebels hadn't started taking over the country from their fellow Mujaheddin tribal warlords until the fall of 1994. Papa was an out-of-date guide, somewhat like a 1970 *Lonely Planet* guidebook. He was essentially going in blind like me. Then there was his hashish habit. We were headed into the most fundamentalist country in the world where they executed you for drugs and my translator was toking up twice a day.

I had switched seats to go up front where there was a little more legroom, sitting to the left of the driver. Then we picked up a little girl in a small village settlement who sat between us. We ate pomegranates for the next few hours, the juices dripping down our shirts. I would break a pomegranate in little bits, feeding some to the girl. Some passengers in the back would pass us apricots and other fruit. Then the girl went to sleep, alternately resting her head on the burly driver's shoulder and mine.

Then the first of many checkpoints. Our driver stopped the vehicle at a checkpoint that consisted of two chairs on opposite sides of the road. A little Afghan boy sat on one chair, stretching a rope across the road at wheel level. Our bus was forced to stop. A Taliban soldier with a long beard jumped aboard and prodded under the seats with his AK-47. He was searching for guns and drugs. Then he checked the driver's paperwork. The soldier moved on to the back of the bus past me. Nothing. Then we were off to the next checkpoint.

We would stop every 20 km as a Taliban checked everyone out. Several times they motioned towards me. Then it was Papa's turn to do the talking. He always asked me to hand over my passport and letter from the Khyber Political Agent. If necessary, Papa asked me to hold up an electronic organizer I kept with me for notetaking. It had a Canadian sticker on the front of it, which seemed to distinguish me from an American more than my passport. The literacy rate in Afghanistan is 31 per cent and getting worse. Quite likely, many of the Taliban couldn't read my passport and recognized the Canadian flag instead.

The country is growing younger every year as the war rages on. Almost half the population of 25 million is under the age of 14. There are fewer adults to take care of a growing number of children. Simply put, war has made Afghanistan an economic, social and political mess. If Pakistan is corrupt, bankrupt and poor, Afghanistan has never come out of the Dark Ages.

As we moved deeper into Afghanistan, I saw the devastation of war. The roads were strewn with burned-out Russian T-72 tanks, armoured personnel carriers and Katushya rocket launchers. Rocks were painted red to warn of areas where the United Nations hadn't swept for landmines. This was the Afghanistan I had read about. Seeing it in person was mind-blowing.

The Russians rolled their tanks into Kabul the morning after Christmas Day in 1979, and Afghanistan has been in a protracted holy war or *jihad* ever since. Ten years later, the Mujaheddin war-lords forced the Russians and their 600,000 troops to withdraw at a cost to the Soviets of $70 billion US. The Mujaheddin leaders started to fight along sectarian lines for control of their country. Then the abuse began. Young Afghan girls and boys were gang-raped by their own leaders. The children's heads were shaved, marking them for all to see, shaming them forever.

The Taliban (religious students turned soldiers) were fed up with the abuse that the tribal warlords were inflicting on the Afghan people. No more than a loose coalition, the Taliban took up arms and rode through many towns "liberating" the Afghans from the Mujaheddin. The Taliban swept through most of the country with little or no opposition. The Afghans, paralysed by a decade of war, were happy to see a new group in control, even if they strictly applied their own form of Islamic purism.

The Taliban were not very organized until three countries saw a chance to exert their influence over Afghanistan. Pakistan, an ally of the United States, had started to feed the Taliban with arms, ammunition and cash. The United States viewed the emerging conflict as an opportunity to get back at their nemesis, the Shiite government of Iran. The Taliban are from the rival Sunni sect of Islam. Soon the war developed into a proxy fight between Pakistan and Iran. Which neighbouring Muslim country would get the spoils once the war ended?

The Americans were also intent on controlling the region because of a proposed oil pipeline that would run from southern Pakistan to Turkmenistan. If Iran brokered a peace deal, the Tehran government might get a say in a new Afghan administration and prevent the Americans from building their pipeline. After three years of fighting, a peace deal was nowhere in the works. As the old captured and abandoned Russian tanks and artillery guns began to break down, the Taliban needed more heavy firepower. Saudi Arabia and the United Arab Emirates entered the fray, rec-ognizing the Taliban government as the legitimate Afghan govern-ment and kicking in a few tanks.

I started to see an increase in the number of bombed-out military vehicles as we got closer to Kabul. It was evening, as our pothole-swerving bus finally made it to the city three flats later. We had only gone 200 km since leaving the border nine hours ago. Papa and I crawled into an abandoned shop. I went to sleep while he brushed his teeth with a piece of wood.

Kabul

Only five people were killed the day we got into town. Kabul was once an Asian Paris. Now it is a gutted hellhole. When Papa and I arrived, most of the city had been without electricity for three years. Families were separated by the ravages of war. Over 30,000 widows in Kabul alone fend for their children. Famine is widespread. Another day, a young girl died when a stray mortar shell inadvertently hit a residential part of town, the shrapnel tearing into her body.

The truth of Kabul was that you saw the effects of war firsthand. In Canada, I had been inundated with violence on television and 24-hour news channels. Now I saw the war all around me, up close and personal. Surface-to-air artillery guns lined a hill in the centre of the city, ready for what enemy aircraft flew by. Few of the factions fighting in Afghanistan have aircraft. Most planes entering the country are C-130 Hercules from the United Nations.

Everywhere I went, I saw adults and children on crutches. Over 400,000 people have been maimed or killed by landmines since war broke out in 1979. Of those victims, 60 per cent were children. In a world where most children go to school to learn about the Internet and multiplication tables, the kids in Afghanistan go to learn about landmine identification. The schools aren't even schools. Most have been shelled. In the larger Afghan cities, mosques act as landmine education centres. Almost every fifth or sixth Afghan family has one disabled person. The drawings of children often reflect this growing amputee society, their stick figure pictures showing one-legged people.

When it is this close, you wonder how war is ever allowed to be romanticized. Papa and I spent a few days around Kabul. We were deciding how to get out to the frontlines when we met a UN demining squad leader. Mohammed Azim was with the UN Office for the Co-ordination of Humanitarian Affairs and worked with the Mine Detection Dog Centre. He had been in Kabul for six months. Over breakfast one morning, he told us that he was on his way out of Afghanistan because funding had dried up. There would be no more mine clearing in Afghanistan. This was a common problem, Mohammed said. They continually had to leave, if not because of finances then because the Taliban would kick them out.

The Taliban have shot UN workers with legendary ruthlessness. They have harassed and killed journalists and kidnapped foreigners (releasing them for $50,000 US). The Taliban carry steel cables to whip people with (it makes it easier to amputate their enemy's limbs). Stadiums are periodically filled with as many as 30,000 people to witness executions. Convicted murderers have their throats cut for all to see in order to avenge crimes. Surprisingly, the Afghan people have put up with this ultra-conservative brand of Islamic fundamentalism, fearing that the alternative is worse.

Women have only recently had to wear the head-to-toe *burqah* veil in Afghanistan and practise *purdah*, where the woman plays a secondary role to the man. But that's where the similarities end among Afghanistan and its Muslim neighbours, Iran and Pakistan. Under a strict interpretation of Islamic law, the Taliban have banned education and work for women. The Taliban have been known to throw acid in the faces of women who don't wear the full veil. Only one woman that I saw didn't have her face covered with the veil, instead choosing to wear the looser shawl-type *chador* pulled down over her shoulders.

The Taliban's hamfisted application of Islam and Sharia law is particularly harsh when it comes to sex crimes and adultery. If a married woman is raped, Sharia law dictates that she is partially at fault for being in the company of such a slimeball. She is stoned — sometimes to death. However, if the woman is single, she only receives 80 lashes. The rapist, on the other hand, is sent off to a Muslim version of Dr. Ruth's marriage counselling seminar and flogged. Definitely no *Ms.* magazines are sold in this country.

When the Taliban marched through the country in 1994 and 1995, television sets were destroyed in many towns (a sign of Western decadence). Other obvious social evils of society such as chess, volleyball, lyrical music and kite flying (a form of gambling) are also forbidden. While much of the Taliban's excesses are non-sensical, some are taken from the teachings of Mohammed. Drinking, smoking and gambling are strictly outlawed. Drug use, an infringement of Islamic law, is the biggest no no.

Although the importing of heroin is legal, the exporting of it is not. The Taliban have only paid lip service to eliminating drugs. Afghanistan is the world's second-largest opium producer after Burma. The best hashish grows in the northern city of Mazar-e-Sharif. During the war with the Russians, the United States turned a blind eye to the heroin shipments that would leave Afghanistan. The Mujaheddin warlords were fighting the Evil Soviet Empire and needed the money to buy arms from the Americans. It was a trade-off. When the Russians left, the US Drug Enforcement Agency again tried to prosecute key heroin smugglers. By that time, it was too late. Hundreds of Afghan villages were completely addicted to heroin. In neighbouring Pakistan, 100,000 people a year fall to the addiction of the deadly drug.

While we didn't see any signs of heroin addicts in Kabul, Papa and I did start to learn our way around the city after a few days. We had been sleeping on concrete floors above storefronts, trying to avoid being checked out by the Taliban who would drive by all night long. The Taliban recruits drove around like well-armed gangsters with AK-47s and grenade launchers in Toyota Tacoma pickups. The picture was reminiscent of rowdy teenagers or football supporters. The Toyotas were tricked out with the latest mag wheels, fog lamps and roll bars. The only thing missing on the trucks seemed to be 16-inch lift kits. They would make the grade on any small-town main street where young men spend three months' wages on the hottest parts out of *Truck World Monthly*.

The vehicles, of course, are stolen or paid for in cash with drug money just like most of the things the Taliban wanted. There is a big business in smuggling goods from Pakistan to Afghanistan and back to Peshawar. Alliances are forged among border officials. The Taliban are bought off to provide protection and approve the shipments. Everything from VCRs to stereos to fridges and cars are hauled between the two countries.

A 10-m-high traffic control tower had become the lynching centre of the city. Papa and I walked by the tower one morning as he explained how a former Afghan president and Russian puppet was the first victim. Then we witnessed one hapless Kabuli being paraded about with black oil on his face. The young Afghan male was terrified. He struggled to get free. It was futile. The crowd was in control. This was an indication of violating some subclause of Sharia law. He was about to have his hand cut off for stealing. A harsh life makes for harsh decisions.

We were headed to the Afghan Foreign Affairs Ministry. For several days, we had refrained from approaching the government for help with heading north out of the city to see if we would be allowed closer to the fighting. Papa thought getting to Kabul was good enough. I thought differently. I wanted to meet the Taliban. We didn't know what the government would do when they found out about us. I was a foreigner, a Western foreigner. Papa was Pathan. He would be fine. Would I be sent back to Peshawar? I would soon find out more about the flow of ideology, guns and drugs in this beleaguered country when we got to the Foreign Affairs Ministry.

The ministry was located in an old brick building with large stately rooms in the centre of town. Over tea, I waited patiently for arrangements to be made. I needed to find out which Taliban military positions outside Kabul were safest to visit. During my wait, a government information officer taught Islamic classes to Taliban hopefuls in a makeshift *madrasah* or religious school. In the end, I had to sign a few papers and interview prospective government translators. Twelve young government employees took turns escorting visiting foreigners in Kabul and acting as buffers should trouble arise with the Taliban. I would have to negotiate a daily fee with one of the translators. The additional interpreter (on top of Papa) was another expense but it was worth our safety for the time we would be out of the city. I found out that I was only the 24th Westerner, except for relief workers, to enter Afghanistan that year.

The deputy foreign affairs minister, Mullah Abas Stanik Zai, told me I had to stay in the Intercontinental Hotel for my own safety. Papa could sleep in the city. The Intercontinental was an old luxury hotel on the outskirts of town and was once used by journalists during the war with the Russians. I obliged with the minister's request and told him I would spend the rest of my stay in Kabul at the Intercontinental as per government regulations. I didn't tell him we had already been in town for a few days.

Despite our remarks to the deputy minister, we only planned to stay in the hotel for one night. I couldn't afford the government translator and the $75 US that the hotel was charging per night. We would be driving to Mir Bacheh Kowt, a small village north of Kabul where the war had reached a stalemate that afternoon. How could I sleep on the floors in the markets if I had to report to the translator every day? I soon made the translator a deal — cigarettes.

Imitation Marlboro cigarettes in Kabul are as common as the Lada and Volga taxis scattered around town. My translator Ranu loved to smoke. He would smoke anything, especially the pack of K2 cigarettes I had brought from Pakistan. Ranu, a young Afghani in his early 20s, agreed to leave us alone after our trip north of the city (all for a few packs of smokes). I just needed the foreign ministry to officially clear my papers and photo identification. I had been travelling this great and mystic Silk Road for several months and was on my way to the Taliban strongholds in Afghanistan at last.

A few hours later, we drove northward out of Kabul in a beat-up old yellow-and-black Volga. My trusty driver, government-assigned translator Ranu and Pakistani confidant Papa Raman were each as nervous as me as we headed 1,800 m up into the mountains. I had three people on my payroll. I soon began to wonder if I was an unwilling participant in some grand scheme to raise the Afghan GDP — courtesy Bank of Fotheringham. The driver came with the car. The foreign ministry wouldn't allow passage to the frontlines without Ranu tagging along and Papa, even with his daily hashish habit, was invaluable. He knew how much to pay for what and how to deal with the Pathan.

We passed scorched tank hulks, howitzers and armoured personnel carriers that sat like gigantic overturned beetles. After an hour's drive, I was able to hear sporadic shellfire. We parked a few thousand metres down the road from a set of tanks up on a hill. Empty tank shells were scattered across the road. It was a signal to go no farther. Out here, the villages were abandoned. Landmines were everywhere and Ranu instructed us all to stay on the pavement. Step off it and we might hit a mine.

Around a bend in the road, I could see the exhaust from a Taliban tank heading towards us. When the tank stopped, Ranu talked with one of the six Taliban soldiers who was riding on top. He said it was all right for us to walk up the hill where the two tanks were and stand behind a sand bunker. Papa, meanwhile, was begging Ranu and me to return to the car. The driver, still in the Volga down the road, sat petrified of the surrounding landmines.

Suddenly, incoming 70mm shells bombarded the hillside. They had just hit short of the Russian and Saudi-made tanks. An acrid smell permeated the air. Shuddering from the reverberations, my instincts told me our 100-m safety buffer was utterly ridiculous. As my heartbeat and adrenaline levels exceeded anything amphetamines ever accomplished, I began to understand this Koran-inspired *jihad*.

Shouts of *allahu akbar* from the gunnery commander echoed with every outgoing volley from the Taliban tanks. Tank rounds and prayer rocketed towards the unseen foe. Papa's sense of fatalism soon translated into mutterings of *insha'allah* ("God willing").

A soldier's head popped out of a hatch in the turret. He

climbed over some smoke dischargers to the top of the tank and peered through a rangefinder lens. He made some notes about co-ordinates and scurried back inside the tank. The green-and-grey striped barrel of the 125mm cannon rotated a few degrees and locked.

"Get down," Ranu shouted.

Then it fired. Boom! The shell must have gone for at least 5 km before it disappeared into a cloud of dust far off in the surrounding hills. Then we waited. Nothing. The back and forth volley of artillery and tank fire wasn't as frequent as I had thought. Then again, we were only a little way out of Kabul. The majority of the fighting was in the north. A year or two earlier, Kabul was under siege. Not anymore.

Then the Taliban quartermaster, Hosain Abdul Qoud, radioed the opposition's field commander and arranged for a ceasefire. I thought I had witnessed a diplomatic breakthrough, but through my interpreter, Hosain informed me that it was just a temporary cessation. The pounding stopped. It was time to pray. Two hours for Allah and reciting the *hadiths* — the recorded sayings of the Prophet Mohammed. Thank goodness both sides are devoted to the same god.

The Taliban had set up some mats and concrete slabs alongside the tanks. Empty shell casings were scattered everywhere around the tank and in one tiny section was their prayer centre. Religion came first. As the religious ceasefire began, Hosain, with a Kalashnikov slung over his shoulder and a few clips around his waist, bent down to pray. Papa went off into the bushes and did the same. He told me he was a little more comfortable away from the machines of destruction.

Both the Taliban and Northern Alliance opposition seemed to spend more time praying for the other's annihilation than they did fighting. This dedication to Islam seemed to preclude any solution to the war. Neither side could advance very far into the other's territory before pausing to carry out their spiritual obligations. Maybe it's my pragmatic outlook on life, but if you're dedicated to pounding the other guy into dust, you don't take five daily two-hour breaks. I felt like handing the Taliban commander a copy of Carl von Clausewitz's *On War* so he could brush up on his strategy. On second thought, these same people held off the Russians for 10 years. Who was I to judge?

Hosain and the rest of his *lashkar* (the small tribal militias of the Taliban) were fighting against the coalition forces led by a former Afghan defence minister. The minister, General Massoud, had been pushed back by the Taliban to Mazar-e-Sharif, 300 km north of Kabul. There, the general (or Lion of Panjir as he's known) was holed up with 15,000 troops, six SU-22 Fitter jet fighters and several Mi-24 Hind helicopter gunships. Until September 1996, he had received his aircraft and ammunition from Iran, Russia and India.

Once prayer break was over, we returned to Kabul. I had taken some great pictures of the Taliban in action and wanted to get some more in the city, particularly of the Afghan women.

Taking Pictures

In Kabul, I saw women walking the streets covered in their red, blue and purple veils. A three-inch-square opening covered with mesh provided the only way to see out. Although the *burqah* was worn in Kabul before the Taliban took control, it was not an enforced dress code. Many women wore scarves that only covered their heads. Now a strict dress code is in effect. The Taliban, enforcing Islam in its most orthodox form, seek to prevent the admiration of women's faces which are thought to tempt fornication.

Had I travelled this far to pass up a photo op? This was an opportunity of a lifetime for me. However, the Taliban prohibit the photographing of women and fiercely enforce the rule. And if I photographed the Taliban without permission, I might be arrested by one of the 400 religious police who cruised the cities in trucks and Jeeps. On the frontlines, I discovered that the younger Taliban men (who ostensibly forbade their photos from being taken) actually obliged when asked. Were their rules about taking pictures more relaxed than I had thought? Ranu told me about a cocky Belgian photographer who had his face bashed in with the butt of an AK-47 in 1996 for taking unsolicited pictures.

For the first time, Afghanistan made me confront the ethics of photographing Muslim women in an extremely hostile country. I had been to other Muslim countries before — namely Morocco — and had just come from Pakistan and western China. Taking photos in those more liberal Muslim areas was different than doing so in Afghanistan. The Taliban shoot people for taking the wrong pictures.

How could I respect the Islamic faith and photograph the Afghan women? I was reluctant to practise my luck in Afghanistan and I wasn't naïve. With many women on the streets out shopping, I knew that patience was my ally. While Papa and I waited outside the Foreign Affairs Ministry for our exit visas, I bade my time until there were very few males around and no Taliban. I was only willing to risk taking a picture behind a woman's back.

I had started practising a few days earlier whenever Papa and I went out to eat. I learned how to take photos in focus, holding the camera at waist level and partially hidden underneath a cloth. This was the best compromise I could think of. Hopefully, I wouldn't be seen, thrown in jail or shot.

Like many things in life, this trip was a calculated risk. Nothing ventured, nothing gained. I made my own ethical choices, assessing each situation, weighing the merits and pitfalls. I made compromises others might not have. With an exhilarating week behind me, Papa and I got ready to take the pothole road back to Peshawar in Pakistan. The best was yet to come.

Dinner with the Taliban

That evening, I ate my liver, pudding and french fries in the gutted Intercontinental Hotel – my one night's stay in Kabul's finest. Papa was sleeping in town. We planned to meet in the morning when a driver would bring him up the winding hill to the hotel. The Intercontinental was the only modern hotel in Kabul or rather the only place that used to be. It was press headquarters when the Russian infidels were tearing apart the country, raping the Afghan women and burning people alive in excrement.

The hotel had been repeatedly shelled; bullet holes lined the walls and windows were smashed everywhere. The dining rooms and banquet halls were closed, as were most of the top floors. Spider webs grew in many rooms. Hall lights were dim. The business office and barbershop were also closed. Only two floors were kept in service, including the bookstore in the lobby. It was the biggest haunted house I had ever seen. If a director were ever going to film an Afghani version of *The Shining*, this would be the perfect setting.

Across the hotel restaurant sat three Taliban soldiers in their dark turbans and grey *shalwar qamizs*. They invited me to join them. Here I was, about to leave Afghanistan the next day, eating with the Islamic world's most merciless killers. Abdul Kahar was a Taliban tank division commander dining with his two medical student cohorts, both Taliban recruits. We shared each other's food, launching into a spirited four-hour conversation. Abdul told me the Taliban ate and slept free of charge at the Intercontinental.

Daod, one of the tank division commanders, attempted to show me the way to nirvana with the usual conversation opener "why you no Muslim?" He was wearing a brown turban with white stripes that draped down to his waist. He had been fighting the opposition forces of General Massoud for two years. This was his 15th year of steady fighting — mostly against the Russians. Abdul and Daod were determined they had won the hearts and minds of the people. They wanted to create a new Islamic nation and rid Afghanistan of the bandits, rapists and thieves. The only opposition were the old Mujaheddin warlords whose time had passed. The Mujaheddin had saved the country from Communism and the Russians, but now they couldn't figure how to keep it out of the toilet.

Through the hours of dusk, our conversation wound its way to women and the punishment for rape. My dinner companions told me their interpretation of the Koran and Islamic teachings were justified. Abdul gestured frantically with his hands, saying that Islam demands a woman must choose her own husband. I pointed out that this wasn't what was happening. Forced marriages were commonplace among Muslims in India, Pakistan and Bangladesh, I said. Islamic law is based on Allah's teachings, Abdul said. People needed to be kept from the degeneration of Western culture. The three of them all questioned the moral wisdom of Americans allowing "naked women" on television and on the covers of magazines. The United States, they said, was morally bankrupt. They did have a point, I thought, but I still had a hard time believing that chopping off a person's hands for stealing was the answer.

After they found out that I wasn't married, they told me that I would lead a healthier life if I found the right woman. I hadn't found that person I told them, even at 33 years of age. Abdul thought I must be truly unhappy, having to live my life without the love of a woman. Then unexpectedly, Abdul began to tell me about how it is all right for a Muslim man to cry.

"I love you," Abdul gushed. "I love all mankind. You are my brother, friend."

"Salaam aleikum," I said in return. Peace be with you.

Then we returned to our adjacent rooms for the night.

The hotel had every modern convenience: dresser drawers, queen-size beds, showers and toilets, mirrors and even a TV, albeit a disconnected one. It didn't work though. I pulled open the curtains and could see Kabul under the moonlight and stars. I could only see one side of town, but since the hotel was up on a hilltop I could make out faint glimmers of light coming from many of the one-storey homes scattered around the city. Much of the town below was in ruins, the larger buildings demolished into piles of brick and concrete. Cement frames of abandoned buildings stood as eerie silhouettes in the night. I lay down for a minute and fell asleep after an exhilarating day. With the help of a co-operative foreign ministry and the Taliban, my brief trip had been more successful than I had imagined. What more could I possibly have hoped for?

The next day, Papa and I left our translator Ranu at the bus station and got ready for the wretched return trip to Pakistan. As our driver packed the Mercedes truck full of luggage and supplies, two scrawny children, a girl and a boy, begged for handouts. The young girl, in a red *chador*, came up to my side of the truck with her hands outstretched, pleading for anything I could give her. As she clutched her mother's hand, a desperate smile broke through her weary look, offset by her beautiful tiny Pathan face. Papa told me to ignore them. There were hundreds of starving families he said. I couldn't help them all.

I ignored his advice though and got out of the truck. I bought some cans of Pepsi and walnuts from a drink stall. Suddenly, I was surrounded by grabbing hands that latched onto my clothes. I couldn't get back on the bus. I tugged, but they wouldn't let go. Their nails dug into my skin. I didn't want to push them, fearing an encounter with a nearby adult. The girl in the *chador* began to sob heavily until her mother and the truck driver intervened, pulling her and the others away. I wanted to help but couldn't. For the first time, the poverty of this desolate war-torn country hit me. Part of travelling to foreign places is finding the unexpected. Hearing the anguished cries of children was too much.

As we left, crammed inside the five-ton Mercedes with dogs, bleary-eyed men and sleepy children, poverty became evident again on the highway. There seemed to be no limit to the capacity of the truck as others clambered onto the rooftop for the harrowing journey to Peshawar.

Under the blazing September sun, young Pathan kids shovelled gravel to fill in the holes left by shelling and tank treads. Drivers were expected to donate a few Afghanis, but no one stopped. Other children in ragged clothes, jury-rigged rubber tubing to roadside waterfalls, selling the water for radiators. Anything for money.

A few hours into our pothole-back-jarring-tank-shredded ride, we stopped at a roadside stall for the men to pray to Allah. I went to get some pomegranates and a warm Pepsi. After the ritual body frisk by the Taliban as I stepped off the truck, someone grabbed my crotch from behind. Instinctively, I turned around and smashed him in his chest with my fist. Bad move. The passengers began shouting in Pashtu and a few Taliban fumbled for their guns. Papa immediately interceded. He started apologizing for me, explaining that I had hit a Taliban. The Taliban soldier who grabbed me, hadn't seen me go through the search and frisk. He was patting me down. He was only checking for heroin in my underwear, Papa said. This incident brought me to the realization that this country was one big tension zone. Everyone suspected everyone. Trust was hard to come by.

That night, Papa and I decided to stay in Jalalabad, 50 km away from the Pakistan border. Another mine-clearing specialist, Farid Homayoun, let us stay at his place overnight. Farid worked for the British HALO demining trust that collaborated with the UN to clear the Russian- and Afghan-laid mines. But we were too tired to talk for long and went to bed early that night. We just wanted to get back to Peshawar.

When we hit the border the next day after a hot and cramped ride, I saw hundreds of women and young girls crossing over into Pakistan. These were not people visiting their relatives in Pakistan for the weekend. They were refugees seeking a new life in Pakistan. Here, women and young girls could go to school and work. Since the last Russian soldier left Afghanistan in February 1989, up to six million refugees have left the country for Iran or Pakistan. One million Afghans alone have set up camp across the border in Peshawar. It is the world's single largest one-time exodus of refugees. The camps have turned into huge squalid cities on the outskirts of Peshawar. Orphaned children from the war are raised among relatives and foster parents, waiting for the day when they can go home. The refugee camps are shocking, but the gun-making town of Darra is truly bizarre.

The Gunshops of Darra

I spent my last day on the Pakistan-Afghan border in a little town just south of Peshawar. Papa and I hired a driver to venture into Darra, a Tribal Area town with watchtowers, fortified homes, smugglers' bazaars and tribesmen armed with AK-47s. Some of the region's biggest gun-runners and drug dealers lived here. The local Pathan carried guns and by guns, I mean big guns. Copies of Chinese- and Russian-made Kalashnikov AK-47 assault rifles and machine guns are as plentiful as Nike baseball hats in New York City.

Out front on the highway, the shops displayed row on row of guns. In the back, highly skilled Pathan tribesmen sat cross-legged on the dirt floors, labouring away as they polished handles and grips with wood varnish. Everything from firing mechanisms to muzzles and handcrafted metal parts were made with lathes and drill presses. Other workers sanded steel parts, smoothing them out to perfection. The much-modified AK-47 (the most widely used weapon in the world) is carried by over 50 armies and is handmade right in this very town. It's said that the British during the 19th century gave the Afridis (the main Pathan group) the right to manufacture arms. In exchange, the British were promised safe passage through the Khyber Pass. Now this pride in workmanship is directed toward the war next door.

The smell of metal shavings and grease permeated the air as we walked through the shops, escorted by a Pathan arms dealer. Some of the gun brokers dealt strictly in the financing of larger arms purchases — the ones where trucks are needed to haul away the goods. A rocket launcher goes for a measly 30,000 Pakistani rupees ($750 US). You can buy grenades like candy bars for 100 rupees and if you want some real leverage, a used Russian AK-47 sells for $150 US. All sales are final. Small handguns, Lee Enfield rifles, semi-automatic rifles, submachine guns: they're here for a price if you've got the cash.

One of the dealers, a large Pathan, offered to let me try a gun. Whether he sensed I was in a shopping mood or just wanted to impress me with the accuracy of his weapons, I didn't know. He gave me a choice of any gun in the shop. That was easy. The

Kalashnikov, of course. I held two or three assault rifles, light machine guns and self-loading carbines to my shoulder, feeling them for balance and comfort. I finally chose the basic 7.62mm AK-47 with a folding grip. The dealer, Papa and I with my weapon, walked over to a hillside where a goat was grazing at the top. I loaded a full clip of 30 bullets. Then, a little target practice.

He encouraged me to aim for the goat on the hill, but the thought of the bloody mess I'd leave if I hit it made me decline the generous offer. The gun dealer assured me the rapid-fire assault rifle had a killing range of 1,350 m, the equivalent of 14 American football fields. I believed him. Firing a few rounds of a semi-automatic machine gun was something I had never done before. I wasn't sure if the recoil would dislocate my shoulder. I started to fire one at a time, a little apprehensive at first. A few rounds bounced off some rocks. The goat winced and bolted over the hilltop.

Then I switched the rifle to automatic mode. A flurry of bullets whizzed through the air, chipping away at the granite boulders up the hill. The empty shells rapidly popped up out of the gun in an endless blur, falling to my side. I was getting the hang of this. A few more rounds on automatic and more shells discharged out of the Kalashnikov. This was fun. I was getting addicted to the power of the weapon with its 30-round magazine. It was sheer brute force. With this AK-47, I knew what it felt like to be that bad ass dude in those Hollywood films. Guns commanded respect. I understood the fear that people had of the Taliban with their guns, now that I held the same weapon in my hands. The way of the Pathan in this outlaw region all made sense now.

These were my last images of Pakistan's Tribal Areas before I had to fly back to Islamabad and pick up my bike. From Islamabad, I was headed to Lahore on the eastern edge of Pakistan where I would bike the short distance across the Indian border. I had caught a glimpse of my first civil war in Afghanistan, but despite the exhilaration of it all, a part of me secretly wished I would never get a chance again. *Insha'allah.*

India: 50 Years Past Midnight

CHAPTER ELEVEN

Arrested Again

Traffic slowed to a crawl. Motor rickshaws, Suzuki vans and ox carts jockeyed for position as they drove around the spoke-like traffic circle ahead of me. A mother carried her toddler precariously on the back of a scooter as she putted past me. Skinny, moustached Muslim soldiers with shiny sabres proudly strapped to their sides stood guard outside the city's massive semi-circular gates. Their vivid purple-and-red turbans were evidence of the city's vibrant character. The city was pulsing with life.

I was in Lahore, the most striking modern-day city in Pakistan. The city of 2.7 million, Pakistan's second largest, has been the capital of the Panjab for the last 1,000 years. Milton praised Lahore in his poetry and Kipling immortalized it in *Kim*. Everyone from Hindu kings, Moghul emperors and Sikh monarchs to British sovereigns ruled Lahore. The British elite made it a favourite stopover on their way to the cooler hill stations in Kashmir, during the era of the Raj. The city became renowned for its courtesans, dancing *nautch* girls, gilded minarets and immaculate Shalimar Gardens with over 400 fountains. By the 19th century, Lahore was the "Paris of India" with a sense of fashion to match.

Compared to Kashgar's slow-paced open markets, Lahore's tiny alleyways were navigational nightmares. They bustled with so much traffic that you had to jump out of the way to let a rickshaw pass. Chipmunks scampered along intricately carved timber balconies overlooking crowded bazaars. Historic Islamic buildings covered in gilded stucco were mixed in with those made of sandstone walls — Hindu-style. The Sikhs, too, had a hand in Lahore's buildings, but they hauled away much of the city's Moghul Gothic architecture to nearby Amritsar after the Muslim empire collapsed in the 18th century.

As I snaked my bike in and out of traffic, I passed a Hindu temple with children begging for money out front. These were no ordinary kids. They were microcephalic children with abnormally small heads and big ears (a result of a rare neurological condition). With their underdeveloped brains, they could well be called the children of a lesser god. Microcephalics are considered holy in Pakistan and receive generous sums from a deeply religious and benevolent public. Their "owners" wait nearby ready to pocket the donations. Others auction the children off to the highest bidder in an underground slave market. Roughly 1,200 rupees ($41) gets you a brain-damaged illiterate five year old to sweep up your garbage at home.

I wanted to stay in Lahore but couldn't. I had to get to Delhi to catch a flight back to Canada in four days. The last 36 hours had been spent trucking, biking and flying my way across Pakistan. When I was landing in Lahore amid recorded prayers invoking Allah's name, I knew I wasn't going to see much of India. Now I was cycling my way out of the city, trying to hook up with the Grand Trunk Road, the subcontinent's main east-west thoroughfare. It was the last leg for me on my Silk Road journey, taking me through a Neapolitan mix of cities on this old imperial highway. The two-lane road runs from Kabul in Afghanistan through guntoting Peshawar, sprawling Islamabad and Moghul-influenced Lahore in Pakistan. It continues across the Indian border in Sikhdominated Amritsar, passing through Hindu Delhi ending up in Calcutta 2,400 km later.

As I slowly rode through the shady bungalows of the military cantonment district, I passed an opening to a walled compound.

I circled around and stopped my bike at an entranceway. Through an open gate, I could see an infantry training ground. Pakistani soldiers were firing at dummy targets, climbing over rope walls and crawling under barbed-wire traps. Twenty metres away, across the broad tree-lined street, a soldier in a khaki uniform eyed me suspiciously as he guarded the gateway opposite.

I straddled my bike, standing over the top tube with both feet on the ground. I reached for my camera in its usual spot in my handlebar bag, ready to take some pictures. This wouldn't take more than 10 seconds, I thought. I could nonchalantly unzip the bag, snap a photo and be on my way. As I fumbled with my camera, the soldier started to cross the road with his rifle in hand. I quickly stuffed my camera back into the bag. It was too late. He grabbed his two-way radio and started to talk into it. Little did I know, but arrest number three was right around the corner.

I turned my bike around and started to pull away, but my weight on the gear made a quick start impossible. I had gone less than a couple metres when the soldier's large hairy arm seized my bike. He held onto the frame while he spoke rapidly into the radio in Urdu or Hindi. I stepped off the bike and held onto it with both hands. I pulled. He wrenched it back. We were in a tug of war. Although neither of us spoke the other's language, we both understood what each other wanted. I yelled at him to let go. I tried to leave, but he firmly held my bike.

Suddenly, a dark green military Jeep screeched around the corner and skidded to a stop beside us. Two Pakistani cadets and an officer in a beret jumped out. I panicked. They immediately went over to the uniformed soldier. I tried to tell them I didn't take any pictures, but they seemed intent on talking to the officer, not me. It was useless. At worst, I thought they would take the film or keep my camera. One of the cadets took my bike while another grabbed my arm and briskly walked me to the Jeep. He pushed me into the back of the open vehicle. I was shoved so hard that I fell on my hands and knees on the floorboards, my cheek grazing the collapsible metal seats. Within thirty seconds, the driver had whisked us away. Everything — my bike and camera — was gone.

This was the first time in two months that I was forcibly separated from my bike. Was I going to lose all my film and belongings? Where was my bike headed? Visions of shelling out hundreds of dollars to my brother (whose bike I had borrowed) flashed through my head. I dreaded explaining to him that the Pakistan Army stole his bike on account of my stupidity. No one spoke English. I had travelled throughout northern Pakistan where communication wasn't a problem. Now I was in the grip of three soldiers who didn't speak English.

Three blocks into our ride, I was getting nowhere as I yelled questions like "Where is my bike?" and "Am I being arrested?" Then I saw a 2 1/2-ton olive green army truck come round the corner behind us. It became clear that the truck was following us as we turned another corner. Through the plastic windows of the Jeep, I could see the handlebars of my bike on the truck. At last, my bike and I were headed in the same direction.

The Jeep and truck pulled into a set of low-slung buildings surrounded by spacious, well-kept gardens. I was escorted out of the Jeep and told to sit in the lobby of the building. It was the headquarters for the Lahore Infantry. Would I like some tea while I waited to see the lieutenant? asked a young male soldier. This pleasant change in attitude immediately gave me confidence that the worst was over. Maybe all I had to do was fill out some administrative paperwork? I could only hope to be so lucky.

A half-hour later, I was ushered into a large office. A ceiling fan whirred above. A short man in army fatigues was talking on the phone when I walked in. He waved me to sit down. When the lieutenant got off the phone, he apologized profusely for my treatment. He pointed to some cookies and peanuts on his desk and motioned me to help myself. Finally, I was able to speak English to someone.

The lieutenant, Rajiv Bhurgari, gently explained that I had forgotten the fundamental fact of Muslim-Hindu politics that led to my arrest. Since the Indian border was situated 30 km away, tension ran high because of the conflict in Kashmir. This month had been particularly strenuous between the two nations, the lieutenant said. Four Westerners had been executed the week before by Kashmiri rebels. Any foreigners who poked their noses where they didn't belong and were dressed like Muslims with a beard, as I was, were asking for trouble.

I apologized to the lieutenant for stirring things up with my camera and then asked for my film back. I was free to go as soon as he heard from his superior, the lieutenant said. But regulations stipulated that he had to confiscate the film. I explained that I had lost a roll or two in China and would really appreciate it if he would compensate me for the cost. No problem he said, as he pulled open a petty cash drawer and handed me a few rupees. In the meantime, was there anything else I wanted? Maybe some Lahore pizza?

After filling out some paperwork with my passport number and address, we settled down to some more tea. The junior soldier who had brought me sugar and cream the first time stood outside the office, ready for any requests from Lt. Bhurgari, including the pizza order. The infantry regiment's staff seemed to operate as efficiently as the British who had originally trained both the Indian and Pakistani armies. Proficiency and promptness were at a premium among these men. Everything was in its place. Mahogany cabinets showed off delicate china and crystal. Over cheeseless pizza and our fifth cup of tea, the lieutenant and I talked about Partition and Muslim-Hindu relations for four hours straight.

I began to think the Pakistanis could teach the Chinese a little etiquette when it came to detaining foreigners. In China, I was heavily fined and treated like a dog, but here in Lahore I was given tea and biscuits. Outside, two soldiers inspected my bike with white gloves, their shiny bayonet rifles glistening in the sun.

Once Lt. Bhurgari found out I was from Vancouver, he jumped to the conclusion that I must know his Sunni Muslim friends in Toronto. Wasn't it a short drive from my house? he asked. I gave the lieutenant a little geography lesson in another room with a wall map. I showed him that Seattle (a place he had never heard of) was the only major city within easy driving distance of Vancouver. We talked in-depth about the history of Lahore and its Sikh and Muslim heritage. If I had time, the lieutenant said, I could find numerous quacks in the city's old bazaars that cured any ailment from aches and pains to sexual dysfunction. No thanks, I said.

When the phone call came allowing Lt. Bhurgari to authorize my release, I knew he would probably be the last person in Pakistan I spoke to at length. The lieutenant, noting I was still hungry despite the biscuits and Lahore-style pizza, ordered the very soldiers who had hauled me away in their Jeep to drive me to Pizza Hut. Outside, we took off my panniers and lifted my bike into the Mitsubishi army truck. Then we headed off along Canal Bank Road to the only Pizza Hut in Pakistan. I hadn't seen a fast-food joint since my first day in Beijing 72 days earlier. Now that I was in the throngs of civilization with all the conveniences of urban life, my stomach began to crave the simple little luxuries that I had gone without for so long.

When I pulled around the corner to the Pizza Hut, there were no teenagers hanging out with their Dr. Peppers. The streets were clean. On one side of the air-conditioned building were rows of scooters lined up in military-like precision. A young boy was washing them with a bucket and soapy water. Their shiny red gas tanks shone under the clear blue sky. At the front door, a soldier in camouflage shirt and pants stood with a semi-automatic machine gun. He wore, per company policy, the standard issue Pizza Hut red cap — the same one worn behind the counter. After two medium pizzas with the works, bloated like a Macy's Day float, it was time to head off down the Grand Trunk Road to the border.

A Woman's Place

"Rape! Domestic violence! Stove Burning! Are you a victim?" the billboard shouted exuberantly.

I was riding on the outskirts of Lahore on my way to Wagah,

the Pakistan customs post, when I saw this sign next to the road. I had heard of the minefields in Afghanistan and the gulags in the Chinese desert, but this billboard shed light on one of the most horrendous domestic issues facing women in Pakistan. Every year, hundreds of young wives are burnt to death, allegedly the victims of exploding cooking stoves. The truth, however, is much more sinister.

Victims, usually from poorer families, are doused in fuel and then set alight. Other women are set on fire by being pushed onto a kerosene stove or having it kicked at them. It is Pakistan's darkest secret. Somehow, the police and doctors always seem to believe that the stove blew up by itself. Burnt women lie on filthy sheets in Pakistan's hospitals, stripped of their skin. They look like macabre exhibits in a waxworks factory. Some hospitals see over 300 victims per year, many written off by the authorities as accidents. In 1998, it was estimated that 888 women in the Panjab alone were killed because of stove burnings by those who wanted to get rid of them.

At the core of stove burnings is the "boys are best" philosophy, so entrenched in the values of many Muslim and Hindu families on the subcontinent. Women are viewed as the property of their male relatives. The honour of the family is tied to the woman. The perception that violence against women by their own families is permissible supports stove burnings and acid throwings (where a woman is killed for real or perceived immoral behaviour). Some families have tried to prosecute. Only one case has ever gone to court in Pakistan. Victims' families complain of corrupt police being bought off by the offenders. If a woman complains to the police, she may be raped and abused, then returned to her family. Of all the women I had seen in Pakistan's Northern Areas, I never imagined the atrocities that were a "feature of feudal society" as the Islamabad government calls it.

If Pakistan's stove burnings are bad, then the problem of female infanticide in India is worse. Babies are aborted in the early months if ultrasound tests reveal a girl. India had to outlaw these "sex determination" clinics in 1994 because of all the backstreet abortions that were being performed. The practice of *sati* (the burning of widows) is similar to Pakistan's stove burnings.

In many Asian countries, a woman's world in the late 1990s feels reminiscent of the late 1890s. In both India and Pakistan, it is a world of inequality and discrimination. Women are treated as property and second-class citizens.

Across the border, the great Hindu nation awaited. I had come to see India, albeit briefly, warts and all.

The World's Largest Democracy

It's called the Zero Line, a no-man's land dividing Pakistan from India. My mountain bike tires rolled over the white line to the other side into India. I was headed into the maze of paperwork that characterizes the jobs of Indian customs officials — Asia's ultimate bureaucratic heel-draggers on the subcontinent.

Cycling through Pakistan customs had been a breeze. I was in and out in 15 minutes. I had opened up my panniers and the Pakistani officer, dressed in his khaki *shalwar qamiz* and sandals, pulled out one or two items. He took a cursory look, sized me up with my beard and told me to repack my things. Almost like a trusting Canadian border official, I thought. I didn't even have to go inside the crumbling customs building. It was like a drive-thru — just plop your luggage on the wood table outside, one foot off the bicycle and show the official your goods.

A few minutes later, I rode the 1,000 m between the two country's customs posts, leaving the dark green Pakistani flag with its crescent moon and star behind. The Indian side of the border was well paved and replete with American-style advertising. Coca-Cola, Nike, Daewoo cars, Nokia cell phones, Johnnie Walker Black Label Scotch, Ray-Ban sunglasses, Kellogg's, McDonald's and Mercedes-Benz — the billboards were all there. I pulled up on my bike to a border guard in a splendid red turban. I was outside the Indian immigration and customs compound. The Sikh guard, whom I recognized by his turban, approached me, rifle in hand.

"You have Pakistan rupees?" he asked.

"No, just the bike and a Visa card," I said, lying.

"Go in then, but take your bags inside. Bike stays out here," he said sternly.

The Sikh, with his wispy moustache, magnificent jet-black beard and sashed waist, ushered me inside the modern customs building. The Pakistan customs office had been about as big as a construction trailer. The Indian building, however, was complete with turnstiles and laminated wood countertops. It looked like a tiny airport terminal. Then the bureaucratic two-step began. A short Hindu man in polyester pants and cotton shirt asked me to take out all my belongings. Piece by piece, I spread them out on the metal table beside the X-ray machine. I grabbed my two Ortlieb panniers, handlebar bag and sleeping bag and laid out everything in neat piles. I even unrolled the sleeping bag.

Out the clothes came. Then my medication, powdered Gatorade canister and bag of film. Then my camera, toothbrush, hiking shoes and Russian bayonet knife I had brought back from Afghanistan. Even some empty shell casings from the AK-47 I had fired and a spent blasting cap from a tank shell. Everything was on the counter. The Hindu officer started to rummage through it all without a care as to what was in which pile. He searched my Uyghur cassette tapes from Kashgar, my medical insurance forms, bike tools, compression sack for my sleeping bag and first aid kit. What were these hypodermic needles doing here? he asked. And how about this? he said, as he held up a can of fire starter paste I had used when camping. What was that for? he would say holding up one item after the other.

For the cyclist, packing is an art. This guy was messing with my well-planned packing system. I usually placed hard items like camping pots, books and heavy clothes on the bottom of a pannier and frequently used items on top. I layered softer things (mainly clothes) in the left pannier, so when I leaned the bike against a building or the ground, nothing would be squished. Food, toiletries and water were stacked in the top of the right pannier for easy access. I wanted to keep all my belongings so I could easily repack them. We had already spent a half-hour going through my stuff, but for what? The customs officer thought otherwise, even after I asked him politely to keep things orderly.

When he saw some political books on Kashmir buried at the bottom of one of the panniers, he pulled them out and called over a co-worker. I had purchased the books in Lahore I told him. Not good enough, he said.

"There are maps in here of military importance," the officer said.

His Sikh superior agreed. "We have to keep the books," he said.

"You can't buy these books in India. They represent the murderous thoughts of the Pak-Muslims. You should have learned that coming from 'Pindi," he said.

Great, I thought. The sign outside said, "Welcome to the World's Largest Democracy!" What democracy, if the government censored basic books on one of the world's longest ongoing conflicts? Although I had never been to India before, I knew the officer was probably lying about the books not being available in Indian bookshops. I felt as though coming from Muslim Pakistan was a signal to do a little foot-dragging by the Hindu-staffed customs agency. God forbid someone should wish to visit "the enemy."

The Hindu officer's boss wanted to go through my things and look at the books — all six of them. This stretched on for hours as the two discussed confiscating the Kashmir books. Noon came and I ate some lamb and *chapattis* for lunch. I read an old copy of the *Hindu Times* for an hour, trying to kill time. Other travellers and tourists came and went as I sat by the window reading. I even suggested that they rip out the pages where the maps were (about 20 pages in all). No good, they said.

I really got frustrated when three hours later, the fourth baggage inspector, another contemptuous Indian customs officer, began to go through my things. For the third time, I was being asked for my passport as they went off into a room to quietly scrutinize it. I had tried to be an ideal ambassador of Canada for three months, four nations and thousands of kilometres. I was a model adventure traveller. My patience and polite mannerisms ran out, though, and I flipped and blurted out more four-letter words than a single episode of *South Park*.

"This isn't a democracy. There's no true freedom of speech in India. You're a bunch of hypocrites in a country that's masquerading as the world's largest democracy," I said, as a few Japanese tourists looked on in embarrassment.

I accused the customs officers of inconveniencing overseas travellers. Didn't they have real smugglers and drug-runners to bother? Didn't they want to give a good first impression to people visiting India? If they kept acting like this, did they expect me to return some day?

"This place is a fucking joke," I blurted out stupidly and began to walk to the door.

"What did you say?" the Sikh officer asked.

"You heard what I said. I'm not going to repeat it," I replied as I turned around.

"Wait right here. Don't leave," the officer said.

Now I had done it. I had just given them reason to keep me here another few hours. The afternoon dragged on as I read my guidebook four times. I couldn't leave. They had my passport. My guidebook said the average border crossing takes four hours — something that should only take 30 minutes. Six hours of gazing at linoleum patterns, weight measuring machines and spider webs later, the customs staff relented. The maps in the books weren't that sensitive after all, the officer said. I could have them back, but first I had to declare my money. I knew my earlier badgering had become ridiculous. It was like beating my head against a wall. Now the long, arduous, boring wait had paid off. I had my books back.

I had been warned that the Indian customs officers were sticklers for preventing Indian rupees from entering the country. They didn't want foreigners buying their currency at a cheaper rate from a Pakistani moneychanger. Customs wanted people to go to the Bank of India and pay the service charges or something like that. It didn't seem like a strong argument to me.

When I came across the border, I was wearing an undershirt beneath my *shalwar qamiz* robe. A pouch had been sewn into the undershirt. The pouch contained 6,000 Indian rupees I had purchased a minute away near the Pakistani customs post. Along with rupees were my debit card, $50 in US funds and a Visa card. I knew from talking to other travellers that if I handed over the Indian rupees with no fuss, I would likely be given 20 per cent of it back. A customs officer would pocket the rest. This was considered *baksheesh*, a tip for making things go through smoothly at the border. My visit to the Indian border had been anything but that.

As another Sikh bureaucrat came up to the counter where I was standing, I sensed a scam and excused myself to go to the bathroom. I quickly took out the 6,000 rupee notes (about $240) and put 5,500 in my underwear. The other 500 rupees were in my pouch. I went back to the counter and showed one of the bureaucrats my credit card, the 500 rupees and US funds. Then he pointed to my stomach. He didn't believe me.

"What is here?" he said poking my stomach with his pen. "Do you have present for me?"

Nothing could fool this guy. I pulled out my debit card and passport, the only things left. I could feel the rest of the rupees in my underwear start to slide down my leg. I squeezed my thighs together to keep the money from falling to my feet. I didn't want anyone to see it and confiscate it. The customs officer asked me to hand over the 500 rupees that I had illegally purchased in Pakistan. I refused to supplement his income. As I was handing the notes to him across the counter, I ripped up the $20 in rupees. The officer's eyes turned to I-want-to-rip-your-head-off-mode.

Then the money between my legs fell to the floor, hitting my sandals. I had $220 lying on the floor. I had pissed off almost everyone in the office over the past six hours and they had pissed me off. I didn't want to give the officers and bureaucrats the satisfaction of having a couple hundred of my dollars. To them, $220 was like $1,000 to me. I was not going to line their pockets one more time. They could wait for the next gullible tourist. As soon as the official turned away, I quickly feigned scratching my shin and palmed the money. Then I was out the door with an armful of clothes, camping gear and panniers. I dropped my stuff to the ground, shoved it in the panniers and rode off.

On to Amritsar I pedalled, half a day late. Visions of voodoo dolls in customs uniforms bristling with pins flashed through my head. I later heard that four guys from France travelling in a Volkswagen van had been detained at the same border for seven days. The Indian autocrats had partially disassembled the muffler and other parts, weighing them, all under the pretence of a drug investigation.

Kashmir and Partition

The best high-altitude soldiers in the world belong to the Indian and Pakistan armies. Ski lifts ferry soldiers across canyons. Others huddle around kerosene stoves, living inside ice tunnels and fibreglass-panelled shacks. Pulley systems lift artillery shells up the mountains and cart human waste back down. The Garden of Eden that is Kashmir is no more.

Since the 1970s, when high-altitude gear made trekking through the Western Himalaya feasible, the two nations have been fighting a refrigerated war 5,400 m (18,000 ft.) up in the Siachen Glacier. Approximately 24,000 people have died since the Kashmir uprising began in 1990 — only 600 of them Indian soldiers, according to the Indian Army. Others estimate double that. The majority are civilians. Another 2,000 were kidnapped (only half were returned alive). Grenades blow up some villagers; others are caught in the crossfire or held hostage. Words like *Line of Control* dominate in the daily papers as the two countries try to gain an extra few kilometres. Minuscule advances are made here and there, as neither side relinquishes ground. The only thing that is conquered is the elements. Some have likened the struggle to two bald men fighting over a comb.

Understanding the social, political and religious complexities of Kashmir is a wake-up call to the realities of visiting the Indian subcontinent. Pakistan loathes India. India seethes with contempt for Pakistan. Muslims hate Hindus who hate Muslims. India has essentially been suppressing Pakistani-supported militias who raid Kashmiri villages around Srinagar. The fighting in Kashmir makes Northern Ireland, Bosnia and Rwanda look like tea parties. Simply put, people die daily because of their religious beliefs and nationality. Kashmir is a paradise turned sour; it's a social time bomb waiting to explode. The two countries have been competing in this ongoing pissing match for 50 years, the result of Britain's impossible task of partitioning its former empire along ethnic lines.

The debate over who controls Kashmir — Muslim Pakistan or Hindu India — is a controversy mired in fanatic religious doctrine. When independence from Britain was proclaimed in August of 1947, two new countries were formed. The question of what to do with this vast agricultural-rich paradise stretching from Gilgit and Hunza on the Pakistan side to Ladakh in India, remained. Did it belong to India because it had a Hindu Maharajah leader? Was it Pakistan's because of its predominantly Muslim population? Kashmiri Muslims and Hindus who had co-existed with their differing faiths side by side for centuries, were now forced by the British to decide whether to join Pakistan or India. A referendum was held weeks before the subcontinent was divided into Pakistan and East Pakistan (now Bangladesh) with mighty India in the middle. The new Muslim country would contain the Panjab, Afghans, Kashmir, Indus, Sind and Baluchistan — their letters forming the acronym PAKISTAN. In the North West Frontier Province, the Pathan, too poor to read, were given a green card for Pakistan and a red card for India. They narrowly voted for accession to Pakistan. Gilgit and Hunza (part of Hindu-ruled Kashmir), acceded to Pakistan shortly after.

The Hindu Maharajah in Kashmir was hesitant to give up his independence. He vacillated in siding with one country over the other. If he took Kashmir into India, he would be forcing the Muslim majority to become minorities in a huge Hindu state. His indecision struck horror into Kashmiri Hindus. Would they become the first state in India where Hindus were a minority? This led to lynching and random attacks on Muslim properties. In the end, the Maharajah took his mountain kingdom and joined India.

On behalf of Pakistan, Pathan soldiers invaded Kashmir while 100,000 Indian infantry troops responded from the east. India claimed all of Kashmir while Pakistan argued Kashmir must decide its own fate, maybe even opt for an independent state. Fifteen months later, the United Nations stepped in and declared a ceasefire line. But what happened in the north in Kashmir was only the beginning.

When Sikhs, Muslims and Hindus found out about the boundaries of their new nations that fateful midnight in August, they panicked. The Pakistan-India border sliced through communities like a giant knife chopping a wedding cake in half. The greatest migration in human history occurred as 10 million people changed homelands. Hindus and Sikhs swarmed east. An equal number of Muslims crossed west through the Panjab in one mass exodus. Trainloads of people fled their native towns for a safer place where they could be in the religious majority. Great columns or *kafilas* of Partition refugees left their homes on foot, carrying what little they could on their backs. One *kafila*, comprising 800,000 people, took eight days to pass through a town.

In the melee, Muslims slaughtered Sikhs and Hindus fleeing for India. In turn, Hindus and Sikhs murdered Muslims escaping for Pakistan. Fearing for their lives, people ate rat poison and committed suicide by jumping into wells, lest they be butchered alive. Children were knifed to death. The vultures grew so fat they could barely fly. The Indian and Pakistan armies, anticipating some sort of disturbances, were ill prepared to deal with the religious hatred and massacres. Some soldiers even joined in the killings.

Sikh farmers in the Panjab lost their priceless farmland to Muslim *zamindars* (landowners) — the new occupants. Muslims lost their houses. The value of the land swap was by no means equal. Traditional administrative occupations, long held by Hindus, were now Muslim jobs in the new Pakistan. Resentment followed. When Hindus realized an independent Muslim nation had come to fruition, their attitudes changed. Respect was gone for the Hindus who remained in Pakistan. They were now *mohajirs* (refugees), considered beneath even the lowest castes. As had happened repeatedly throughout history, new states were carved up with little concern for the ethnic or religious makeup of towns. It's estimated that 500,000 people were brutally killed in the weeks after Partition.

I had read about Partition and how it tore a nation apart. For Pakistan and India, it was their Holocaust. I couldn't put a face to the stories of a half-century ago. It all seemed so long ago for me, something that should be left to the history books and forgotten. I didn't realize how wrong I could have been. Then I met Salah Udeen, a Muslim who had lived in Amritsar in 1947.

Salah told me the story of how he escaped westward in a truck bound for his new homeland in Pakistan. At the border near Lahore, a police officer ordered the vehicle to stop. As all the young men were ordered out of the truck, the Muslim officer said, "You want to see Lahore, don't you?" Across the road at a nearby station, two Amritsar-bound trains jam-packed with departing Hindus were waiting eagerly to cross the border into India.

"Nobody goes to Lahore until you kill every single Hindu on these trains," the policeman said.

The officer then waited patiently as Salah and 50 young men complied with his order. When the massacre was done (mostly with machetes), the Muslim men, blood on their shirts and hands, were given a tour of Lahore and granted shops in one of the prestigious business districts. Ironically, many of Salah's friends are Hindu to this day.

What happened in the Panjab over a half-century ago cannot be easily explained. Sadly, those born right after Partition — the so-called midnight's children — could only ask one question. How could two communities that had lived together for centuries, shared the same language, sang the same songs and danced together at common shrines, do what they did to each other?

Three wars later (two over Kashmir), Pakistan and India are divided by a 10-m-wide barbed-wire fence running the length of their northern borders. Along the Grand Trunk Road, truckers stretch their legs at roadside *dhabas* where they eat a little *dhal* (lentil soup) and rice. I rode my bike another hour through the old caravan staging posts of centuries ago. This portion of the Grand Trunk, now an endless metalled highway, is where the Moghuls once sank wells in the road. Barefoot wayfarers still walk from city to city. Donkey carts or *ekkas* head to markets as their combustion engine counterparts rumble past. Two wheels, three wheels, two feet, four feet, eight wheels; everyone travels the GT. Kipling called it the "river of life." True indeed. This last leg to Amritsar was the end of my cycling leg on the Grand Trunk Road. After that, the bike would be packed up in Delhi and shuttled from airport to airport on the final journey home.

Amritsar

No one will ever say Islamabad or Beijing has charm. Amritsar, on the other hand, oozes it. I had cycled into Amritsar for two days of rest. I had heard that the Sikhs were some of the most polite and generous people in India, unfettered with the hatred that afflicts so many Muslims and Hindus over Kashmir.

Amritsar, the Sikh capital of the world, is home to the magnificent Golden Temple, a two-storey marble building with inlaid flower motifs, encircled by a sacred pool. I entered the temple where thousands of people were literally camped out on the premises, sleeping on cots or the tiled floor. A Sikh group from Birmingham, England, was donating the funds to re-gild the holy shrine with 100 kg of pure gold.

Outside the temple, women crowded around market stalls, craning their necks to choose their favourite buttermilk or yoghurt drinks. *Lassis* (sweet and sour versions of thick milkshakes) had become a favourite of mine since I had passed through Pakistan. The people of Amritsar regard these milk-shake-like delicacies as a source of energy, just as they do ghee, the Indian version of butter. Cream versions of the drinks, as thick as curd, became my daily fix and journey to hardened arteries. The drinks, as well as the many curried foods and *puris* (fried pancakes), were a sign for me that I was heading into southern India. I stopped filling up with watered-down Sprite and Fanta and began to drink *lassis*. In the West, chewy chewy chocolate chip and maple walnut are about as diverse a selection of milk-shake flavours as you'll find. Here, there are *lassi* specialists called *halwais* that could give Dairy Queen or Ben & Jerry's a run for their money any day. From arriving in Lahore to my departure in Delhi, I never once ordered the same drink. As popular as the *lassis* are, juicebars were equally widespread throughout Amritsar. You can drink *chicku* shakes, order a *kulfi pista* and mix *mosoumi* or mango juice with all of the above. I was glad to be gaining the weight back after nearly three months on the road.

I found out, along with an American cyclist from Georgia, that the Golden Temple's food and lodging was free for three days. Those who can afford a small donation do so when leaving. All faiths were allowed into the temple, provided you take your shoes off and cover your head. Volunteers serve up to 30,000 people a day in a massive kitchen and dining hall. We hauled our bikes into the temple grounds and registered our names. Every square foot seemed to be covered with hundreds of people sitting, sleeping, changing their turbans or breast-feeding their babies. In and out everyone went. It was like a spiritual version of a rock concert without the music.

For two days, I would cycle into the city markets, browse the bookshops and marvel at the architecture, influenced by the Hindu and Muslim cultures as much as the Sikh. Then it was back to the temple where, as a foreigner, I was segregated into a separate unit with the other backpackers and cyclists. The Sikh guards who roamed the temple kept the sprawling shrine safe, their brightly coloured turbans contrasting with the white complex around the pool.

For many years, security wasn't a serious issue. But in 1984, Prime Minister Indira Gandhi sent the Indian Army's tanks into the holy compound. The government was trying to hunt down Sikh extremists hiding in the temple. After two days of shelling, the temple walls were riddled with bullets. The outrage at sending the army into the holiest of Sikh places led to Gandhi's assassination four months later by her own Sikh bodyguards. Riots erupted outside Delhi, as Hindus retaliated against Sikhs for murdering their leader. Over 3,000 Sikhs in Delhi alone were doused in kerosene and set alight.

Just around the corner from the Golden Temple is Jallianwala Bagh, the ornately adorned gardens where 150 British soldiers opened fire upon 20,000 Hindu, Sikh and Muslim protesters in 1919. They killed 372 people and wounded 1,200. I walked through the brick entranceway and peered down the wells where people had jumped to avoid the bullets. The massacre helped propel the independence movement at a time when opposition to the British Raj was mounting. A young lawyer name Mohandas K. Gandhi had organized the demonstration, the first of many.

Delhi

The roads of Delhi are arranged like the spokes on a great Ferris wheel, winding ever inward through concentric circles of tree-lined streets. The dusty metropolis peels away like a red onion; each successive layer weaves a path through forts, mosques and colonial mansions. I was sandwiched inside a black-and-gold motorized rickshaw. My bike hung out the side, its front wheel spinning in the wind as we passed residential enclaves, diplomatic missions and roadside *dhabas*. The bike's handlebars stuck into the rubber fabric of the roof. This caused the driver to check continually over his shoulder in case the roof tore. Consequently, the three-wheeled vehicle would gently swerve back and forth each time he turned his head around.

We were clattering along the crater-pocketed Ring Road, the rickshaw's engine sounding like a decrepit lawnmower. We had come from Indira Gandhi International Airport through what Salman Rushdie calls the "bone-dry heat of Delhi." Up ahead, a grey veil of carbon monoxide hung over the city. Somewhere I had read that a day in Delhi was the equivalent of smoking 20 packs of cigarettes. Asthmatics beware. As we passed India Gate, a stone arch memorial to the campaigns fought by the Indian Army, shoeshine boys contested for business alongside masseuses and ice cream vendors. When we reached the columned façades of Connaught Place, Delhi's commercial centre, the air seemed thicker, the people more frenzied.

Originally designed as a horseshoe, Connaught Place buzzed with snake charmers and hucksters trying to sell everything from train tickets to delicious green bananas. A woman held onto a little boy's hand, her left hand balancing a copper urn atop her head. She paused for a moment, squatted in the street without pulling up her dress and urinated. Then she continued on. No one noticed. Nothing unusual had taken place. This was Delhi. Welcome to India.

Delhi is one inescapable spinning mass of humanity — a byword for poverty. Like most other Indian cities, there are the tin-roofed shacks, garbage dumps and tangled electrical wiring. Complacent cows sleep on traffic medians oblivious to the bullock carts, Maruti pickups and Ambassador sedans speeding past. The olive-coloured skin of men and women contrasts pleasantly with their bright white *dhotis* and brilliant yellow *saris*. Delhi, however, is rife with the signs of Western pop culture.

Pretty Hindu girls clad in halter-tops and Levi's ride Honda scooters. The latest Prada look-a-like purses hang from their shoulders. Disco-dancing teens pass by street beggars on their way to burger joints. Familiar logos from Toyota, Nike, Motorola and Pepsi dot the streets. KFC is king in India. Going to Pizza Hut or McDonald's is considered an evening out. This was once a country where half the population couldn't even sign their own name. The country exists in several timeframes at once — some in the late 20th century, the others centuries earlier.

When I was in the Chinese desert, I was far enough away from the majority of the population centred in the southeast. India, however, was a constant stream of people. You notice it everywhere from the cities and villages to the countryside. I didn't know the meaning of the word *congestion* until I set foot in Delhi. India has the highest growth rate in the world. The numbers speak for themselves. India at one billion is three and a half times more populous than the United States and is expected to surpass China in population by 2035 — all this on one-third the real estate of the US. Family planning is all but a vague notion. Of women between 17 and 19 years old, 60 per cent are mothers. Female literacy runs at 37 per cent, limiting most women to a life of housework and labour in the fields.

Indians, however, have a plan to get them out of the mess their nation is in. They have a messianic faith in technology. I saw this after I checked into the Sunny Guesthouse in Connaught Place. Stereos, VCRs, cell phones and fax machines — all from major manufacturers, changed hands over counters. Wads of rupee notes were piled high in the cash registers. Automatic teller machines, a rarity in Pakistan, were located throughout the city core. Forget the spice markets, Islamic bazaars and poultry and fish markets — Indians want what the West already has. What's more, India has the purchasing power to buy the goods they see on television.

Bill Gates is famous for stating that South Indians are the brightest people in the world after the Chinese. This has given India hope — particularly in Hyderabad, the Silicon Valley of the subcontinent. A quarter million highly skilled workers have created a demand for basic commodities, and this in turn provides jobs for others. India is poised to become the next Asian Tiger economy. So far, the country has succeeded in becoming one of the world's 10 largest emerging markets, churning out a $5 billion software industry each year. Now it is India's turn to pull itself out of the developing world.

Hyderabad has separate commercial zones where generators

supply reliable power to towering glass offices. Beside these gated high-tech dot-com companies, Muslim and Hindu shantytowns make do with eight hours of electricity per day. As a tiny part of India discovers commercial success on the Mumbai stock exchange, the rest of the country toils away, scouring floors and shuffling paperwork in entrenched bureaucracies.

Delhi, too, has gone upscale. Everywhere I went, from the Don't Pass Me By breakfast joint to Keventers (a milk bar), the Kwality Restaurant and Domino's Pizza, merchants were embracing the Electronic City shops to the south and the world of fast food, french fries and Adidas shoes. But not all of India sees its future in selling computer chips and Nokia cell phones. One astute entrepreneur in the Chawri Bazaar in Old Delhi held a cardboard sign in front of his pile of brass Buddhas. The correct price scrawled in felt pen was written on one side and a higher price on the other. As he bartered over prices with an elderly Hindu woman, he flipped the sign around and continued his rant.

The day before my flight back to Canada via Malaysia, I visited Humayun's Tomb, Delhi's precursor to the Taj Mahal in Agra. The interior echoed as I walked through the vaulted 38-m-high ceilings, inlaid with black-and-white marble. Nearby on the same grounds is the first tomb of Babur, the great Moghul Emperor. As I wandered around the lush green grounds dotted with tiny footpaths and palm trees, I came upon some small storage compartments outside the base of the tomb. Peering inside, I recoiled from the caustic smell. Bat shit! I never smelt anything so putrid. Not even camel dung in China. Competing for architectural elegance was the 12-sided marble white petals of the Baha'i Temple, reminiscent of the Sydney Opera House. Over in Old Delhi, a few kilometres to the north, is the 350-year-old red sandstone Lal Qila or Red Fort.

Then there is the caste system. Caste is what distinguishes the street sweeper from the politician. Indians are born into the Brahmins (the priest class), the administrative and artisan classes, or the Sudras (the peasants) at the bottom. The untouchables,

India's downtrodden, are below even the Sudras. They have no caste and perform the most menial tasks. Gandhi tried to be more inclusive of the untouchables, who have been renamed the Dalit. A person's caste decides who they are till they die, where they work, what they eat and wear, how they piss, where they live and who they marry. I saw people scrubbing office and hotel floors with dirty worn-out rags. In this nation of airplane and computer chip manufacturers, the mop seemed to be an alien invention. But gone are the days when caste rules dictated that a low-caste member couldn't serve food to a high-caste person.

In a country where money, favour and privilege make the system work, India's claim as the world's largest democracy is called into question. At the airport I handed over my camera batteries to the customs officer (a customary antiterrorist measure) and walked to the Boeing 737 the old-fashioned way — across the tarmac. An Indian Army soldier, in his regal uniform and beret, stood at attention in the blazing midday sun, watchful of my every move. Even here, India's religious nationalism and fractured past were indelibly stamped on people's minds. India needs new hope; the people deserve another past.

My last week on the subcontinent exploring the metropolises of the Grand Trunk Road were everything and more I had hoped for. It wasn't hard to imagine Kipling's Kim and his companion Hurree Chunder Mookerjee astride the great bronze cannon Zam-Zammah in Lahore.

And then there was nothing for me to do but step aboard my plane in Delhi and take my seat in 19F. I smiled at the flight attendant in her beautiful indigo *sari* as she packed my bags in the overhead rack. My mountain bike was tucked away in the belly of the cargo hold; it was dusty with a few Canadian stickers fastened to the frame. The memories of the past three months would be with me for a lifetime. I ignored for a moment the bustling bazaars, barren deserts and funky old men eating apricots as I closed my eyes.

The Silk Road Today

As a young boy, I used to run my hands over a globe as if it were a Braille *Penthouse*, following borders and tracing mountains. I let my fingers rest in exotic places — Rhodesia, French Indochina, Morocco, Afghanistan, Cairo — they all seemed enticing. Now I had travelled through places I once only dreamed of. Tajik farmers, tribal warlords, Afghan tank commanders, child beggars and Chinese police — they had changed the way I look at other cultures and myself.

When I began my trip in Beijing, I thought the desolate Takla Makan desert and snow-capped peaks of the Karakorams would be the highlight of my 5,000-km journey. The mountains of the Pamirs, Karakorams, Hindu Kush and Himalaya — these were the forbidding landscapes that Marco Polo dared venture to cross with camel caravans 700 years ago.

Three months after finishing my trip in Delhi, it was the people more than anything else that had made my trip memorable. I would never forget the strangers who brought me into their lives; I shared bread and water in a Kyrgyz yurt, lunched with the Mir's family in northern Pakistan, negotiated my way through Afghanistan with Papa and had pizza with the infantry lieutenant in Lahore. The Sikh temple guards, Muslim nomads and Pathan tribesmen of Pakistan and Afghanistan had all helped me in some small way.

In many ways, so little has changed on the Silk Road from its glory years. The desert oases in China, the village hamlets in Kashmir and the hot plains of the Punjab are still there. The same goods are carried to the same markets by the same means. Time has passed them all. Today, places like Kashgar and the villages of northern Pakistan remain trapped in time, largely unfettered by pop music, cable television or the automobile. Western culture is only a faint murmur as foreigners pass through on their tour buses and mountain bikes. The sound of the muezzin still wafts through the mosques, calling the masses to prayer as it did a thousand years ago.

Although largely a trucking route now, the Silk Road retains many of the mystical and romantic trappings of centuries past. Camels graze by the road while Kazakh herdsmen tend their sheep. Canvas yurts covered in cotton quilts dot mountain valleys. Kids throw rocks, and dogs larger than wolves (called Kurt-Kopegis) chase you as though you're their take-out dinner.

The old Silk Road routes in China now act as economic gateways to the former Russian republics. Entrepreneurial traders take advantage of trans-border routes, bartering their goods in the new Central Asian states. Camel caravans have been replaced by diesel trucks hauling their wares to markets in Almaty, Kashgar, Gilgit and beyond. Everything from melons, spices and strings of garlic to washing machines, Abba CDs, clock radios and silk stockings are sold. Mongolians trade with Han Chinese. Tajiks trade with Pakistanis. Kyrgyz women hitch rides to the Muslim markets of Kashgar. The Karakoram Highway has brought them all together. The Silk Road is reborn.

Big business is even poking its nose into the massive natural gas fields of China's northwestern province, Xinjiang. Invaluable to the Chinese government, Xinjiang's petroleum resources have triggered interest in constructing pipelines across to Uzbekistan and the Middle East. American petroleum companies are waiting in the wings to grab up contracts when things settle down. The political instability of Afghanistan and other Muslim nations, however, has not made this a viable project.

The modern Silk Road is even a conduit for the vices of our modern society — porn tapes, cocaine and guns. The Pakistan-Afghan border is a maze of donkey paths where gun-runners smuggle rocket launchers and AK-47s to feed the civil war in Afghanistan. The Pamir Mountains that straddle the Afghanistan and Chinese borders are now home to some of Central Asia's biggest drug smugglers. Centred in Osh, Kyrgyzstan, opium and heroin are transported on horseback and trucked from Afghanistan through Uzbekistan.

Over in Kyrgyzstan, waiters can quote the going rate of opium to their customers. One kilogram of cocaine sells for $1,000 US in Osh, up from $140 US in Afghanistan. When the coca leaf is refined into the final product, a kilogram of cocaine sells on the streets of Moscow for $11,000 US. Heroin, an incredible cash machine with Afghanistan supplying 75 per cent of the world's supply, can fetch up to $140,000 US per kilo. But even that may change since the Taliban ordered a halt to all poppy cultivation in July of 2000. Farmers are now forced to try to subsist on wheat and vegetables at a fraction of the price they got for opium. Some think the Taliban are trying to drive heroin prices up by creating a shortage in the market. As of August 2001, the ban on cultivation of poppy seeds remained.

Meanwhile, China, a withering Communist state, struggles to keep up with a world gone high-tech. Awarded the 2008 Olympic Summer Games in Beijing, the Chinese are delirious with pride; the world's most insecure society is eager to show it has come of age and can play with the big boys.

China's Muslim tribes, once the gatekeepers of the Silk Road, still move contentedly at their own glacial pace, far removed from cell phones and an Internet-obsessed world. But the Middle Kingdom is on a resurgence, albeit slowly. Give China another hundred years and it may become the most influential economic power on the planet. Will China's economic growth gradually weaken the patriarchal family structure, empowering women and creating independence for many as it has in South Korea?

Pakistan today is still furious-paced, drug-hazy and drunk with nuclear power. Its hatred for its larger, more prosperous Hindu neighbour has wasted much money and valuable resources. In May 1998, eight months after I returned to Canada, both Pakistan and India tested nuclear weapons. The genocide of the Kashmiri-Muslims by the Indian Army and the sporadic terrorism by Pakistani-sanctioned freedom fighters have segregated the two countries along religious lines, turning the Indian subcontinent into one giant nuclear-armed powder keg.

Pakistan has failed to define a national identity in its first half-century as a country. A few hundred land-owning families still control most of the wealth. In a nation of 150 million, less than 1 per cent of people pay income tax. Pakistan's political system is fraught with corruption and endures an inferiority complex towards India. The military returned to power in late 1999 when one of its generals appointed himself president after a bloodless coup, exiling Prime Minister Nawaz Sharif.

Under Islamic fundamentalism, Afghanistan — where the penalty for beardlessness is 10 days in jail — is no longer the hippy getaway it was in the seventies. For me, it was the epitome of the unconventional. As it has for hundreds of years, Afghanistan struggles against illiteracy, against landmines, against poverty and an indifferent world, battling the aggressor — this time itself. The *jihad* lives on.

Afghanistan is losing its best and brightest, as well as its culture. Two giant Buddha statues, carved into a cliff face 1,400 years ago, were dynamited in March 2001 by the ruling Taliban who decided the statues were objects of worship, a contravention of the Taliban's interpretation of the Koran. Today, hundreds of thousands of Afghan refugees flee the civil war and cross the border into the squalid camps at Jalozai near the Khyber Pass in Pakistan.

India, nonetheless, is confident in its cultural roots dating back a thousand years before Christ and is poised to leap-frog out of the 17th century straight into the 21st century. It's just a matter of time. India is sure of itself, despite recently passing the one billion mark. Even more so than China, India is well on its way to economic success. It has the brains and the middle class, and it isn't hampered by a decrepit dictatorship or a Communist system. Part of India will rise beyond the developing world. The country already has tripled its literacy rate and doubled the life expectancy of its people to age 60 since independence a half-century ago.

In the end, my Silk Road odyssey put me face to face with some of the most fascinating peoples in the world. I had caught a glimpse into other lives, other times. My trip was not just an adventure on a mountain bike. Travelling along the Silk Road in Central Asia had taught me something more — a lesson in self-discovery.

Marco Polo, whose Silk Road journals were without question the original adventure book of the modern world, said it best on his deathbed, "I didn't tell half of what I saw, because no one would have believed me." So true.

September 2001

Selected Bibliography

1. Byron, Robert. *The Road to Oxiana*. (London: Macmillan, 1937 [rpt. 1981]).
2. Felton, Robert Young. *Fielding's The World's Most Dangerous Places*. (Redondo Beach, CA: Fielding Worldwide Inc.).
3. Fleming, Peter. *News from Tartary*. (London: Abacus, 1936 [rpt.1994]).
4. Hopkirk, Peter. *Foreign Devils on the Silk Road*. (New York: Oxford University Press, 1980).
5. Keay, John. *Explorers of the Western Himalayas: 1820–1895*. (London: John Murray, 1977).
6. Naipaul, V.S. *Beyond Belief: Islamic Excursions Among the Converted Peoples*. (London: Little, Brown & Co., 1998).
7. Polo, Marco. *The Travels of Marco Polo: Complete Yule-Cordier Edition*, Vols. 1–2. (Toronto: General, 1993).
8. Rushdie, Salman. *Midnight's Children*. (London: Jonathan Cape, 1981).
9. Schofield, Victoria. *Kashmir: In the Crossfire*. (London: I.B. Taurus & Co. Ltd., 1996).
10. Tharoor, Shashi. *India: From Midnight to the Millennium*. (New York: Arcade Publishing, 1997).

Glossary

asalaam aleikum	peace be with you (Arabic greeting) used by all Muslims
baithak	sitting rooms in Pakistani homes
baozi	Chinese steamed bread filled with meat, mutton or chicken, wrapped in a round dumpling about the size of a small tennis ball (breakfast delicacy)
bheja masala	devilled brains
binguan	guesthouse hotels for Chinese and foreigners (usually more expensive)
bishtek	Russian hamburgers
buzkashi	hybrid version of polo where the headless carcass of a goat is used as the "ball" in Afghanistan
cha	green tea in China
chai	tea in Pakistan
chapatti	bread (India and Pakistan)
chogas	woollen robes worn by men in Pakistan
chukka	polo period
dhabas	roadside stalls in India
dhal	lentil soup
dhoti	loincloth pulled up between the legs and worn by Hindu men
dupatta	scarf, usually worn over a woman's head
ekkas	donkey carts
gush nan	Muslim meat pies (costing about 10 cents)
halwais	specialists who make lassi yoghurt drinks
Han	dominant ethnic group in China
haveli	mansion
hutong	alleyway in Chinese city
imam	officiating priest in a mosque

jirga	group of Pathan elders
kafilas	columns of refugees from Partition escaping for the newly formed Pakistan and India during Partition in 1947
karahai	cast-iron pan like a wok
Kazakh	Muslim herders originating from Kazakhstan, many living in canvas yurts in the mountains
khagina	boiled eggs scrambled in chilies with garlic and ginger
kirpan	sabre
kuai	slang for yuan (Chinese official currency)
Kyrgyz	Muslims originating from Kyrgyzstan, many living in adobe (mud and straw) homes
lamian	noodles and broth
lao wai	foreigner in China
lashkar	armed militia
lassi	fruit-flavoured yoghurt drink common in Pakistan and India
luguan	bottom-end Chinese accommodation hotel
madrasah	religious school in Afghanistan
mohajirs	refugees
muezzin	a crier who calls Muslims to prayer over a loud speaker in the early morning hours
murraba	sugary (carrot) stew with almonds
nan	bread (India and Pakistan)
nautch	girls (dancers) in Pakistan
ni hao	hello in Mandarin
pagri	turban worn by Pathan tribesmen in Afghanistan
pilaf	Muslim fried rice and meat
pita manta kawaps	Muslim shish kebabs
poshkal	crepe-like treat filled with yoghurt-relish mixture
pulau	fried rice
puri	fried pancake
raita	a mint-flavoured yoghurt sauce (Pakistan)
ravaps / tamburs	Muslim long-necked lizard-skin guitars with elaborate inlaid wood
sari	long toga-like garment for women with one end draped over the shoulder (India)

shalwar qamiz	tunic and loose trousers
Sharia	the Islamic code of law
shashlyk	Muslim kebabs
shukria	thank you (Punjabi)
Tajiks	Muslims originating from Tajikistan
tangmian / chaomian	Chinese noodles
tongas	horse-drawn carts
tutor	two-stringed Muslim guitar
Uyghurs	dominant Muslim group in Xinjiang province
wai bin	rich foreign guest in China
yuan	Chinese official currency
yurt	canvas tepee-like domed home used by Kyrgyz and Kazakh nomads
zamindars	landowners